D0060027

WORKPLACE WELLNESS THAT WORKS

WORKPLACE WELLNESS THAT WORKS

10 Steps to Infuse Well-Being and Vitality into Any Organization

LAURA PUTNAM

Cover image courtesy of Laura Putnam
Cover design: Wiley

Published by John Wiley & Sons, Inc., Hoboken, New Jersey.
Published simultaneously in Canada.

For general information on our other products and services or for technical support, please contact our Customer Care Department within the United States at (800) 762-2974, outside the United States at (317) 572-3993 or fax (317) 572-4002.

Wiley publishes in a variety of print and electronic formats and by print-on-demand. Some material included with standard print versions of this book may not be included in e-books or in print-on-demand. If this book refers to media such as a CD or DVD that is not included in the version you purchased, you may download this material at http://booksupport.wiley.com. For more information about Wiley products, visit www.wiley.com.

Library of Congress Cataloging-in-Publication Data:

Putnam, Laura, 1965-
Workplace wellness that works : 10 steps to infuse well-being and vitality into any organization / Laura Putnam.
pages cm
Includes index.
ISBN 978-1-119-05591-4 (cloth); ISBN 9781119055730 (ePDF); ISBN 9781119055723 (ePub)
1. Employee health promotion. 2. Organizational behavior. 3. Well-being.
4. Industrial hygiene. I. Title.
RC969.H43.P87 2015
658.3'82—dc23

2015007711

Printed in the United States of America

10 9 8 7 6 5 4 3 2

For Bill Baun, a great mentor and a big brother to me,
and for my dad, Sam

CONTENTS

Preface ix
Acknowledgments xi
Introduction An Overview of Workplace Wellness xv

Section I START IT (WORKPLACE WELLNESS THAT EXCITES) 1

Step 1 Shift Your Mind-Set from Expert to Agent of Change 3
(The Changemaker Imperative)

Step 2 Imagine What's Possible 27
(The Imagination Imperative)

Step 3 Uncover the Hidden Factors 57
(The Culture Imperative)

Step 4 Start with What's Right 85
(The Optimism Imperative)

Section II BUILD IT (WORKPLACE WELLNESS THAT GROWS) 103

Step 5 Take a da Vinci Approach to Change 105
(The Interdisciplinary Imperative)

Step 6 Go Stealth 133
(The "Sneakiness" Imperative)

Section III MAKE IT LAST (WORKPLACE WELLNESS THAT WORKS) 157

Step 7 Create Meaning 159
(The Engagement Imperative)

Step 8 Design Nudges and Cues 191

(The "Make It Easy" and "Make It Normal" Imperative)

Step 9 Launch and Iterate 215

(The Experimentation Imperative)

Step 10 Go Global 245

(The International Imperative)

Pull It All Together 269

About the Author 275

Notes 277

Index 299

PREFACE

My approach to workplace wellness has always been "different." Perhaps that's because I come from a different background than most who are in the field. For years, I was a public high school teacher. My job, in fact my calling, was to engage every one of my students. Every day, I needed to design and facilitate a classroom experience that taught, motivated, and inspired, and that ultimately led my students to *their* calling.

Now I'm CEO of Motion Infusion, a well-being consulting firm, and I'm finding that I'm doing exactly what I did as a teacher—but with adults, and, specifically, with adults in the workplace. My job today, or *calling*, is to engage, energize, catalyze, and to promote lasting behavior change, moving people toward their higher purpose.

The workplace is essentially school for adults. Just as schools are uniquely positioned to foster positive growth and change in young people, workplaces are uniquely positioned to do the same with adults, especially in the areas of health and well-being.

The numbers clearly demonstrate that the traditional wellness model—one that overly relies on medical and behavioral sciences—is simply not working. What's the missing ingredient? A meaningful and lasting engagement of employees. We need to widen the lens and use a more interdisciplinary approach to promote wellness that works in the workplace, applying thinking from psychology, education, design thinking, and even advertising. To bring sustainable wellness to the workplace, we need to get creative: Imagination is the key to bringing research-based theories to life in real-world settings.

Evidence shows that effective employee engagement doesn't come from compliance-based programs with scary statistics. Lasting engagement stems from a *movement* that appeals to the emotions and inspires people to get "in motion." A movement focuses less on the individual employee and more on changing the overall culture and reshaping the work environment so that healthy choices become the easy and "normal" choices.

By exploring the latest research and multidisciplinary best practices from a number of related fields in conjunction with real-world examples and case studies, I will show what every organization can do to sustainably increase the well-being of its employees so that employees can experience vitality on a daily basis.

This book builds on what I've learned over the past 10 years as a practitioner in the field of workplace wellness, along with my formal training as an educator, my experience in public policy and advocacy, and my passion for movement as a nationally competitive collegiate gymnast and professional dancer.

There's still a lot to be explored and discovered in the field of wellness. I like to refer to the field of workplace wellness as "the Wild, Wild West" as there are still so many questions with unclear answers. The challenges of obesity-related disease, poor health outcomes, and health care costs are as daunting as ever. But having the courage to seek input from unexpected sources may lead us to the solutions.

My hope is that by reading this book you'll discover new ways of looking at wellness and that you'll have step-by-step plans for implementing wellness programs that fit with your organization. In short, my goal is that you'll have the tools to create Workplace Wellness That Works.

Let's get started!

ACKNOWLEDGMENTS

First and foremost, a very big thanks and acknowledgment to Karen Murphy, senior editor, for making this whole project possible. She took a leap of faith and provided superb guidance.

Thanks to the people who helped me with the actual writing process. MeiMei Fox got me started, kept me going, and made it all seem possible. Thank you to Leonard Gross who provided inspiration and mentorship. Thanks to Destiny McCune for her speedy and enthusiastic transcribing. Thanks to Peter Wolff for his excellent research work. Thanks to Michaele Kruger for her research assistance and transcribing. Thanks to Micaela Scarpulla for also helping out with research and fact-checking. Many thanks to Mari Ryan, Heidi Kuhn, and Christian Kindler for their helpful editing advice. I'm very grateful to Judy Howarth, who patiently and expertly edited the book in its first round. I am also appreciative of the additional team members for their follow-up editing, marketing, and assistance: Shannon Vargo, Michael Friedberg, Tiffany Colon, and Lauren Freestone. A very special thank you to Gray Pard Ponti for her amazing, lifesaving editing and proofing. Thanks to Madeleine Eiche who originally designed the "Motion Infuser" that appears on the book jacket and throughout the book. Thanks also to Megan Clark and Maria Guerriero for designing most of the graphics in the book.

This book would not have come to life in the way that it did without the many people I interviewed who shared their insights, expertise, and stories. Each is a great example of an agent of change. Thanks to Flip Morse, Allison Rouse, Francis Scarpulla, Amy Schoew, Sheryl Niehbuhr, Marjorie Schlenoff, Sheri Snow, Jennifer Flynn, Bill Baun, Jacqueline Szeto, Robin Oxley, Casey Chosewood, Sig Berven, Tim Blouche, Alexandra Drane, Amanda Parsons, Toni Parks-Payne, Emily Markmann, Susan Ganeshan, Alex Chan, Deb Smolensky, Denis Hayes, Jeff Coles, Dee Edington, Matthew Coan, Mike Radakovich, Lynn Vojvodich, Leslie Ritter, Emily Tsiang, Laura Young, Whitney Smith, Maggie Spicer, Josh Levine, Jennifer Pattee, Jennifer Pitts, Tom Drews, Joel Bennett, Marnie Ellison, Duane Bray, Firdaus Dhabhar, Lance Dublin, Mari Ryan, Marianne Jackson, Michelle Segar,

Vic Strecher, Rosie Ward, Mike Ward, Paul Terry, Elizabeth Cushing, Judi Hennebry Wise, Julie Shipley, Mike Yurchuk, Kara Ekert, Douglas Burnham, Eric Stein, Patty de Vries, Tess Roering, Jay Powell, Cale Feller, Ryan Picarella, Jim Golden, Paul Johnson, and David Hunnicutt. I am particularly grateful to Firdaus Dhabhar who shared his work and kindly permitted me to include a model that he created.

There is a whole group of individuals who connected me with others and provided assistance in gathering information. A big thanks goes to Miriam Senft, who put me in touch with so many great people. Thanks to Seth Williams for connecting me with Clarabridge, along with Katie Clark and Andrew Lovett-Barron at IDEO who connected me with Duane Bray. Thanks to Anthony Mosse for connecting me with Robin Oxley at Virgin America. A thank you also goes to Lyta Hamm, Barbara Brown, and Matt Davis with Solano County for helping out with sending out a survey that provided helpful information for the book. Thank you to Sherri Novak, Stefan Gingerich, Heidi Vivolo, Debra Amador DeLaRosa, Gary Pinkus, Jackie Charonis, and Julie Kaufmann for their assistance.

In writing this book, I drew on the research and insights of many academics including (in addition to those interviewed): Kelly McGonigal, Robert Lustig, Howard Gardner, Edward Deci, Ron Goetzel, Jon Robison, Alfie Kohn, Michael O'Donnell, and Dean Ornish. I also am grateful to thought leaders who helped to shape my thinking for the book, in particular Marcus Buckingham, Daniel Pink, Patrick Lencioni, Arianna Huffington, Michael Gervais, and Chip Conley. A special thank you also to Chip Conley for agreeing to share his model in the book.

A very special thanks goes to Jessica Grossmeier, who generously contributed an enormous amount of time lending her expertise, offering editing advice, and very kindly connecting me with so many experts. Thanks also to Joel Bennett and Bill Baun for their time and helpful advice.

A huge thanks goes to Angelique Pera, who kept me sane and hopeful and inspired to think big. I am also deeply grateful for having had the chance to learn from Ted Sizer, an innovator in educational reform and former professor of mine, whose enduring wisdom guided and inspired me to think differently about education and engagement—and whose perspective shines throughout the book. Thanks to Logan Wales who shared good coffee and good humor, along with Amanda

Corzine and Cassie Hanson at Two Skirts who offered a respite from my writing, and a big shout-out to my favorite fellow procrastinator: Melvin Thomas at Peets.

Lastly, I am enormously grateful to my family: my sister, Elicia; my brother-in-law, Roger; my fiancé, Chris; and my mom, Betsy. All of them tirelessly read through many, many drafts, offering their incisive thoughts, amazing editing, and endless support and love.

Introduction An Overview of Workplace Wellness

People are designed to move. As hunters and gatherers, we moved up to 20 miles a day. We *had* to move to survive. We're also designed to eat food—real food, not processed food. We're designed to perform under pressure and then renew. We're designed to love and be socially connected. And we're designed to find happiness and meaning in life. These essentials are at the root of what we've been seeking through the ages, told through the voices of philosophers like Aristotle and Viktor Frankl to poets like Pablo Neruda to pop singers like Lady Gaga. Today, more than ever, we're talking about these ageless questions, but grasping to find the answers.

Wellness, at its core, is about getting back to doing what we naturally do. Increasingly, however, we're being *culturally* asked to do things that we're not biologically designed to do. We're born to move, but we're culturally mandated to sit. We're biologically programmed to eat whole foods, but our busy schedules and toxic environments prompt us to eat processed foods that are immediately gratifying, but *never* satisfying. We're hardwired to alternate stress with relaxation, but the society we live in idolizes being busy and always on the go. We're born to be with others, but many of us are feeling isolated in a sea of hard-driving competition, despite our ever expanding virtual social networks on Facebook and LinkedIn. We live in a world that exerts pressure to be available 24/7 and dishes up professional demands that are ever more unrelenting, with less time to rest and replenish. It's no wonder that so many of us are feeling depleted and worn out.

In this petri dish of biological-cultural mismatches, workplace wellness initiatives have been gaining both popularity and notoriety. Workplace wellness, one might say, is any kind of organized effort to support employees in being more human at work: moving more, eating more natural foods, finding balance, building meaningful connections, and working toward a higher purpose. Done well, workplace wellness has the potential to offset the ill effects of the increasingly demanding and toxic environment and culture we live in. Done poorly, workplace wellness can feel like another top-down compliance initiative that has little to do with well-being and everything to do with checking boxes and taking tests.

Workplace wellness should not be complicated and controversial—and yet, it has become just that. In truth there are a number of really simple, inexpensive practices that *any* organization—and any person within the organization—can do to create an oasis at work that nurtures well-being *and* benefits the bottom line. Every organization already has the capacity and the resources right now to achieve Workplace Wellness That Works. This is exactly what this book is about.

Applying promising practices from workplace wellness, along with principles from related fields like education, learning and development, organizational development, psychology, and even a discipline called "design thinking" (think like a designer to devise creative solutions), we *can* make a difference in employees' health and happiness, and we *can* promote an overall culture of well-being at work. We can create Workplace Wellness That Works, and we can help employees achieve their higher purpose.

A Guide to Using This Book

This book is designed for anyone who is tasked with or is interested in workplace wellness. You could be the designated wellness liaison or a manager in human resources, a safety coordinator, a senior executive who wants to bring wellness to the entire organization, or even an external consultant or broker. The book assumes no prior background in the wellness field, but even wellness veterans may be interested in the chapters that highlight innovative thinking from other industries.

This book provides tips that can be applied to any stage of a wellness program, whether the program is just getting started or is long-standing—and it can be applied to organizations of any size. You will find that what I write about goes beyond standard wellness programs. Be prepared, because a lot of organizations and decision makers are not ready for this. For many organizations I work with, the first challenge is to move decision makers forward on how they perceive wellness. In some cases, you will have to work around limited views of workplace wellness, or you may have an organization that is completely wellness-averse. In these cases, you might consider "going stealth"—sneaking wellness into non-wellness initiatives—being sure *not* to call it wellness.

In still other cases, you may enjoy the full support of senior leaders and managers who are ready to jump on board and a receptive group of employees who are waiting to join the wellness movement. Whatever the case, you'll need to tune into what your organization is ready for—and this book will help you identify where your organization is right now and how to get started, given your current reality.

Let's step back first, though, and take a look at the larger context.

WE ARE FACING A TIDAL WAVE

We are facing a tidal wave of obesity, chronic disease and conditions, lots of stress, and too many missed opportunities for each of us to reach our full potential. The statistics are overwhelming. By and large, this tidal wave stems from the massive biological-cultural mismatch that we have collectively created in the United States, and increasingly as a global community.

In the United States, more than a third of us are obese, and another third of us are overweight—double the rate in 1980.[1] If trends continue, almost half of us will be obese by the year 2030.[2] Nearly one in two Americans has at least one chronic disease or condition.[3] Heart disease continues to be the number one killer.[4] According to the Centers for Disease Control and Prevention, over 1 in 10 Americans has type 2 diabetes and more than a third of American adults are in the early stages of diabetes.[5] If we continue on the same trajectory, a third of us will be diabetic by year 2050.[6]

The cost of this tidal wave is enormous. It's estimated that obesity alone costs over $300 billion annually in medical costs, disability costs, premature death, and lost productivity.[7] About 75 percent of our national health care expenditure goes toward *treating* largely preventable diseases. Meanwhile, less than five percent goes toward prevention.[8]

Our economy simply cannot sustain these skyrocketing expenditures. Almost 20 percent of our gross domestic product goes toward health care costs, and we spend over two and a half times more than any other country in the world on health care. Sadly, we have little to show for it. In a controversial World Health Report released in 2000, the United States was ranked No. 37 in the world in terms of overall health performance—behind countries like Morocco, Dominica, and Costa Rica.[9] According to a 2013 "Most Efficient Health Care" Bloomberg report, the United States ranked 46th in a group of 48 nations. The authors of this report noted, "Among advanced economies, the U.S. spends the most on health care on a relative cost basis with the worst outcome."[10] More important than money, though, is the human cost. This tidal wave is shortening our life spans, diminishing our quality of life, and limiting our potential.

Perhaps most devastating is the impact this tidal wave is having on our children. Nearly one in five children in the United States today is obese.[11] It's estimated that at least one in four children born after the year 2000 will acquire type 2 diabetes sometime in their lifetime. For some populations, it could be even higher—30 percent, 40 percent, even 50 percent.[12] And, for the first time ever in history, there is evidence to suggest that our children will have shorter life expectancies than we do—unless we do something.[13]

So the natural question is, "What can I, as just one person, do to stand up to this colossal tidal wave?" The answer: *I can make better choices.* The fact is that the onset of most of the chronic diseases and conditions we face today—heart disease, stroke, type 2 diabetes, obesity, arthritis, and certain cancers—could be prevented, if only each one of us made better choices.[14]

Let's break this down a little further. The American Heart Association has identified a list of seven criteria needed to support a healthy heart. Called the "Simple Seven," the list includes eating a healthy diet, getting at least 150 minutes of moderate physical activity each week, being a nonsmoker for at least a year, along with maintaining a healthy weight, healthy blood pressure, healthy cholesterol levels, and healthy blood sugar levels.[15] Seems straightforward enough. When I speak to groups about this, I then pose a follow-up question: "According to one large study, out of a pool of 17,820 adults between the ages of 45 and 98, how many do you think met the Simple Seven?" Usually, the guesses are in the percentages—ten percent, five percent, or, for those who are feeling more pessimistic, two percent. Then comes the shocking answer: "two people."[16] We can do better than this. The question is: How?

THE BILLION-DOLLAR DILEMMA

According to David Katz, director of the Yale Prevention Research Institute, the tidal wave we're facing can be boiled down to three simple words: "feet, forks, and fingers." We need to get more active (feet), we need to change what we eat (forks), and we need to stop smoking (fingers).[17] The need to make these healthier choices is made painfully obvious by the scary statistics, but what the scary statistics don't tell us is how to motivate and empower ourselves to make these healthier choices.

With shockingly few exceptions, each of us *knows* what changes we should make, but very few of us are able to actually put these changes into practice. We know we need to eat more vegetables, avoid smoking, get more exercise, maintain a healthy weight, get a good night's sleep, manage stress, and make time for our family and friends. But, very few of us are able to put this knowledge into practice. This is what I call the "knowing and doing gap." Not only is this gap causing a huge level of unnecessary pain and suffering; it's costing us a lot of money—in the billions of dollars every year.

We see examples of the knowing and doing gap all the time. For instance, every trained nurse is well aware of the health risks associated with obesity, yet surprisingly, some studies have found that the obesity rate for nurses is actually *higher* than the national average, 40 percent as compared to 35 percent![18,19] Another great example of the knowing and doing gap is the annual ritual of setting New Year's resolutions. Every year, many of us resolve to lose weight, quit smoking, or perhaps join a gym in an effort to improve our well-being. Amazingly, statistics show that 88 percent of these resolutions fail.[20]

The issue for most of us is not *what* to do, but *how* to do it. The explosion of books, blogs, and talks on behavior change and habit formation illustrates a growing demand for answers. When I was a Pilates instructor, for example, clients, friends, and even strangers would often ask, "How do I lose weight?" "Well," I would say, "You need to eat healthier foods and get more exercise." Invariably, their response was always, "Yeah, yeah—I know that!" I eventually realized, they weren't asking, "*What* do I do?" They were asking, "*How* do I do it?"

CHANGE IS HARD

Making a change seems seductively simple—and yet, it is anything but. For starters, our brains are hardwired to resist change. Making a short-term change or participating in a one-time event is easy. But making a permanent change is difficult, as it requires ongoing motivation and self-regulation. Respondents to a recent survey conducted by the American Psychological Association reported that the number one barrier to making a lifestyle change was a lack of willpower.[21] For so many of us, we know what we want to accomplish—say, losing weight or getting on a regular exercise program—but the willpower we're counting on seems to dissipate when we need it most.

There's a lot of research to suggest that our ability to stay motivated and exert willpower is actually a limited resource. The thinking and decision-making part of our brain, called the prefrontal cortex, is responsible for a variety of tasks: focusing, processing short-term memory, and solving abstract problems. The prefrontal cortex is also responsible for motivation and resisting temptations, and this is where we run into trouble.

When we overload our prefrontal cortex—which is par for the course in most knowledge-based jobs today—we simply don't have much leftover prefrontal capacity for staying motivated in resisting temptations, despite our best efforts. This helps to explain why so few of us are able to keep a New Year's resolution. In our busy, overloaded lives, our prefrontal cortex is simply maxed out and doesn't have the remaining capacity to exercise restraint.

Roy Baumeister, social psychologist, called this phenomenon "willpower depletion." In a seminal study, he demonstrated how willpower and high-level focus are linked. Two groups of participants were given two different sets of instructions when entering a room with warm, freshly baked cookies and a plate of cold radishes. Half of the participants were instructed to help themselves to the cookies and the other half were asked to refrain from eating the cookies, and stick to the radishes. Shortly afterward, each of the participants was given an unsolvable puzzle. The radish eaters—the ones who had to exert willpower to not eat the cookies—gave up within 8 minutes (on average), while the cookie eaters persisted and kept at it for an average of 19 minutes. Baumeister concluded that the willpower needed to resist the cookies depleted the brainpower needed to persist in solving the puzzle—and that the two therefore must come from the same source.[22]

Professor Baba Shiv and a group of researchers at Stanford University followed up on Baumeister's work. This time, however, the researchers issued the brain challenge first. Two different groups of students were given two different numbers to memorize. The first group was asked to memorize a seven-digit number, and the second group was asked to memorize only a two-digit number. Afterward, each group was given a choice: chocolate cake or a bowl of fruit. Net result? The group given the bigger prefrontal task (memorize the seven-digit number) was twice as likely to choose the chocolate cake. The conclusion from this study, consistent with Baumeister's findings, is that a cognitive overload (such as memorizing a longer number) makes it more difficult to self-regulate or resist the unhealthy choice.[23]

A lot of the habit-formation solutions that have been put forward are effectively clever ways to outmaneuver our change-resistant brains. These include techniques like monitoring our behaviors and keeping track, arranging our environment to make the desired behavior the easy choice, using mindfulness to notice what's happening internally every time we make a choice (good or bad), setting goals that focus on specific behaviors within a set time frame, linking new behaviors with old triggers to accelerate the automation of a desired habit, finding a friend so that we're accountable to somebody else, treating ourselves to timely rewards, and decreasing the amount of motivation required through "tiny habits" that eventually result in big changes over time.[24,25,26,27]

Problematically, all of these techniques target the individual—and this is where I believe many wellness efforts have gone astray. Personal choice and willpower, while important, are small parts of a much larger equation. Widespread and sustainable change can only happen if we shift the focus away from the individual and toward the larger, surrounding forces, like environment and culture.

THE ISSUE IS BIGGER THAN THE INDIVIDUAL

For workplace wellness to truly work, we need to address the culture and the environment first, and then the individual. Collectively, for example, we have constructed an environment in which movement is abnormal and sitting is normal. Together, we have built environments that are more designed for driving than they are for walking. As John Ratey, author of *Spark*, characterizes it, "In today's technology-driven plasma-screened-in world, it's easy to forget that we are born movers—animals, in fact—because we've engineered movement right out of our lives."[28]

In terms of our dietary habits, our societies have supported massive food infrastructures that are undeniably unhealthy. As highlighted in the recent documentary *Fed Up*, our policies—from farming subsidies started under the New Deal to pressure by the Bush administration to alter a 2003 World Health Organization report on the dangers of sugar consumption—have repeatedly supported the agricultural-industrial complex at the cost of our health.[29]

Here's where workplace wellness steps into the picture. Up against brains that are hardwired to resist change, a massive disconnect between what we know we should do and what we actually do, and a larger environment and culture that is designed to diminish rather than amplify our health, just the *idea* of workplace wellness is an act of courage.

The workplace is where most adults spend the vast majority of their waking hours, so if there was ever a time that we *needed* effective workplace wellness programs, it's now. Workplace wellness can provide an exit out of a collectively unhealthy lifestyle and an entrance into a collectively healthy lifestyle. Good idea, but how do we actually do it? Let's start with taking a look at the prevailing tack we've been taking to promote well-being in the workplace.

The Classic Model for Workplace Wellness

The 2013 RAND Workplace Wellness Programs Study report, the most comprehensive study to date on the impact of workplace wellness, outlined the customary protocol for standard workplace wellness programs: assessment, feedback, programs, and incentives (represented by the stars in the graphic) to motivate people to join and then stay in the game. This is what I call the "classic model."

The Classic Model

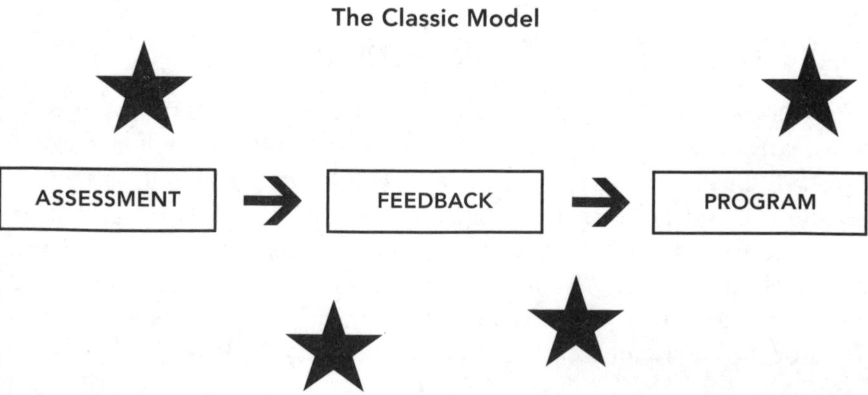

The goals of the classic model are to (1) establish a baseline both for the individual as well as the organization; (2) stratify employees according to levels of health; (3) inform employees of their "risk factors," or attributes and practices, that increase their likelihood of developing chronic disease; (4) encourage employees identified as either "healthy" or "at-risk" to participate in lifestyle management programs, or activities and resources that focus on prevention and health promotion; (5) guide employees who are already in a disease state toward disease management programs, or activities and programs that help to manage and slow down the progression of a chronic condition; (6) enable employees to achieve positive health outcomes; and (7) also benefit the organization.

A Breakdown of the Classic Model

Assessment Phase

The assessment phase, which provides a benchmark, typically consists of the following: health risk assessments (HRAs) and biometric screenings. These are used to assess health status, health risks, behaviors, attitudes toward health, and readiness to change.

Many employers also conduct additional assessments:

- **Needs and interests survey:** What are employees' needs and what types of wellness activities are they interested in?
- **"Culture of health" audit:** Does the culture and environment support health and wellness at work?

Feedback Phase

Typically, each participating employee receives a report with his/her individualized calculated risk score. Meanwhile, the aggregate results are reported back to the employer to help in the design of the wellness strategy. There are a number of ways

(*continued*)

(*continued*)

that this information is communicated back to the individual employees:

- **Health/wellness coach:** A coach delivers the results to the individual, face to face, telephonically or digitally.
- **Web portal:** The information is delivered through a Web portal, which creates a dashboard for each participating employee.

PROGRAMS PHASE

There are two broad categories of programs: lifestyle management and disease management. Below are some common examples of each.

Lifestyle management programs:

- **Weight control programming:** Common programs include Weight Watchers, weight loss contests, and education on diet and nutrition.
- **Fitness:** Some organizations provide on-site fitness facilities, classes, and training; others provide subsidies for outside memberships.
- **Wellness coaching:** Coaching can occur face to face, telephonically, even digitally. A coach (or virtual coach) supports individual employees in setting health-related goals and taking measures to meet these goals.
- **Lunch 'n' learns/on-site seminars:** These are information sessions on health-related topics, generally provided by experts, often outside consultants and trainers.
- **Tobacco cessation programming:** This is programming that provides support for smokers wanting to quit.
- **Wellness resources:** These are any kind of information sources, in forms of newsletters, e-mails, posters, or blogs, that are generally focused on raising awareness.

- **Online programs/engagement platforms:** Technology-based solutions that provide information to employees, enable employees to enroll in programs, encourage virtual interaction among employees, and provide tracking support.
- **Challenges:** Employees compete individually or as part of a team against one another. Common challenges include walking, weight loss, or weight maintenance.
- **Drug/alcohol abuse programming:** These services are often provided through Employee Assistance Programs.
- **Stress management programming:** Typical programs include building skills in areas such as mindfulness, compassion, gratitude, or yoga.
- **Prevention services:** Services include on-site vaccinations, exams, preventive screenings, or education on preventive care.
- **Healthy food options:** These options include availability of healthy choices in vending machines, food served during meetings, as well as healthy options in the cafeteria (if applicable), which are often subsidized.
- **Nurse line:** A 24-hour support line assists employees in making informed decisions regarding their care.

Disease management programs:

- **Health coaching:** A health coach serves as a support in helping an individual employee to better understand, manage, and slow down the progression of a chronic condition.

Evaluation Phase

Evaluation, which loops back to the assessment phase, is usually based on participation rates and employee feedback, along with changes in behaviors, risk factors, and health outcomes. In addition, employers sometimes measure organizational outcomes, such as medical costs, workers compensation costs, disability costs, absenteeism, productivity, and turnover.

Is the classic model working? In the case of a company like Johnson & Johnson, the answer is actually "yes."

The Story of an Early Pioneer in Workplace Wellness

In 1979, James Burke, CEO of Johnson & Johnson, decided to do something radical. He decided that it was a good idea to invest in the health of his employees. It was the right thing to do, he thought, and healthy employees could amount to good business. This idea evolved into Johnson & Johnson's "Live for Life" wellness program, a program that was one of the catalysts of what is now purported to be a $6 to $10 billion industry.[30]

The Johnson & Johnson wellness strategy has, by and large, followed the classic model: assessment, feedback, programs, follow-up evaluation, and incentives to encourage participation.

For over three decades, Johnson & Johnson has continued not only to provide wellness for employees, but also to *measure* the impact of wellness (which is actually very difficult to do). The company's internal studies, corroborated by outside research teams, have demonstrated that participating employees have achieved health outcomes in terms of improved blood pressure, weight, physical activity, and tobacco use—and that the company has saved on costs. The savings generated come to $565 per employee, with a return on investment (ROI) up to $3.92 for every dollar invested into the program.[31]

The Johnson & Johnson story certainly gives credence to the classic model, but for most companies, the classic model is simply not working. Most organizations are not reaping the hoped-for benefits—especially when it comes to saving on health care costs. In fact, some workplace wellness programs are leading to *additional* costs related to unnecessary tests and needless care.[32]

To make matters worse, there are a growing number of stories about companies and wellness vendors overstating, misleading, and in some cases, making outright false claims. Safeway famously bragged about the health care costs it saved through a leading-edge wellness incentives program. Unfortunately, it turns out that the savings in health care costs happened *before* the program actually launched.[33] It's not surprising, therefore, that we're seeing headlines like "Do Workplace Wellness Programs Work? Usually Not."[34]

THE CLASSIC MODEL IS NOT WORKING WELL ENOUGH

Wellness is top of mind for many organizations these days. In fact, more than half of employers with 50 or more employees now offer wellness programs and more are joining the wellness bandwagon, according to the RAND report. This translates to about 75 percent of employees in the United States having access to wellness at work. The RAND report also states that employers overwhelmingly believe that their programs are having a positive impact—despite the fact that these programs are rarely formally evaluated. In addition, the study found that workplace wellness programs have led to meaningful improvements in exercise, smoking habits, and even weight control—*for those who are participating.*[35]

This is where the bad news starts. Employers are struggling to get people in the door, and they're having an even harder time *keeping* them there. In the initial assessment phase, less than half of eligible employees are participating. Come time for the actual programs, most organizations are down to a participation rate of less than 20 percent.[36]

"Program participation rates are considered a leading indicator of successful worksite health promotion (WHP) initiatives," writes Jessica Grossmeier, CEO of Verity Analytics and vice president of research for the Health Enhancement Research Organization (HERO), in a recent article in *The American Journal of Health Promotion.* "Even the most effective programs will not be effective at a population level unless enough of the right people are attracted to participate. Unfortunately, most employers do not appear to be experiencing the participation rates needed to yield the expected health outcomes and health care cost savings that motivate employers to offer WHP programs."[37]

Indeed, what the workplace wellness industry has repeatedly learned is that the *Field of Dreams* "build it and they will come" mantra just doesn't hold true. Rather, the industry has experienced *just the opposite*: If you build it (as in a workplace wellness program), they (employees) will *not* necessarily come. Just having a wellness program is not enough, and having an ill-conceived wellness program is often worse than not having one at all.

Vexingly, wellness programs, even well-designed ones, may not actually lead to a cost savings on health care spending. A celebrated and repeatedly cited Harvard meta-analysis reported that workplace wellness programs can generate a return on investment of $3.27 for every dollar invested in terms of medical costs and $2.73 for every dollar invested in terms of absenteeism costs.[38] But subsequent studies have not supported these results.

The RAND study and another large study of PepsiCo's celebrated wellness program demonstrated that there is *not* a significant difference in health cost savings between participants and nonparticipants in lifestyle management programs. However, according to the PepsiCo study, there does appear to be a significant difference in health spending as a result of the disease management programs, largely due to a reduced number of hospital visits.[39]

The reality is that the potential medical savings incurred from lifestyle management programs (which are the kinds of activities we typically associate with workplace wellness) are likely too far off in the future to translate into any kind of meaningful savings for the employer. If an employer is interested in a broader *value*, on the other hand, then investing in workplace wellness is worthwhile. The RAND study, along with a multitude of studies, shows that workplace wellness done well *can* positively impact employee health, boost engagement and job satisfaction, enhance productivity, and help an organization to become an employer of choice. While these outcomes are harder to measure, they are certainly worthwhile.[40]

THE FACTORS THAT MAKE THE DIFFERENCE

It goes without saying that all workplace wellness programs are not created equal; some are clearly better than others. While every organization has different needs and goals, below are some universal, key success factors to consider:[41,42]

- **Leadership Engagement on All Levels:** Leadership is, perhaps, the most critical factor in determining the success of any workplace wellness initiative. All levels of leadership, from executives to middle management to informal leaders within the organization, need to be not only supporting— they need to be actively participating.

- **Alignment:** Workplace wellness strategies must be aligned with the organizational core mission and values, objectives, operations, and cultural norms.
- **Opportunities for Engagement:** Employees need to feel like there are opportunities to engage—in terms of time, accessibility and perceived sense of permission.
- **Leveraging Existing Resources:** I repeatedly see examples of underutilized resources, especially those available through an employer's health plan. Organizations that have built effective wellness programs are good at leveraging both internal and external partners and resources.
- **Communication:** Communication and messaging is vital for the success of any workplace wellness program and needs to occur through multiple avenues. Done well, strong communication can even serve as a powerful motivator and can help to reduce an organization's dependency on incentives to encourage participation.[43]
- **Continuous Evaluation:** Engaging in ongoing assessments in an effort to improve can lead to higher levels of success—even if the evaluations are informal. Simply gathering input and feedback from employees, managers, and leaders, for example, can provide valuable insights. Beyond evaluating, however, organizations need to apply these lessons learned.
- **Quality of Programming:** The programming itself needs to be excellent and something that people *want* to engage with—not something that they *have* to participate in. Too often, programming, which is the "doing" part of workplace wellness, gets the short end of the stick. Far more resources are going toward incentives rather than toward creating top-notch initiatives.

WIDENING THE LENS

Moving forward and ensuring that workplace wellness does work is really a matter of widening the lens. Workplace wellness is much broader than the classic model would suggest.

Below are some ideas on how to get started:

Shift the Conversation. Shift the conversation from a focus on just physical risk factors (like weight and blood pressure) and health behaviors (what we eat, how we move, and the quality of our sleep) to a more holistic sense of *well-being and living with vitality*. Ultimately, what matters—and what is more immediately meaningful to people—is quality of life. Creating a life that matters encompasses a range of elements, such as physical, emotional, financial, social, career, community, environmental, creative, and even spiritual dimensions.

Elements of Well-Being

PHYSICAL Energy	**EMOTIONAL** Resilience	**FINANCIAL** Resource management
SOCIAL Love & connection	**CAREER** What you do	**COMMUNITY** Where you live & what you give
ENVIRONMENTAL Good for the earth is good for you	**CREATIVE** Authentic expression	**SPIRITUAL** Sense of a higher purpose

Infuse Well-Being. Make workplace wellness more than a single program. Instead, think about *infusing* well-being into every aspect of your organization. Incorporate wellness into business objectives and core values. Discuss wellness at meetings, from staff meetings to executive and annual planning meetings to team-based retreats. Make wellness a part of performance reviews. Build well-being into individual career planning and goal setting. In short, make wellness a regular part of your organization's practices, policies, and norms, built into the culture, and intentionally designed into the environment. Your goal is that everyone in the organization is living and breathing wellness—from the administrative assistant to the CEO.

Stretch the Boundaries. Any organization, of any size, in any industry, in any part of the world, can benefit from

Workplace Wellness That Works. Whether your organization is a tech startup in San Francisco or a Fortune 500 company in Cincinnati or a manufacturing plant in South Africa or a small nonprofit in India, Workplace Wellness That Works is well worth the time and commitment. Generally speaking, smaller organizations have the disadvantage of having smaller budgets than larger organizations, but have the advantage of greater agility in creating new policies and shifting the culture. While there are differences, there are also universal factors that apply across all organizations.

The wellness challenges we face are immense. To overcome these hurdles, we need to continue evolving, innovating, and sharing best practices across organizations and even across national boundaries.

Workplace Wellness That Works Is a Movement

Addressing the billion-dollar dilemma—behavior change—calls for much more than a mundane series of behavior-change solutions. Another program is not going to solve this dilemma. It needs to be much bigger. Workplace Wellness That Works, in my view, needs to be a *movement* that captivates the hearts and minds of leaders, managers, and employees. Your job will be to start this movement, build this movement, and make this movement *last*.

To tackle this Herculean task, I've organized the book into 10 steps that are divided into three main sections. Keep in mind that putting these steps into practice will likely be more of a juggling act than a linear set of tasks. Don't be surprised if you find yourself going back to some of the steps more than once. Getting leadership buy-in, for example, is not a one-time event. Engaging employees and creating the conditions in which they are more likely to be motivated and enabled to make sustainable change is also likely to be an ongoing process.

Steps 1, 2, 3, and 4 constitute Section I, the "Start It" section. In this first section, we'll explore the key elements to starting Workplace Wellness That Works in an organization. Steps 5 and 6 constitute Section II, the "Build It" section. In this second section, we'll explore the building blocks of effective workplace wellness programs. Steps 7, 8, 9, and 10 constitute Section III, the "Make It Last" section. In this final section, we'll examine what it takes to make wellness an integral and lasting part of a workplace.

Together, these steps will lay the groundwork for Workplace Wellness That Works, and maybe even, perhaps, enable the voices of Aristotle, Victor Frankl, Pablo Neruda, and Lady Gaga to sing in one of the most central parts of our lives—the workplace. Like these artists, however, I encourage you to be creative in how you apply these steps. They are a series of notes and rhythms that can be arranged and rearranged in order to create the best harmony for your particular audience.

Section I

START IT (WORKPLACE WELLNESS THAT EXCITES)

Our first four steps focus on how to *start* a wellness movement in your organization.

Step 1: Shift Your Mind-Set from Expert to Agent of Change discusses how the movement starts with *you*. This step helps you explore new ways to expand your wellness leadership skills by becoming an agent of change. As an agent of change, you'll have a better shot at influencing other leaders in the organization. But even if you're "going solo," you'll have the tools to spark a bottom-up wellness movement in your organization.

Step 2: Imagine What's Possible discusses how to leverage the power of Maslow, a psychologist who dared to imagine what could be. With this paradigm in place, you can transition the conversation from just physical health to one about well-being and living a life of vitality. This chapter will help you bring a powerful vision and sense of purpose to your wellness movement, both critical elements to building effective workplace wellness.

Step 3: Uncover the Hidden Factors helps you better understand the *organizational culture* you're working in. This chapter helps you identify the inherent strengths in the culture of your organization, as well as the elements that may undermine your efforts. With this knowledge, you'll have the tools to implement a wellness movement that fits the culture, which research shows is an essential component of any long-term and sustainable workplace initiative.

Step 4: Start with What's Right offers an overview on how to build wellness momentum with *positive energy*, empowering people to begin with an optimistic mind-set. We'll discuss how you can apply a strengths-based approach, as opposed to a deficit-based approach. With optimism as the foundation, you'll have a solid and far more successful platform for initiating your wellness movement.

STEP 1

Shift Your Mind-Set from Expert to Agent of Change

(The Changemaker Imperative)

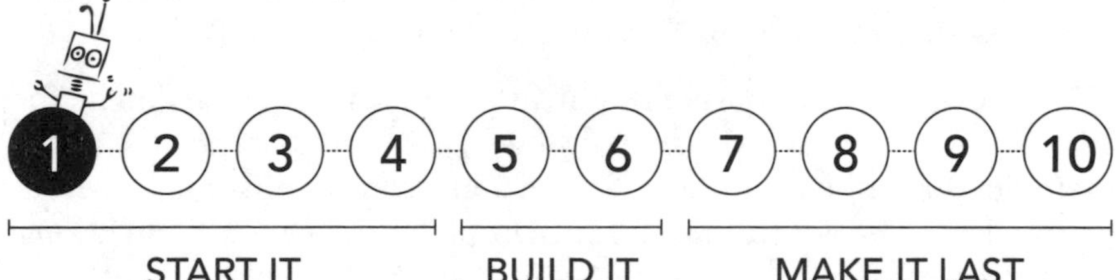

What do Oprah Winfrey, Morgan Spurlock, and Michael Pollan have in common? All three are agents of change, and none of them is an expert on health. Without any special credentials in nutrition, exercise physiology, or even psychology, all of them have influenced the choices of millions of people in the area of health and well-being. All three have set movements in motion.

Oprah is one of the most influential people in America today. A talk show host, actress, and philanthropist, she has an uncanny ability to influence the choices of millions of people around the world, whether it's what books to read, which diets to consider, or which leaders to believe in. In a 1998 PBS NewsHour broadcast, for example, Oprah spoke candidly about the risks of eating beef, exclaiming, "It has just stopped me cold from eating another burger!" This one interview, disgruntled cattlemen claimed, led to the lowest dip in cattle prices in a 10-year period.[1]

Morgan Spurlock, documentary filmmaker and activist, charmed and activated us in his irreverent 2004 documentary *Super Size Me*. Galvanized by a failed lawsuit against McDonald's, Spurlock took action outside of the courtroom, waging his own campaign against the megacorporation. In his film, Spurlock led viewers on his odyssey of a super-sized McDonald's-only diet, a regimen of physical activity restricted to fewer than 5,000 steps a day, and visits with health professionals to measure the effects—all to illustrate the deleterious effects of fast food.

At the beginning of the film, doctors laughed at his idea. Within less than a month, however, Spurlock gained 24½ pounds; his cholesterol jumped to 230; and he developed the beginning stages of fatty liver condition. The same doctors who had laughed were now begging him to discontinue immediately or risk losing his liver.

Although it took Spurlock 14 months to lose the weight he had gained, his unhealthy stunt was an enormous success. The film won best documentary at the Sundance Film Festival, was nominated for an Academy Award, and six weeks after the debut of the film, McDonald's removed super-sized items from their menu.

Michael Pollan, journalist and author of several books, including *The Omnivore's Dilemma*, *In Defense of Food*, and *Cooked*, is another example of an unlikely leader of health and wellness. His simple, seven-word advice has gotten more play than perhaps any other nutritional advice out today: "Eat food, not too much, mostly plants."[2] It's not unusual to see experts like Dean Ornish, world-renowned cardiologist and founder of the Preventative Medicine Research Institute, quoting his line regularly in his talks, or to see scientists at the Centers for Disease Control and Prevention spilling into an overcrowded theater to hear Pollan himself recite these same seven words.

How are these *nonexperts* having more of an influence on our wellness choices than *experts* with their slew of scary statistics and depressing data? Each of these nonexperts is an agent of change, and we need more agents of change to turn the tide on our rising health care and well-being challenges. Without a doubt, we need experts, we need research to move the field forward, and we need to take an evidence-based approach toward health promotion. But we also need to augment this expertise with an *activist*-based approach to health promotion.

Experts speak to our brains and tend to overload us with facts—using scary statistics and depressing data. Agents of change, on the other hand, speak to our hearts—and they *move* us. In the words of Seth Godin, best-selling author and marketing expert, "It's not about being the smart guy in the room; it's about making things happen."[3] We need to speak to people's hearts and *move* people to inspire widespread and sustainable change in wellness. This is why your first step in starting your movement will be to shift your mind-set from just being the expert to becoming an agent of change.

In this chapter, we'll discuss:

1. The key elements of being an agent of change,
2. Preparing for the challenges that you will face in getting your movement started,
3. How wellness movements can get started—top down and bottom up,
4. Obtaining leadership support—by devising a business case and an *emotional* case, and
5. Building bottom-up support.

YOUR STEP 1 CHECKLIST

- ☐ Build your story bank.
- ☐ Sharpen your changemaker edge.
- ☐ Form your core action team.
- ☐ Make the case—both logical and *emotional*—for your wellness movement.
- ☐ Issue an initial call to action—to leaders *and* employees.

FROM EXPERT TO AGENT OF CHANGE

In the opening of his most recent book *Eat Move Sleep*, best-selling author Tom Rath clarifies that he is *not* the expert. "Let me be clear, I am not a doctor. Nor am I an expert on nutrition, exercise physiology, or sleep disorders."[4] And yet he's writing a book on eating, physical activity, and sleep—and loads of people are buying the book. Why? Because he's an agent of change with a cause that people—lots of people—want to be part of. Beginning with his personal story of a life-threatening health challenge, Rath confides that he, like his readers, is a patient—and he's on a quest to find the right answers on how to build a life of vitality, one small step at a time. He asks us (the readers) to join him in this movement.

In his book *Leading Minds: An Anatomy of Leadership*, Howard Gardner, educational psychologist at Harvard University, provides an academic perspective on this important notion of expert versus agent of change. By examining the traits of leaders such as Margaret Mead, Martin Luther King, Jr., and J. Robert Oppenheimer—he identifies each as either a domain-specific or a general leader. Very simply, a domain-specific leader embodies characteristics associated with an expert, a leader within their field, while a general leader manifests elements of being an agent of change, a leader who transcends their domain to reach a broader audience. Gardner describes how Margaret Mead, a leading anthropologist, shifted from being an expert known and respected within her field to becoming a household name. She made this transition by adopting characteristics of an agent of change.

YOUR NUMBER ONE JOB

Regardless of what's in your job description or the task that's been assigned to you, whether you're internal to the organization or external, your number one job will be to persuade and influence. In other words, you'll need to be an agent of change.

Framing your efforts as a movement is a great way to win the hearts and minds of both decision makers and employees. Chesapeake Energy, an Oklahoma City-based energy company, is refreshing its wellness platform, moving from the classic model to a "Join the Movement" model, which emphasizes intrinsic motivation, focus on culture, and a more interdisciplinary and collaborative approach to wellness. When Amanda Parsons, employee health analyst, presented the new platform to the senior leaders, the response was supportive. She successfully accomplished getting buy-in from the top, in part by connecting wellness to a higher purpose in addition to business relevancy. These elements are both critical, as we will discuss shortly.

Starting a movement begins with *you*, meaning that you need to be thinking about what it takes to lead change within your organization. It's no coincidence, therefore, that Leslie Ritter, head of the well-being initiative at Eileen Fisher, a New York City-based fashion company, has the title of "wellness leader." Regardless of your title, your mind-set needs to shift to being a leader and an agent of change.

ELEMENTS OF BEING AN AGENT OF CHANGE

Let's break down what's actually involved in becoming a changemaker.

1. **Agents of change know their why.** Leaders who move us have a deep sense of purpose and a deep sense of conviction. *They know their why*. When they model this, they encourage others to do the same, and they create a ripple effect of change in their wake. The clearer you are about your personal why—why you do what you do and what moves you on the deepest level—the more people will want to follow you.

   Shane Valentine, chef and activist, models leadership that starts with his personal why. He's leading Kids Cook with Heart, an American Heart Association program that's teaching and inspiring kids and teens to cook healthy meals. Under his leadership, the program now reaches over 4,000 kids and teens. Valentine's why is a startling statistic: So few kids in America are meeting the American Heart Association's Simple Seven criteria for a healthy heart that the total number is statistically equivalent to *zero*. The breakdown? Unhealthy diet.[5] When he shares his why, he inspires others to join him in his movement to "cook with heart" in a way that data alone never could.

2. **Agents of change speak to the heart.** Agents of change are emotional geniuses; they value emotional quotient (EQ) over intelligence quotient (IQ). And they're right to do so. According to Daniel Goleman, author of *Emotional Intelligence*, "After analyzing 181 competence models from 121 organizations worldwide, we found that 67 percent of the abilities deemed essential for effective performance were emotional competencies. Compared to IQ and expertise, emotional competence mattered twice as much."[6]

   Any marketing and advertising professional knows that we buy with our hearts and later justify with our minds. Perhaps one of the greatest examples of how much an emotionally charged advertisement can shape our choices is the MasterCard "Priceless" commercial that first aired during the 1997 World Series. This campaign single-handedly catapulted MasterCard from a distant second to neck and neck with Visa.

   Jonathan Haidt, psychologist and author of *The Happiness Hypothesis*, originally proposed the metaphor of the "rider" and the "elephant" to help illustrate the power of our emotional side over our thinking side. When making a change—or trying to influence others to make a change—we cannot speak only to the rider (our thinking side), and ignore the much larger elephant (our emotional side). Whether it's change on an individual level, a team level, or an organizational level, we need to get the elephant on board first. Only after the elephant is on board can we "direct the rider." If we don't have the elephant on board first, it'll be an uphill battle from the start.

3. **Agents of change are great communicators.** Motivating the elephant—and gaining this emotional buy-in—starts with being a great communicator. Agents of change deliver compelling messages that we want to follow, and these messages are often short, exceedingly simple, and filled with metaphors. In his memorable "I Have a Dream" speech, Martin Luther King, Jr. moved his listeners through metaphors like "Let freedom ring" in lieu of statistics. Communicators also create powerful *experiences* for their followers, usually in the form of stories.

   This means that agents of change need to master the art of storytelling and, more important, *value* stories over statistics. "Stories are just data with a soul," said Brené Brown, speaker and author.[7] As leader of a wellness movement, you're now in the business of persuasion, and storytelling is one of the most powerful ways to wield influence.

   Bill Baun, longtime leader in the field of workplace wellness and wellness officer at MD Anderson Cancer Center, a Houston-based medical center, always leads through storytelling. In delivering talks around the world and in moving people and organizations to embrace wellness, he shares stories, including his own as a cancer survivor. He understands that a movement starts with the heart.

   Researchers like Uri Hasson at Princeton University have studied the science behind what storytelling does to the listener's brain. Hasson's research has shown that when we hear compelling stories, parts of our brain actually light up in brain scans (that would not light up with statistics alone). This leads to what Hasson refers to as "brain to brain coupling" (between storyteller and listener).[7] To get people on board with the wellness movement you're starting, you'll want to catalyze brain to brain coupling. Good storytelling is the only way to make this happen.

Action Item

Story Bank

Build your story bank. I always encourage wellness leaders to recall stories, keep a tally of these stories, and use these to build a story bank. These stories—much more than the statistics—are what will move people.

4. **Agents of change embody their stories.** "It is important that a leader be a good storyteller but equally crucial that the leader embody that story in his or her life," writes Gardner.[8] This means that as the leader of a wellness movement, you're going to need to take action in your own well-being. This is exactly what Arianna Huffington did. After collapsing in her office due to exhaustion, Huffington made a commitment to always get a good night's sleep. Success, as she now defines it in her most recent book *Thrive*, is more than just money and power. Rather, the "third metric" of success encompasses well-being, wisdom, wonder, and giving back.[9] Huffington's sharing and embodiment of her story is what awakens and activates others to follow her movement.
5. **Agents of change do whatever it takes.** Chade-Meng Tan, Google employee turned Nobel Peace Prize nominee, anointed himself "Jolly Good Fellow" and volunteered himself as the official greeter at Google. U.S. Rep. Earl Blumenauer has been known to dress up in a chicken suit and deliver stand-up comedy. And, Oprah boldly danced onstage with Tina Turner for 5 minutes and 27 seconds. Becoming an agent of change requires great courage, and doing whatever it takes to move people to join your movement.
6. **Agents of change don't wait for permission.** Agents of change do whatever it takes to make a difference, and they

don't wait for permission. This is perhaps the most critical component to becoming an effective agent of change. The classic model for workplace wellness calls for obtaining senior leader support first, but as an agent of change, you can start a movement *without* waiting for permission. Spark a bottom-up movement that builds more organically (perhaps one team at a time), nurture it so that it gains momentum, and *then* bring senior leaders on board.

Malala Yousafzai, recent recipient of the Nobel Peace Prize, didn't wait. She stood up to the Taliban and in doing so started a worldwide movement to support girls' education. Vivienne Harr, founder of Make a Stand, also didn't wait for permission, nor was she deterred by what most would see as a barrier: her age. At the tender age of nine, she started her own nonprofit—or "giveness" (as opposed to business)—with the goal to end child slavery. She set up a lemonade stand and asked people to give "what was in their hearts." Within six months, she successfully raised over $100,000. In her view, being an effective agent of change requires "thinking like a kid."[10,11]

To follow in the footsteps of change agents like Oprah Winfrey, Morgan Spurlock, and Michael Pollan, you'll need to do the following: (1) be very clear about your personal why, (2) hook people on an emotional level first, (3) communicate your message through metaphors and stories, (4) embody your message, (5) do whatever it takes, and (6) most importantly, don't wait for permission.

ACTION ITEM

8 ACTIVITIES TO SHARPEN YOUR CHANGEMAKER EDGE

1. Ask yourself, "What is my why?" While words are good, often images are better. I suggest you use images or creative instruments like colored chalk or markers or even crayons. Try writing out your why on a chalkboard, and then ask a friend to take a picture.

2. The next time an employee asks for advice, consider responding with a compelling question. Instead of telling people what to do, help people to find *their* why.
3. Instead of "selling" leaders, managers, and employees on wellness, design *experiences* for them. Experiences move people, as we saw with the ALS Ice Bucket Campaign. By simply tying the ask (for a donation) with a dare to dump a bucket of ice water over one's head, the ALS Association tripled its annual fundraising to the tune of $115 million.[12]
4. Remember that becoming an agent of change is a process. Everyone has it within them to become a powerful agent of change. You are no exception.
5. Being an agent of change means finding and sharing your voice. Channel Rep. Blumenauer to explore creative—even outlandish—ways to share your voice. What will be your version of dressing up in a chicken suit to deliver a stand-up comedy act?
6. Stop gathering statistics and start collecting stories. Buy a notebook, label it "My Story Bank," and get started!
7. Instead of themes, organize campaigns around big questions.
8. Use metaphors to light the fire for your movement. Metaphors like "placing the oxygen mask on yourself before your child" help leaders to understand better why their personal well-being matters so much to their people.

GET READY FOR A CHALLENGE

Let's be clear, leading a wellness movement is not for the faint of heart. You'll have lots of hurdles to clear, and here are some that you can expect:

- **Buy-in from decision makers:** To have a broad impact, it's vital that decision makers see the value of investing in employee health and well-being. Your challenge will be to win their support.

- **Management engagement:** Leaders and middle managers may support wellness, but it's best if they actually participate in the wellness programs. Your challenge will be to empower them to take part.
- **Employee engagement:** The more engaged the employees are, the more likely they are to participate. Your challenge will be to create the conditions in which employees are likely to motivate themselves, feel inspired, perceive value in well-being, and authentically commit to their own health and well-being—as well as the well-being of others.
- **Culture:** A healthy, vibrant culture will buoy your wellness movement. Your challenge will be to slowly build a culture that supports well-being and makes it "okay" to take part in wellness activities.
- **Environment:** The environment creates the opportunity—or lack thereof. Your challenge will be to help build an environment that makes it easy to invest in one's health and well-being.
- **Accountability:** You'll need the right mix of accountability (on both sides—organization and individuals). Your challenge will be to build this over time.
- **Changing behaviors:** Behavior change is what many consider to be the Holy Grail of workplace wellness. Your challenge will be to build a strategy and devise programs that actually move employees, managers, and leaders to form new well-being habits.

ACTION ITEM

FORM YOUR CORE ACTION TEAM

To help you to navigate these challenges, pull together your inner circle. Who are one or two others within your organization who can join with you to form a "core action team" to start the movement?

WELLNESS MOVEMENTS CAN START AT THE TOP

Yvon Chouinard, founder of Patagonia, issued a call to "Let My People Go Surfing," stirring a movement within his organization, daring other companies to follow, while laying the foundation for an organization that is built on well-being and vitality.

The Cleveland Clinic's best-in-class Total Care Wellness Program is the embodiment of another movement that started at the top. The program is based on an ethos of belief: belief that change is possible for every individual and that these changes can happen as a result of workplace wellness. To reinforce this ethos, every month in an address that goes out to all 43,000 employees, CEO Toby Cosgrove highlights stories of coworkers who have transformed their lives by taking part in the company's wellness program.

These monthly talks are part of a larger strategy, primarily led by chief wellness officer Michael Roizen that emphasizes supportive culture and environment, quality programming, and incentives. Since 2008, over 3,000 employees have registered to participate in the on-site yoga classes, over 30,000 employees have enrolled in the online coaching program focused on healthy eating and weight maintenance, and an average of 30,000 visits are made every month to the on-site fitness center. In 2013, the company's health care costs actually went down by 0.6 percent.[13]

Nintendo, a multinational consumer electronics company, is another example of an organization with a wellness movement that started at the top.

THE STORY OF NINTENDO

"All you need is at least one person who is willing to champion it," Flip Morse, senior vice president of corporate resources of Nintendo, a leading electronic entertainment company, explains about his company's wellness program.

(*continued*)

(*continued*)

"It only takes one executive who is at a high enough level to influence policy. And you need to have an executive team that either supports it, as we have at Nintendo, or, at the very least, will not resist it."

The key piece here is that Flip and his fellow Nintendo executives *believe* in wellness—and they recognize it as a value, as opposed to a transactional equation. "Not only is wellness the right thing to do—employees are happier, they're more productive, they show up more regularly for work. But also from strictly a financial perspective, it's crazy not to offer it," he says. "You can pay a lot of money to consultants for teambuilding, or you can go to one of [our] events, where . . . employees are riding or running together, standing together in a tent talking about road conditions, having conversations you'd never have otherwise with coworkers in a work setting. You're all the healthier for it, and the next time you see them at work, you have a new bond with them."

Here are some of the ways that Nintendo's commitment to wellness has paid off:

- 94 percent of its workforce declare themselves to be tobacco-free.
- Of the 6 percent that admitted to using tobacco, two-thirds of them elected to enroll in a tobacco cessation program.
- Of those that chose to enroll, about 25 percent were successful in quitting tobacco use.

Source: Flip Morse, interview with author, October 31, 2014.

For Nintendo, Patagonia, and the Cleveland Clinic, investing in wellness is more than just a program; it's a movement. It's more than numbers; it's a belief system that encompasses a way of being at work and in the community.

WELLNESS MOVEMENTS DON'T ALWAYS START AT THE TOP

While it certainly makes it a lot easier if the leader of the movement is a CEO, company founder, or member of the executive team, the truth is that *anyone* within an organization can spark a wellness movement.

Bill Baun, wellness officer at MD Anderson Cancer Center, describes a bottom-up movement he witnessed in one organization. A group of employees organized a pickup basketball game during lunchtime. This was their idea and they certainly hadn't asked for permission. Over time, this lunchtime activity gained momentum—and eventually caught the attention of senior managers. Inspired by what they saw, the senior managers took the initiative to build a gym to encourage these employees to keep playing basketball and to support others in getting active during lunchtime.

At Schindler Elevator Corporation, a leading global manufacturer of elevators, escalators and moving walks, another bottom-up wellness movement is taking hold.

THE SCHINDLER STORY

Julie Shipley, manager of general training at Schindler Elevator Corporation, hatched an innovative idea to incorporate well-being into a leadership-training workshop for the leading managers in the company. Naming it "Leadership Odyssey," Julie wanted every participating manager to embark upon a personal journey of well-being and understand how this connects with what it means to be an effective leader.

To make it happen, she started a movement and then began building it. She got her immediate supervisor on board, Mike Yurchuk, director of organization development, along with the vice president of human resources. Then she asked our company, Motion Infusion, to help out. In a collaborative and participatory

(*continued*)

(*continued*)

fashion, all of us worked together to build a two-day leadership-training workshop. The workshop combined personal well-being experiences, such as yoga, walking meetings, and well-being self-assessments with leadership development and culture change training.

This workshop single-handedly started a movement. Says Mike, "I never experienced something like this in any program or any type of work experience. I think my expectations were that people would gain another perspective, but I never expected that people would believe in it to the point where they would become agents of change."

What Julie started was not just another program. Rather, it was a *movement* that continues to grow. Participants are sharing success stories on an ongoing basis, many are leading their teams in stretches or encouraging walking meetings, and some are now using standing desks. They're encouraging team members to invest in rebuilding their energy, and they're engaging in deeper conversations about emotional and social well-being. Most importantly, all of the managers now look at their team members through the lens of well-being—and this has shaped how they now lead their teams.

The vice president of health and safety at Schindler recently "got the bug" and requested the same workshop, but geared toward his team of safety area managers. Following the workshop, called "Safety Odyssey," each of these managers, in turn, has gone on to build a movement within *their* respective teams. It's even spreading internationally, with some global offices starting similar wellness movements. What we see here is a great example of the power of a *bottom-up* movement, sparked by one person's idea, that is working its way up and infusing itself into the fabric of the organization.

Source: Julie Shipley and Mike Yurchuk, interview with author, December 12, 2014.

MAKING YOUR CASE

Whether your movement is top-down or bottom-up, at some point, you're going to need to make a compelling case to leaders as to why the organization should invest in workplace wellness.

Let's now look at the nuts and bolts of building your case. Below are some strategies you can employ that will help you to move leaders beyond the singular, cost-oriented return on investment (ROI) mind-set to see the bigger picture and value of workplace wellness.

Strategy 1: Focus on the costs *beneath* the surface. Quantifying direct reductions in health care costs generated by wellness programs is notoriously difficult, especially when the program is in its infancy. It turns out, however, that there are much greater costs—and opportunities for savings—*beneath* the surface. The indirect costs related to poor health and diminished well-being include absenteeism, disability, and presenteeism—all resulting in a net loss in productivity.

One study showed that absenteeism due to disability and illness is costing the U.S. economy about $468 billion annually.[14] The biggest cost, however, is what's called "presenteeism," which means showing up in body but not being fully present. There's an abundance of evidence to suggest that the costs of presenteeism (due to distractions from illness or disability) are higher than the costs of absenteeism (due to illness or disability). In other words, it costs the company more money to have checked-out employees come to work than if they were to just stay at home![15]

According to a study conducted at Bank One, direct medical and pharmaceutical costs to a company only account for 24 percent of total costs associated with employee poor health. On the other hand, presenteeism costs account for a whopping 63 percent of total costs to the organization.[16] A recent study found that almost a quarter of employees are reporting that they're not fully present on the job due to chronic illness, adding up to 2.5 billion impaired days per year in the United States.[17]

Your job will be to help senior leaders make the connection between employee well-being and productivity at work—and that direct health care costs are only the tip of the iceberg.

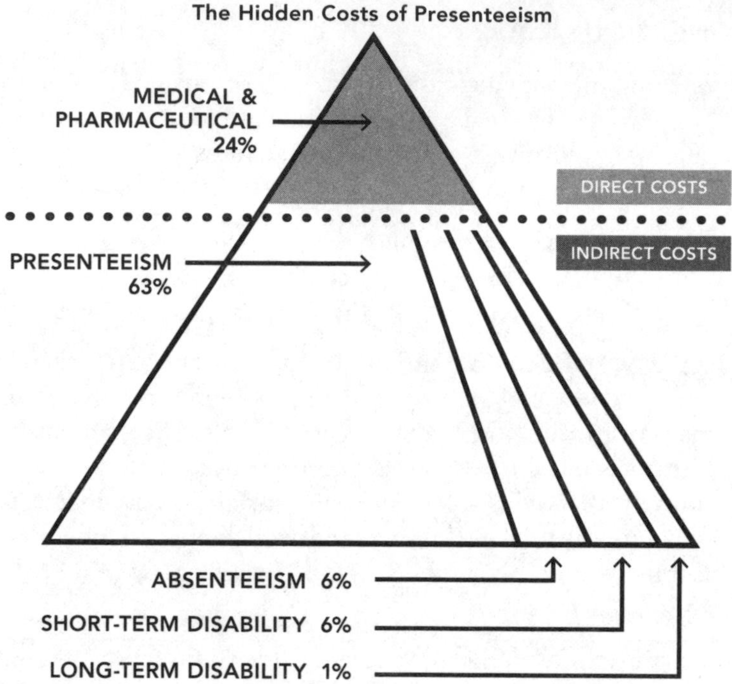

Source: Bank One. Adapted and reprinted with permission from "Presenteeism: At Work–But Out of It," by Paul Hemp. *Harvard Business Review*, 2004. Copyright 2004 by Harvard Business Publishing; all rights reserved.

Strategy 2: Focus on the *value* instead of return on investment. Given the controversy of the ROI conversation, there is now a shift toward presenting the "value proposition" of wellness, or "value on investment" (VOI). The latter focuses more on the broader benefits—and doing something that's good for employees. Wellness, particularly a more holistic *well-being* platform, can help to build a thriving, vibrant workplace that boosts morale, fosters engagement, enhances human performance, and attracts and retains top talent. An increasing number of workers, especially millennials, now *expect* potential employers to care about them—and this includes offering workplace wellness.

While these broader benefits are more difficult to measure, this value-based rationale for workplace wellness can help to create a better culture around the program itself. This enhanced culture, in turn, can increase the likelihood of employees' authentic engagement with the wellness offerings. If an organization's primary focus is on ROI (doing what's good for shareholders), employees are likely to feel that any workplace wellness program is something that is being "done *to*" them.

Focusing more on the *value* of wellness, on the other hand, can make workplace wellness feel like something that is being "done *for*" employees. Generating this perception is absolutely critical for sustainability.

Strategy 3: Build a business case based on specific organizational needs. Every organization has different needs. Key to your success in winning over top management support is tailoring the message to fit the core objectives of your organization. Celina Pagani-Tousignant, president and founder of Normisur International, a global consulting firm that specializes in corporate social responsibility, and Asako Tsumagari, founder and CEO of MEvident, a wellness services provider, suggest applying a four-part "Value Creation Framework,"[18] developed by McKinsey & Company and the Boston College Center for Corporate Citizenship, to build a case for workplace wellness based on organizational need.

Value Creation Framework

Marketing Creation (focus on innovation and launching new products)	Efficiency in Operations (focus on efficiency and cost containment)
Risk Management (focus on safety)	Leadership Quality (focus on leadership development and retention)

Source: Adapted from Value Creation Framework chart, created by Celina Pagani-Tousignant and Asako Tsumagari in "Designing an Effective Corporate Wellness Strategy." Used with permission.

Companies, like Safeway, a national supermarket chain, that are operating at a relatively low profit margin, are most concerned about operational efficiency and cost containment. With this kind of company, you'll need to focus on increased productivity (to enhance efficiency) and containing medical and workers compensation costs. Companies like Con Edison, a utility company based in New York, on the other hand, are largely focused on risk mitigation. With this kind of company, you'll need to demonstrate the connection between wellness and safety. Companies like Google are generating a much higher profit margin per employee. Therefore, their focus is less on containing medical and workers compensation costs and more on innovation and launching new products. They're looking to wellness as a way to help spark collaboration, creativity, and energy. Finally, companies like

Cisco Systems, a multinational company specializing in networking equipment, are focused on developing leaders over the long term. In a case like Cisco, you'd be wise to focus on talent attraction and retention.[19] In general, for companies that have a younger demographic and are in an industry where they are competing for talent, attraction and retention is a huge selling point to senior leaders.

Strategy 4: Make the emotional case. Up to this point, we've focused on cost-benefit analyses for gaining decision makers' support for a wellness movement. Let's not forget, however, that even CEOs and CFOs are moved by their hearts, not just by logic. In fact, I would argue that each is moved just as much, if not *more*, by the heart. That's why it's critical to make an effective business case *and* an effective *emotional* case. The best way to make the emotional case is through stories—particularly stories specific to the organization.

TIP: HOW TO RALLY THE LEADERS

You need to show leaders that workplace wellness is both the right thing to do (appeal to the heart) and the smart thing to do (appeal to the brain).

Strategy 5: Connect wellness with a higher purpose. A singular focus on ROI is only part of the picture and misses the larger point—namely, making a difference in people's lives. Investing in workplace wellness is about *doing the right thing*. According to Dee Edington, longtime leader in the field and author of *Zero Trends*, "We [wellness providers] were forced into making the ROI proposition to get decision makers on board with health promotion in the workplace."[20] Fortunately, this is changing.

Robert Safian, editor and managing director of *Fast Company*, writes about "a rising breed of business leaders who are animated not just by money but by the pursuit of a larger societal purpose."[21] Mission-driven companies like Patagonia are increasingly becoming the norm. You can ride this wave to lift your call for workplace wellness to a higher purpose.

Ultimately, workplace wellness is about people, not just costs, and an increasing number of leaders are catching on to this. For leaders like Jamie Dimon, throat cancer survivor and CEO of JPMorgan Chase, workplace wellness comes from the heart and is about doing the right thing. In a recent memo, he reminded his employees, "As always, and especially since my diagnosis, I followed the advice I give to others—take care of your health first—nothing is more important."[22]

CHECKLIST TO BUILD YOUR CASE

To help organize your thoughts, below are some prompts to get you started on building both the logical and emotional case for your movement.

Your personal why:

How this initiative builds on your why:

Your organization's mission:

How this initiative supports the mission:

Your organization's values:

How this initiative supports the organization's values:

Your organization's core business objectives:

How this initiative supports these core business objectives:

What people want:

How this initiative supports these wants:

What people need:

How this initiative supports these needs:

The *logical* case for the initiative:

The *emotional* case for the initiative:

SPARK "MINI-MOVEMENTS"

Finally, you want to think about how you can generate a widespread movement, sparked by a series of "mini-movements." One tool that has gotten a bad rap in workplace wellness is the good old-fashioned lunch 'n' learn. As a former teacher, I always bristle when I hear that education doesn't work when it comes to changing behaviors. The truth is that *good* education can work. *Bad* education, on the other hand, doesn't work—and that's what I've seen in most lunch 'n' learns. Below is a classic example of bad education in action.

THE STORY ON HEALTHY AGING FOR WOMEN

I was asked by a nonprofit organization that supports women entering and reentering the workforce to deliver a talk for their clients on the topic, "Healthy Aging for Women." This was part of a yearlong "Love Your Body" campaign. A couple of weeks before the presentation, the organizer sent me a prepared slide deck on the topic. "Here's a PowerPoint you can use for your talk," she explained. The presentation was packed with all kinds of scary statistics: leading causes of death, number of older women living with a chronic condition, number of older women with skin disorders, number of older women who are depressed. The slides continued with an array of all kinds of terrible things to expect with aging: hardening arteries, creaky joints, saggy skin and lots of wrinkles, liver spots, shrinking bone structure, impaired memory. Ugh! The underlying message was, "Shoot me now!" Finally, at the very end, after a download of demoralizing data, the presentation issued a call to action: "Make the right choices."

Just reading through the slides was enough to make me feel like *I* needed a drink. The presentation painted a bleak future; it certainly didn't motivate me to "make the right choices." This slide deck was not prepared by agents of change; it was prepared by agents of terror!

A lunch 'n' learn done well, on the other hand, *can* inspire change and pave the way for a mini-movement. In one case, I delivered a lunch 'n' learn for a large insurance company that was in the beginning stages of launching a wellness program. Before my talk, the wellness coordinator confessed that she was having difficulty recruiting employees to join the newly formed wellness committee. Only three had volunteered up to that point. During my ensuing talk, I issued a call to act: Join the wellness committee. One week later, the wellness coordinator called to tell me that 26 had committed to join!

Recently, I delivered a lunch 'n' learn called "Please, *Don't* Have a Seat!" at the Kimpton Hotels & Restaurants headquarters. Following the presentation, an inspired participant, Whitney Smith, created her own makeshift standing workstation in the middle of the common area. When curious coworkers asked why, she shared, "I just learned about the benefits of sitting less, so I'm standing more and already feel a lot better!" Her bold mini-movement is now inspiring others to get out of their chairs and build their own standing workstations.

Your goal is to move people, and there's nothing wrong with explicitly calling this out. In fact, I often start my lunch 'n' learns with the advice: "What I say doesn't matter. All that matters is what you actually *do* when you walk out the door at the end of the session." Inspire and give people the tools to engage with the movement once they walk out the door. This means delivering key calls to action, crafting a message, and delivering it in a way that's emotionally compelling.

To reinforce this call to act, I usually end my lunch 'n' learns with a reminder that each of us can be an agent of change, and in fact, we already are. Every one of us is part of a social network, and within this network, every personal choice we make can spark a social contagion effect, or ripple effect. Our habits influence our friends, our friends' friends, and even our friends' friends' friends![23]

To bring meaning to this phenomenon, I often ask participants to recall Kennedy's speech in which he urged us to "ask not what your country can do for you—ask what you can do for your country." One of the very best things that each of us can do, I tell my listeners, for ourselves, our friends, our families, our coworkers, our communities, our country, and even for our world, is to begin with ourselves and simply make better choices. In issuing this reminder, I am asking each of the participants to join me in "being the change" to change the world, one mini-movement at a time.

Simple Tips to Build a Better Lunch 'n' Learn:

1. **Create an emotional experience.** It's always much more powerful to open with an emotional hook—a story, a video

(*continued*)

(*continued*)

clip, even a movement-based or interactive activity—that builds empathy and emotional engagement.

2. **Less is more.** Remember that your goal is to inspire people to take action. The point is not to deliver a boring health lesson, with lots of frightening facts and boring statistics. Don't go overboard on data, or you will quickly lose your audience.
3. **Issue a call to act.** I'm always surprised at how long it often takes lunch 'n' learn speakers to get to the point. Many times, they wallow in information overload. Don't make that mistake. Issue the call to act right away, frame it in language that inspires action, and repeat it throughout the lunch 'n' learn. Just like your goal is to be an agent of change, encourage participants to also feel empowered as agents of change.
4. **Encourage social activism.** It's helpful to use titles like "Stand Up for Being the Change." Remind participants that their personal choices are actually not so personal. For some people, investing in their health and well-being feels selfish. Remind them that it's just the opposite. Behaviors spread like viruses through social networks, so every time we make a positive choice, we're positively influencing the choices of friends, friends' friends, and even friends' friends' friends.
5. **Give them something to do.** Less information means more time for interaction. If you want to increase the likelihood of generating change, you need to create more opportunities for participants to make sense of the material on their own terms. This means less lecturing and more doing. Provide time for participants to draw from their own experiences and their own knowledge base through small group work.
6. **Be a coach.** Step out of trying to be the expert and source of all information. Think more about *facilitating* a learning process. A great coach is someone who not only delivers information, but also creates emotional hooks to motivate and

inspire. This means asking more questions and encouraging participants to learn from one another and from themselves, not only from you.

Final Thoughts

Being an agent of change is not just about delivering information and demonstrating expertise; it's about moving people and giving them the tools to transform themselves. While you certainly want to get up to speed on the latest research and best practices in the field of workplace wellness, you also want to think about how you can adopt the elements of a changemaker. Beginning with your personal why, your task is to courageously move forward with sparking a movement of well-being within your organization. Stories and emotional connections are what will lend persuasion to your call to action.

Step 2

Imagine What's Possible

(The Imagination Imperative)

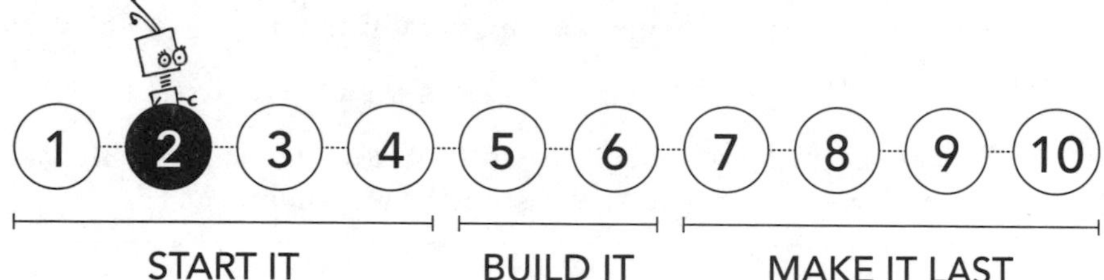

In 2014, the Seattle Seahawks won their first Super Bowl title. The real story behind the headlines was Mike Gervais, the team's sports psychologist. To inspire peak performance, Gervais began every initial conversation with the question, "What's possible?" Then he worked with each player and coach to develop a practice of mindfulness, helping each to shift from seeking *the* moment (of a winning play) to being in *every* moment. In a talk at the 2014 Wisdom 2.0 Conference, the interviewer asked Gervais, "How do you know when the players are actually getting it?" Gervais hesitated for a brief moment and then shared the story of a large defensive player who made a fantastic play. The player stormed off the field, ran up to Gervais, and shouted, "THAT'S what I'm f'ing talkin' about!"

Agents of change imagine what's possible—and then paint a picture of a desired future state that's worth working toward. This is exactly what you need to do in conceptualizing and leading the wellness movement within your organization.

In this chapter, we'll discuss:

1. Creating a vision for what's possible,

2. Abraham Maslow, an early pioneer in focusing on what's possible over what's wrong,
3. Leveraging Maslow to move workplace wellness beyond "health,"
4. Research showing that our health is more than a physical checkup, and
5. The multiple dimensions of well-being.

YOUR STEP 2 CHECKLIST

- ☐ Create the vision for your wellness movement.
- ☐ Identify the key well-being elements for your movement.
- ☐ Create a tracking system to ensure that your programs address your identified dimensions of well-being.

CREATE THE VISION FOR THE MOVEMENT

In Step 1: Shift Your Mind-Set from Expert to Agent of Change, you identified your personal why. Now, let's take it a step further. What's the why behind your *wellness movement*? A compelling why usually stems from an inspiring vision. Creating this vision begins with looking forward, and imagining the myriad of possibilities and benefits that infusing well-being and vitality into your organization could produce. As you create the vision, it's important to stretch your mind beyond "health" and even beyond "wellness." Push yourself to think of a workplace environment where everyone is becoming their best selves and living to their full potential. Imagine what that might look like—for individual employees and for the larger organization.

ACTION ITEM

BUILD A VISION USING IMAGES

Don't overthink the vision. Instead, embrace your creative side. A great way to tap into your creativity is to build a collage of images. Tear out pages from magazines, download images from bigstock.com or istock.com, or ask your organization's marketing department if they have inspiring visuals on hand that you can use. As you and your core action team select images, ask yourselves, "Which images capture what's possible for our organization?" Just go with your gut.

After you've built your collage, add in some words. Words like "inspiration," "freedom," "vitality," or "well-being" might come to mind. You'll notice that in going through this process, you're also starting to create the brand, or identity, for your movement.

Once you've created your collage, post it on a wall and use it to guide you. This process helps you lay the foundation of what's possible for your wellness movement.

EARLY PIONEER IN IMAGINING WHAT'S POSSIBLE

Abraham Maslow was a renegade in the field of psychology. He took the lead in shifting the focus on what's *wrong* with people, to instead focus on what's right—or better yet, what's *possible.* At a time when the field of psychology only valued the study of pathology as opposed to potential, Maslow wasn't interested in schizophrenia, depression, obsessive-compulsive disorder, or other mental disorders. Instead, he was inspired to study *optimal* psychological states.

Maslow was convinced that each of us is born with a desire and ability to reach our full potential. His life-long study focused on exploring what this personal best looked like—and how we could achieve it. He studied Eleanor Roosevelt, Albert Einstein, Frederick Douglass, and others who he felt had achieved or had come close to achieving their full potential. He then developed a roadmap, or hierarchy, of needs required to reach this level of self-actualization.

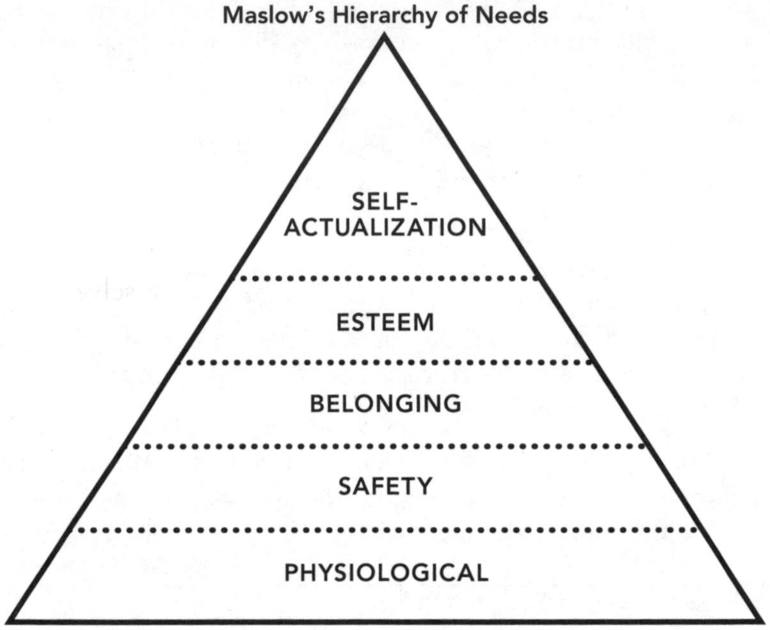

Level 1: An individual has basic survival needs, such as food, water, shelter, rest.

Level 2: Above these basic needs, each individual requires safety and security.

Level 3: Next, every individual wants to belong and be in connection with others.

Level 4: Next, each individual has a need for esteem and a sense of achievement.

Level 5: Finally, each individual has a need for "self-actualization," or reaching one's full potential in life.

VISUALIZING WHAT'S POSSIBLE

When asked how she felt about the upcoming slalom race at the 2014 Winter Olympics, Mikaela Shiffrin, gold medalist, cooly responded, "To everybody, this is my first Olympics. But to me it's my thousandth."[1] In other words, she had *visualized* skiing in the Olympics a thousand times. Great athletes use visualization to win races. We can do the same to win better health and well-being. Ultimately, your goal in this step is to empower employees to visualize what's possible.

This is exactly what Teresa Snyder did with her team.

BECOMING OUR BEST SELVES

Teresa Snyder, team leader of a group within a leading multinational financial institution, decided that she wanted to give her team the tools to fully thrive and become their best selves. She wanted to start from the place of *what's possible.* To do so, she launched what became an award-winning program that combined soft skills training focused on work performance outcomes with well-being programming organized around the principles of Maslow's hierarchy of needs. Her goals were to help a team of hardworking, performance-driven, technically oriented engineers recognize (1) the value of soft skills; (2) the value of investing in self-care; and (3) the connection between the two.

I worked with Teresa to provide the Maslow-inspired, seven-part "Get Vitality" well-being series. Each session served as the kickoff for ensuing soft skills training. The series started with the basics—eat better and move more—and then ascended Maslow's hierarchy of needs to explore higher order needs like resilience, happiness, innovation, and leading with purpose.

One of the key messages throughout was that our personal choices are actually not so personal. Because of the social contagion effect, our choices impact others around us, so each of us is already "being the change." Therefore, by enabling ourselves to become our best selves, we naturally empower others to do the same.

Source: Teresa Snyder, interview with author, December 15, 2014.

LEVERAGE MASLOW TO MOVE BEYOND "HEALTH"

"Good health is a crown worn by the healthy that only the ill can see." This Arabic proverb illustrates a common reality: disease prevention is not inspiring for most—especially for those who are lucky enough to be in good health. On the other hand, fully thriving in life *is* inspiring for most. As long as our health is not immediately in jeopardy, most of us are more focused on other priorities, or higher-order needs like achieving success in our careers, forming meaningful relationships, or even making the world a better place. If we were to look to Maslow's hierarchy of needs, these needs would be considered "higher-order" needs. It turns out that these higher-order needs are actually vital to our health and well-being.

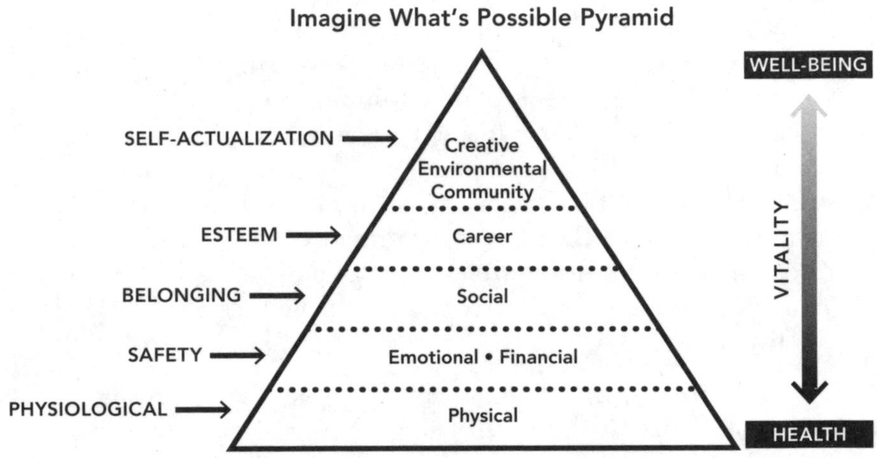

HEALTH IS MORE THAN A PHYSICAL CHECKUP

For many of us, we associate "health" with going to the doctor to get a checkup on a limited battery of factors: "You have high blood pressure. You need to watch your weight. Eat more fruits and vegetables." Rarely is there a conversation about other factors that impact our well-being, such as our jobs, our relationships, or our financial standing. In some cases, we're told that there's nothing wrong with us—and that's the end of the conversation.

When I was living in New York pursuing a career as a dancer, I went to the doctor for an annual checkup. As he wrapped up the appointment, he asked me if there was anything I wanted to discuss. I said, "Yes, I feel really tired. Do you have any suggestions?" He retorted, "Welcome to New York!"—and that was that. Cartoonist Randy Glasbergen sums it up nicely in a cartoon that shows a doctor speaking with a patient: "You have a rare condition called 'good health.' Frankly, I'm not sure how to treat it."

Health, in the full sense of the word, encompasses far more than just the absence of disease. It's more than just eating vegetables and getting enough exercise. Rather, there are multiple factors that play into our health and well-being—and some of them are surprising.

Zip code. There is irrefutable evidence that our zip code matters a lot more than our genetic code. Zip code indicates our socioeconomic bracket, and this plays a big role in our health, life expectancy, well-being, and overall vitality. How long we live and how well we live may be determined by the distance of a couple of subway stops, according to a study commissioned by the Robert Wood Johnson Foundation. As an example, babies born in Washington, D.C., have a shorter life expectancy by *seven years* than babies born in nearby counties. In New Orleans, the difference between babies born only a few miles apart is as much as 25 years![2]

Level of education. Education can also have a huge impact on life expectancy. The difference in life span between those with a PhD versus those with less than a high school diploma may be as much as 10 years[3]—and the effects of education may outweigh other well-known factors such as income, race, or even access to health insurance.[4] So if we really want to improve health, researchers like James Smith, a health economist with the RAND Corporation, and Adriana Lleras-Muney, an economist at the University of California at Los Angeles, argue that we would be wise to focus more of our efforts on improving our *educational system* over improving our health care system.

The social factor. Loneliness is no fun—and it's also bad for our health. An abundance of evidence suggests that we should be paying as much attention to our social calendar as we do our diet, exercise, or sleep. Studies have shown that social isolation can increase early mortality risks by 45 percent.[5] Conversely, those who have strong social ties are 50 percent less likely to die young.[6]

There's even evidence to suggest that social connections can override other risk factors. Researchers have long been stumped by a well-documented "Hispanic Epidemiological

Paradox" in which Hispanics tend to outlive their non-Hispanic counterparts in spite of having risk factors that typically lead to shorter life expectancy, such as lower levels of education, lower income, or even hypertension and weight. Studies show that the strong social-support networks of many Hispanic communities may well explain this phenomenon.[7]

The "unmentionables." The term "unmentionables" was coined by Alexandra Drane, founder and chairman of the board of Eliza Corporation and named as a "Woman to Watch in 2014" by Disruptive Women in Healthcare. The "unmentionables" are the things that we don't like to talk about but that actually matter a lot to our health. These things include the quality of our relationships, our perceptions of our financial situation, whether we're in a caretaking role, our stress level at work, even how often we have sex (and how satisfying it is).

"We tend to think of our health as directly tied to a particular disease or condition, but if there is one thing that we've learned in our years of research, our over one billion interactions, it's that we need to consider more than just the traditional definitions of health," Drane says. "Real life has health consequences above and beyond what you talk about in your doctor's office—things like financial stress, caring for an aging parent, stressful work environments—in fact, these often 'unmentionable' factors can actually be more predictive of our well-being and overall health and productivity than traditional health factors." Drane and her team's research suggests that these unmentionables may be quintupling our national health costs.[8]

KEYS TO LIVING WITH VITALITY

"We know," explains Dee Edington, coauthor of *Positive Health as a Win-Win Organizational Philosophy*, "that there are stratifications within a risk-stratification. You line up a bunch of low-risk people. Are there some healthier than others? I think the answer is yes."[9] Edington believes these differences in health stem from attitudes, spirituality, work, family and friends, and where we live.

So what are the key elements to consider in building a wellness movement that infuses well-being and vitality throughout your organization? Based on a survey conducted in over 150 countries, Gallup researchers identified five essential elements of well-being, as outlined in Tom Rath and Jim Harter's book *Wellbeing: The Five Essential Elements*. Their findings suggest that career well-being, social well-being, physical well-being, financial well-being, and community well-being are the keys to not just surviving, but fully thriving. The findings of this research show that people who are excelling in all five areas are not only happier, more engaged, and more productive, they also have lower medical costs—by more than 40 percent—compared with those who are doing well in two areas or less.[10]

Taking a more holistic and multidimensional understanding of wellness is not new—and in many ways revisits earlier wisdom. The mind-body-spirit trifecta has long been held as the foundation for a classic education. In the 1970s, Bill Hettler with the National Wellness Institute identified six key factors for optimal well-being and vitality in his "Six Dimensions Model." These six factors include physical, social, intellectual, spiritual, emotional, and occupational factors.[11]

WHAT SHOULD YOU CALL IT—HEALTH, WELLNESS, WELL-BEING?

This is exactly what the field is trying to figure out. What do you call it? While some strictly define "wellness" as pertaining only to physical health, others define "wellness" more broadly, to include multiple dimensions. In many cases, the word "health" is used to refer to these different components. Some even refer to the different elements as "energy." Don't get caught up in semantics; use whatever term you think will work best in your organization.

For clarity's sake, I refer to the larger field as "workplace wellness," the general concept as "wellness," and the elements that compose it as "well-being." I tend to use the two terms "wellness" and "well-being" more interchangeably than some. There are many ways to define and parse out the multiple elements of total

(*continued*)

(*continued*)

well-being. The key is to figure out what is meaningful for your organization—and what is likely to get employees engaged in achieving a higher level of well-being and vitality.

Let's take a look at Brocade, a global technology company based in San Jose, California, that has designed its wellness program around multiple dimensions of well-being.

A LOOK AT BROCADE'S 5 PILLARS OF WELLNESS

Brocade's "WellFit" program is taking workplace wellness to a higher level. Initially sparked by employees requesting wellness for the new corporate headquarters, the CEO of Brocade, Lloyd Carney, fully embraces well-being at work. "We take employee well-being extremely seriously," he noted in a recent interview. "For Brocade, WellFit is an essential part of our DNA."[10]

Led by Jacqueline Szeto, wellness program manager, the programming addresses five dimensions of well-being, which they refer to as their "5 pillars of wellness":

Physical health and wellness: Brocade covers the basics and more at their San Jose headquarters—expansive fitness facility, stairs that are accessible and well-lit, on-site athletic field, and healthy options in the cafeteria.

Emotional and mental health: Brocade conducts monthly campaigns to raise awareness on various wellness topics. As part of a monthly theme on stress awareness, employees were encouraged to do daily "stretch-your-stress-away" activities at work.

Financial health: To support financial health, Brocade offers seminars to employees on topics such as managing personal finances, planning for children's college, and making preparations for retirement.

Sustainable health: Brocade's "BGreen" initiative draws the connection between being good to our bodies and being good to the earth. One of the most popular programs is an active commute program. Recently, over 200 employees participated in the annual "Global Bike Challenge."

Family health: Brocade invites employees to bring their family members to company wellness events. In addition, the company encourages employees to bring well-being practices into the home. According to Jackie, initiatives like the "Global Family and Friends Challenge" encourage families to "go for walks after work and read before bedtime."

Source: Jacqueline Szeto, interview with author, November 11, 2014.

A Look at the Different Elements of Well-Being

With input from employees, managers, and leaders, you and your core action team need to identify the components for your overall wellness strategy. What dimensions will you focus on to foster well-being and vitality for all the stakeholders within your organization—and even for stakeholders outside your organization? Here are some elements to consider:

Physical Well-Being = the Basics

Donning a T-shirt that read "Everyday I fight,"[11] the late Stuart Scott, ESPN anchor, spoke about investing in his health in order to have the energy he needed to fight his battle against cancer. His story was and is a powerful reminder of what it means to invest in the basics—and how it can serve to not only build energy, but also help make each moment of life fully count. In accepting the ESPY "Jimmy V" Award, Scott said, "If I die, I haven't lost the battle. It's more about why you live and how you live it."

Physical well-being is what we might consider as the foundation for overall well-being. Going back to Maslow, physical well-being can be equated with our survival needs. These basics are what we traditionally associate with health: getting enough physical activity, eating well, not smoking, and getting enough rest. This is where most workplace wellness initiatives focus their efforts.

Let's talk about the big three elements related to physical well-being: healthy eating, physical activity, and sleep.

- **Healthy eating:** Healthy eating has become convoluted and a battleground of competing dietary solutions. It's no wonder that Michael Pollan's seven-word advice, "Eat food, not too much, mostly plants" has become so popular. People are tired of an overcomplicated and over-politicized conversation. The reality is that there is no "best diet" and in fact, research shows that these different diets are more *similar* than they are different. "Healthy eating" is a matter of doing what we already know:[12] Load up on fruits, vegetables, whole grains, nuts, and seeds. Eat fish, go easy on red meat, and minimize the bad stuff—sugar, salt, fried foods.

  An acronym I like to follow is "SOUL": seasonal, organic, unadulterated, and local. As much as possible, eat fruits and vegetables that are in season. Organic is good (but don't get overly hung up on this), and local is even better. The biggest and most impactful step we can take is to simply buy food that is unadulterated—meaning food that has not been processed. Try this one idea: Buy only food that's available along the perimeter of the grocery store such as fruits, vegetables, dairy, and meat, and avoid the food that's in the center (where most of the processed food lives). Your body will be delighted.

  Let's take a closer look at why processed foods are so tough on our system. Processed foods, by and large, are designed to immediately gratify. But these "ultrapalatable" foods, as characterized by David Kessler, former FDA commissioner and author of *The End of Overeating*, are hard to resist and nearly impossible to stop eating once you start. Even worse, these foods will leave you wholly *unsatisfied* and actually wanting more. And so the cycle continues.

  You *can* fight back against the cycle of processed foods. Try building "satisfaction snacks" that combine the perfect combination of healthy fat, healthy protein, and healthy carbohydrate. For example, apple (carbohydrate) combined with almond butter (protein and fat) will give you more lasting energy than just an apple on its own.

- **Get moving:** When it comes to getting enough physical activity, the number one perceived barrier I hear is, "I don't have enough time." I always respond with, "You *do* have enough time if you consider two simple concepts: EAT and NEAT"—two acronyms coined by obesity expert James Levine, professor of medicine at Mayo Clinic. EAT, which stands for *exercise activity thermogenesis*, is any type of intentional workout, such as going to the gym or playing a sport. This is what we typically associate with "physical activity." NEAT, or *nonexercise activity thermogenesis*, is any *incidental* movement throughout the day.[13]

  Over the past several decades, our NEAT levels have plummeted—contributing to the obesity epidemic and rise in chronic diseases (like heart disease) that we're facing today. Levine's call to action is for all of us to stop sitting so much and start doing whatever it takes to move more throughout the day: standing desk, treadmill desk, walking meetings, or doing more household chores.

  On average, Americans are sitting 9.3 hours a day.[14] Referred to as the "new smoking," too much sitting may be as little as three hours a day![15] Within a shockingly short span of time (a couple of hours), our bodies experience changes on a cellular level that put us at much greater risk for a litany of frightening outcomes: shortened life, heart disease, diabetes, disability at a younger age. Surprisingly, research shows that exercise does not offset the negative effects of too much sitting.

  Getting up and out of our chairs is much easier said than done. Our culture in the United States, and increasingly around the world, is built around our chairs. When someone comes to visit us in our office or home, we politely invite them to "Have a seat!"—a custom that we learn at an early age. Insidiously, before children learn their ABCs, they're taught to sit. One of my favorite cartoons depicts an out of shape, middle-aged man getting an annual checkup. The doctor advises him, "For years your teachers have been telling you to sit still and be quiet—you can stop now."[16]

GETTING PEOPLE MOVING ON THE JOB AT PRIMED

While onsite fitness classes are standard, one company, PriMed Consulting Services, Inc., decided to address the other side of the coin: NEAT, or more movement throughout the *rest* of the day.

Already addressing the EAT component with robust offerings of fitness classes, including a monthly "fitness day," Judi Hennebry Wise, wellness and education services director at PriMed, and her team took action. To encourage employees, managers, and executives to sit less and move more, Judi and her team promoted activities such as the following:

- Taking the stairs
- Standing up every 30 minutes
- Walking to a farther bathroom
- Communicating with colleagues in person rather than sending e-mails
- Engaging in small stretches at one's desk
- Engaging in "mini-workouts" at movement stations
- Holding standing and walking meetings
- Taking advantage of the nearby public trail for breaks and walking meetings

Source: Judi Hennebry Wise, interview with author, December 17, 2014.

- **Get sleep:** Author E. Joseph Cossman once wrote, "The best bridge between despair and hope is a good night's sleep." Sleep is perhaps the most overlooked area of physical well-being, but potentially the most essential. There's new disturbing research suggesting that lack of sleep can literally shrink our brains! According to Clair Sexton, with the University of Oxford, "We found that sleep difficulties (for example, trouble falling asleep, waking up during the night, or waking up too early) were associated with an increased rate of decline in brain volume over three [to] five years."[17]

Some simple tips that we can each use to improve our sleep include creating a device-free, work-free, pet-free oasis in our bedrooms, creating a series of pre-bedtime relaxing rituals, and setting a regular pattern of sleep—and sticking to it even on the weekends.

Emotional Well-Being = Resiliency

Moving up Maslow's hierarchy of needs, we might say that emotional well-being is equivalent to the next level up—our need for a sense of safety and security. Emotional well-being is less about what happens to us in life and more about how we *respond* to what comes our way. It's about resilience. Resilience, defined by Merriam-Webster's Dictionary, is the "ability to recover from or adjust easily to misfortune or change."[18]

In *Man's Search for Meaning*, neurologist, psychiatrist, and Holocaust survivor Viktor Frankl explained that while we may have little control over our personal circumstances, we have infinite power in how we *respond* to these circumstances. This, he described, is where our power lies and is the key to our "inner freedom."[19]

Perhaps one of the greatest examples of resilience is Nelson Mandela. While in prison for 27 years, the famous leader leveraged his "inner freedom" by focusing on what he could do rather than what he could not do. Among other efforts to cultivate change, he learned Afrikaans, the language spoken by the prison guards, and befriended them. This ability to cross over and form bridges is what enabled him to endure during his time in prison and subsequently was crucial to his political success when he was elected the first president of post-apartheid South Africa in 1994.

The biggest obstacle we face in building resiliency is stress—*or so it seems.* We've all learned that stress is bad. But new studies, largely led by neuroimmunologist and associate professor of psychiatry and behavioral sciences Firdaus Dhabhar at Stanford University, are now showing that stress can actually be good and even "beautiful." Dhabhar asks, "What if stress is not always bad for us? What if it's even good for us at times? If so, how can we harness it to benefit us in unexpected ways?" His research has shown that short-term stress can actually enhance immune function, in contrast to previous findings, and can also increase performance.

What we *don't* want is long-term stress. This is what Dhabhar characterizes as "bad" stress, which is definitively deleterious for our health. The question is, what can we do to prevent short-term stress from becoming long-term stress? One step that we can each take is to do the same, but *differently* (as in a more relaxed, Type B manner). Cardiologist Meyer Friedman, one of the early researchers to start looking into the effects of stress, focused on the link between personality style and heart disease. His book *Type A and Your Heart*, released in 1974, popularized the conversation about the mind-body connection. His prescription: Practice "Type B" behaviors more often. These behaviors include being nice to people, smiling more often, intentionally choosing the longer line at the grocery store, driving in the slow lane, and reading good, long works of literature.

In his "Staying on the Good Side of Stress Spectrum," Dhabhar suggests that we actually *sharpen* short-term stress. This is what he calls "optimizing good stress." This means increasing our levels of stress in the short term can be *good*—and can be a great source of energy. The key, though, is to then offset these short-term bouts of stress with what he calls the "green zones." This is when we (1) zero in on practicing the basics—sleep, food, and moderate exercise; (2) leverage our psychosocial buffers—which includes activities like spending time with friends, practicing gratitude, and being nice to others and to ourselves; and (3) engage in restorative activities—things like meditation, yoga, music, art, and walking.[20]

© 2015, Firdaus Dhabhar, All Rights Reserved. Adapted from: Effects of Stress on Immune Function: The Good, the Bad, and the Beautiful. Dhabhar, F.S. (2014) Immunol Res, DOI 10.1007/s 12026-014-8517-0.

Mindfulness is a "green zone" practice that has taken the country by storm. Even politicians are taking to it. Tim Ryan, U.S. Rep. from Ohio, is leading mindfulness sessions on Capitol Hill and in schools; he's encouraging unlikely advocates, including NFL football players and veterans, to join him in his efforts to spread the movement, and he's introducing legislation like the Veterans and Armed Forces' Health Promotion Act of 2013 which includes provisions to promote mental health through practices like mindfulness. In his recent book, *A Mindful Nation*, Rep. Ryan wrote, "The mindfulness movement is not quite as dramatic as the moon shot or the civil rights movement, but I believe in the long run it can have just as great an impact."[21]

Mindfulness, as defined by Jon Kabat-Zinn, professor emeritus of medicine and creator of the Stress Reduction Clinic and the Center for

Mindfulness in Medicine, is simply "paying attention in a particular way; on purpose, in the present moment, and nonjudgmentally."[22] The research shows that the benefits can be enormous: Mindfulness can help to recalibrate our brains, increase our creativity capacity, and improve our problem-solving skills.[23]

A broad spectrum of companies are joining the wave of promoting mindfulness in the workplace. Technology companies like Apple, biotechnology companies like Genentech, management consulting companies like McKinsey, financial services companies like Goldman Sachs, consumer goods companies like Procter & Gamble, food manufacturers like General Mills, and even automobile manufacturers like Ford are offering mindfulness teaching and practices to their employees.[24]

ACTION ITEM

TIPS ON PRACTICING MINDFULNESS

Here are some simple tips to get started on practicing mindfulness. You can try them out and pass them along to build a calm and centered energy for your wellness movement.

- **Focus on one thing at a time.** In a world of multitasking, this can be a challenge. A common technique is to focus on the breath. The biggest distractions are often the voices in our heads. With practice, though, it gets easier. I've heard Arianna Huffington refer to these voices as the "annoying roommate in my head."
- **Take a break between tasks.** Too often we launch from one task to the next. Stop for a moment and be mindful: Detach from the work at hand, take a few breaths, and simply tune into what is happening right here, right now.
- **Find your inner freedom.** Remember that you always get to choose how you respond to every circumstance that you

encounter. Slowing down to reflect and be present in the moment is a good way to shift from reacting to achieving greater clarity.

Financial = Effective Management of Resources

Without financial security, it's hard to feel safe and secure. This element of well-being also fits with Maslow's level of safety and security. Financial well-being, beyond covering the basics, is really about being smart about how we spend our money—and also how we *feel* about our finances. Research shows, for example, that (a) spending money on experiences over things and (b) spending money on others (instead of ourselves) can increase our financial well-being.[25]

FINANCIAL FITNESS IS ON THE UPTICK

An expanding number of organizations are now helping their employees get financially fit: reduce debt, save for retirement and children's college, plan for emergency expenses, and manage daily finances. More than 75 percent of employers polled in a recent Aon Hewitt survey indicated that they have plans to begin providing or expanding upon their current financial wellness offerings.[26]

In addition to the usual offerings—individual counseling, classroom education, and online information—companies like Staples are leveraging gamification to help their employees take charge of their finances. To encourage more employees to invest in the 401(k) plan, Staples launched "Bite Club," a game that allows employees to imagine they're vampires needing to make financial decisions as they manage a nightclub. Due to popular demand, Staples is now launching a second game called "Farm Blitz," to empower employees to reduce debt and save for emergency funds.[27]

The natural question is—can money buy happiness? The answer to the question is yes, and no. Yes, there is a correlation between life satisfaction and having enough money to live. We certainly need a baseline level of resources to prevent pain and suffering. And we certainly feel better when we have good systems in place to manage our finances. On the other hand, a phenomenon known as the "Easterlin Paradox" shows that while the average income has risen over the past 50 years in the United States, our levels of happiness have remained flat.[28] So what's going on here?

Once we've met our basic financial needs, the real issue seems to be one of *comparison*. Studies have shown that we are happier when we are making more than others around us, and less happy if we are making less than others around us—even if we're getting paid more on an absolute scale. It's really a "keeping up with the Joneses" phenomenon—and this, of course, is a race we can never win. There will always be someone who is wealthier than we are, has a bigger house than we do, or has fancier clothes than we do. This insatiable desire to have more can set in motion a "hedonic treadmill": We make more money (so that we can keep up with the Joneses), we get used to a higher standard of living, we're still not satisfied, and then we need even more money to continue to live the good life—and happiness is still out of reach.[29]

The way out of the unhealthy hedonic treadmill is, first of all, to change our perceptions and tell ourselves that we already have enough. Second, we can simply divert our efforts to elevate other areas of well-being—such as social well-being.

Social Well-Being = Love and Connection

A couple of years out of college, I spent seven months in a small village in Ghana, West Africa. When I arrived, one of the first questions my hosts asked was, "What day of the week were you born?" At the time, I had absolutely no idea, but it turns out, I'm a Friday baby, and in keeping with Ghanaian tradition, I was officially given my day-of-the-week name: "Efua." In Ghana, babies are not given an individualized, Christian name until they're two weeks old. Many Ghanaians prefer to go by their day-of-the-week name, even into adulthood.

For an American raised in a culture that reveres individualism, this was hard to fathom. But I later appreciated how this day-of-the-week naming tradition reflected a culture that honored community over individualism. Not surprisingly, loneliness is not common in Ghana, but is endemic to American culture. According to a recent survey, the rates of loneliness in the United States have doubled from 20 to 40 percent since the 1980s.[30]

Social well-being can be equated with the next level up on Maslow's hierarchy of needs: the need for belonging. In *Connected*, researchers Nicholas Cristakis and James Fowler write, "How we feel, what we know, whom we marry, whether we fall ill, how much money we make, and whether we vote all depend on the ties that bind us."[31] In other words, our social network impacts every aspect of our lives, especially our health, our well-being, and our overall level of vitality. Their research demonstrated that we are impacted by our immediate social contacts, and also by our larger social network—by a measure of up to three degrees.

As we discussed earlier, social well-being is vital to our health. People with stronger social connections, on average, have lower blood pressure, lower obesity rates, and better immune responses.[32] Social isolation, research shows, can create a downward spiral of negative choice making. Those who are lonely have a harder time self-regulating and are more likely to give into destructive habits, such as overeating or alcohol abuse.[33] To maintain a high level of social well-being, studies show that we should be spending six hours a day with others.[34]

Career = What We Do

Having just a "job" is bad; not having one at all is even worse. One study looked at the effects of long-term unemployment and found that, over time, this can be more devastating than the loss of a spouse.[35] Career well-being is what we do every day—and the corresponding level of fulfillment that we experience. This element of well-being is what we can equate with the next level up in Maslow's hierarchy of needs: the need for esteem and achievement. This may well be the element of well-being that matters most. According to Gallup, people who are thriving in their careers are 50 percent more likely to be thriving overall—and are much more likely to live into their nineties.[36]

Fran Scarpulla, 73, a leading antitrust attorney in San Francisco, exemplifies what we should strive for in career well-being. The satisfaction he derives from his work radiates through everything he does. He runs circles around his younger colleagues and has won numerous peer awards. Known as the "Titan of the Plantiffs Bar," he works hard, but he also makes a point of actually having a life. Nearly every weekend, he heads out of town to enjoy the open space of his ranch in Humboldt County, five hours north of San Francisco.

Dedicated to his wife and family of five children, and committed to his friends, he also carves out time to mentor up-and-coming young lawyers during the week. Fran enjoys his life, and he is thriving in all dimensions of well-being. This is not surprising. Research shows that people with a high level of career well-being are more likely to be enjoying their lives at work—*and* their lives at leisure.[37] Fran, unfortunately, is an outlier. According to Gallup, only 20 percent of us enthusiastically report that we like what we do.[38]

However, companies like Starbucks understand the importance of career well-being for their employees—and are willing to invest in it.

THE STORY OF NICK DAVIDSON

Nick Davidson, a 10-year employee at Starbucks, is taking a "career coffee break," or yearlong sabbatical. This is one of *many* benefits he enjoys as a Starbucks employee: adoption assistance, robust Employee Assistance Program, discounts on wireless service, flowers, gym memberships, concert tickets, rental cars, to name a few. Even as a part-time employee (a minimum of 20 hours a week), he is also eligible for their Total Pay package: full medical, dental, and vision.

In addition to this stunning array of benefits, Starbucks employees now have the opportunity to take advantage of an incredible career-boosting perk: a heavily subsidized education. Launched in June of 2014, Starbucks College Achievement Plan is helping employees like Nick to leapfrog into a new career with a stellar education. During the first two years, Nick received a partial reimbursement for his education. Now, as a junior (and continuing through his senior year), he will receive *100 percent* reimbursement. "As a user of the benefit," he says, "I'm the first to say, 'It's fantastic!'" Nick is on his way to becoming a software engineer, and has Starbucks to thank for it.

Source: Nick Davidson, interview with author, January 3, 2015.

"Are you in a job, a career, or is this your calling?" This is a question that business leaders like Chip Conley, founder of the California-based Joie de Vivre Hotels, and Tony Hsieh, CEO of Zappos, an online shoe company, are asking their employees. I've asked this question in workshops and have found that it always generates lots of conversations, sometimes heated. In one workshop held at a financial services corporation, I asked participants to describe their work situation by placing dots on a flipchart that had "job," "career," and "calling" written into a pyramid. Most of the dots hovered between "job" and "career." During the follow-up discussion, the room crackled with heated comments like, "How can you expect us to feel like this kind of work is a 'calling?' It's a job!" When I came back a few months later, I learned that a couple of the participants were no longer with the company. That single conversation at the workshop had inspired them to go out and find their calling. That's what I would call a success!

ACTION ITEM

JOB, CAREER, OR CALLING?

This provocative tool can help employees to think more critically about their current level of career well-being and engage in a lively discussion.

Here's how you can do it. Draw a triangle, divided into three parts: job, career, calling. Then, ask participants to place a

(*continued*)

(*continued*)

sticker dot on the level that best applies to where they are (individually). Follow this up with discussion.

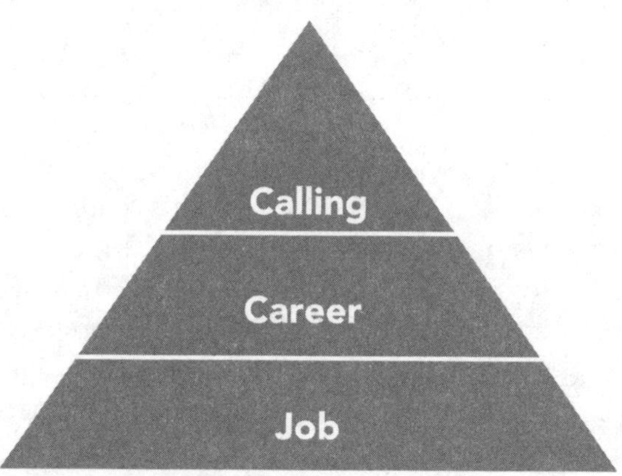

Source: © 2015 Chip Conley, All rights reserved. Adapted from *PEAK: How Great Companies Get Their Mojo from Maslow*. Permission granted to use.

This simple technique allows each employee to retain anonymity, but still share their "voice" in creating a composite of the group's level of engagement with their work. Just seeing the formation of dots can spark an interesting discussion. You might want to open this interaction with a "pair share," in which participants turn to a partner and share thoughts. After a few minutes, you might transition into a discussion with the larger group. If you're operating in a low-trust culture, you might consider just having employees *think* about where they are on the pyramid and then perhaps journal some thoughts about it.

For a full-group discussion, here are some useful questions to debrief the activity:

- What do you *see*? (Encourage participants to share just what they see, without interpretation. For example, "I see that most of the dots are in the category 'career.'")
- What do you *think* about what you see? (Now, encourage participants to start making interpretations and analyze what they see. For example, "I think that this feels like a career for

many of us because we're given a lot of opportunities for growth in this company.")

- What do you *wonder*? (Now, encourage participants to ask questions based on what they've seen and some of the insights they've gained. For example, "I wonder if discussions about purpose might help more of us to feel like this is our calling?")

Community = Where We Live and What We Give

At age 75, Betsy Warriner is thriving more so than she ever has. What's made the difference? She's found a community in Bend, Oregon, that reflects her values and embraces her. As the leader and founder of a nonprofit organization called Volunteer Connect, she is giving back to her community every day. The satisfaction she derives from running a successful nonprofit, and her high level of community well-being, fuels other areas of her life. She's part of a tennis group, attends a myriad of social events, sings and performs with a community chorale group, lives close to one of her daughters, and walks everywhere. Betsy is living a *great* life.

Community well-being is what Rath and Harter describe as "the differentiator between a good life and a great one."[39] This area of well-being fits in with Maslow's top level: self-actualization. On a very basic level, community well-being is about feeling safe where we live, having places to play, and being part of a community that reflects our values and preferences.

On a higher level, it's about giving back, which studies show is really, really good for us. A survey by UnitedHealth Group of more than 3,351 adults found that volunteering provides mental, social, and physical benefits. After a volunteering experience, the vast majority of respondents reported feeling healthier, in a better mood, less stressed, more connected to their purpose in life, and having a higher level of self-esteem.[40] For those who are giving more than 100 hours a year, the health benefits are astounding. One study showed that those who are giving live longer compared with those who are not.[41] Studies have also shown that those who volunteer regularly experience greater life satisfaction and are less susceptible to depression.[42] A study conducted by researchers at Johns Hopkins found that senior citizens engaged in volunteering lowered their risks of developing Alzheimer's disease.[43] Our brains literally light up when we give back, and we reap a multitude of well-being benefits.

Environmental = Good for the Earth, Good for Us

Denis Hayes, national organizer of the first Earth Day, now runs the Bullitt Foundation, which is dedicated to supporting environmental efforts in the Pacific Northwest. Hayes oversaw the planning, design, and construction of the Bullitt Center, which houses the foundation and other commercial tenants. The goal of the project was to build the greenest commercial building in the world that would support not only the environment but also employee well-being. The underlying assumption was that what's good for the earth is good for us (and vice versa).

Throughout construction, Hayes and his team found ways to avoid many of the toxic substances that are normally used—about 350 altogether! The building was designed with oversized windows to allow for plenty of natural light and fresh air. The stairs are prominently positioned, with windows looking out on the city's skyline, making them a far more appealing option than the elevator. To encourage active commuting, the Bullitt Center has a *bike*-parking garage, along with a shower in every bathroom.

Focusing on environmental well-being provides many benefits. First, it's good for the environment; second, it's good for our health; and, third, it's motivating for a growing group of individuals, especially millennials. Homing in on this area of well-being can serve as a powerful way to connect with our higher need for self-actualization. There's exciting research that suggests that individuals may be more motivated to make changes in their health habits when the focus is on environmental benefits as opposed to health benefits. We'll talk more about this in Step 6: Go Stealth.

Creative = Authentic Self-Expression

"If I could say it—I wouldn't have to dance it," said Martha Graham, who is often credited as the inventor of modern dance. Ultimately, well-being and living with vitality are about finding our own unique and authentic form of creative expression. This element definitely ties in with Maslow's highest level: self-actualization. Creative well-being, in the truest sense, translates into living life on our own terms. According to Bronnie Ware, an Australian hospice nurse who worked with dying patients for years, the number one regret she heard was, "I wish that I'd had the courage to live a life true to myself, not the life others expected of me."[44]

Too often I encounter organizations that "value" creativity and innovation but effectively don't *allow* for it. Employees aren't given time for creative thought, nor are they given the resources to act upon any ideas they come up with. Often, a company's idea of "innovation" is having employees execute the ideas of *others* (such as integrating new technologies that are brought into the company).

Creativity, which is tightly associated with autonomy, is something that is inherently motivating—even for those who don't consider themselves to be creative. If we are to live up to President Obama's call to action in his 2011 State of the Union Address "to out-innovate, out-educate, and out-build the rest of the world," employees must be given more leeway and opportunities to enhance their creative well-being at work. Incorporating creative well-being into your wellness movement can provide a powerful and lasting impact by empowering employees to experience greater levels of autonomy.

LEVERAGING MASLOW TO DRAW THE CONNECTIONS

While each of these elements is important singularly, what matters most is the *interaction* among the multiple dimensions. Each element feeds off of the others and all are interdependent. Those who have a high level of social well-being are almost 50% more likely to be thriving in their careers. To fully thrive in life, we need to meet all five areas. Unfortunately, only 7 percent of us are thriving in all five areas, according to Gallup.[45] Therefore, in thinking about devising your workplace wellness strategy, it is critical that you look for ways to promote multiple areas of well-being and, ideally, in combination.

I find it's helpful to leverage Maslow in order to more clearly highlight these connections. Beethoven exemplified how these different areas of well-being can connect. His daily ritual was a morning walk (physical well-being). In addition to providing exercise, the walking is what generated his creative thinking for the day. With a notebook in hand, he would record his thoughts and then return to his studio, ready for a day of composing (creative well-being).

"When we move," I often tell people, "we get healthier, we get happier, and we even get smarter." Like Beethoven, each of us can use movement to accelerate our creative thinking and spark our inner genius. The benefits to the brain are enormous: More circulation and more oxygen, more synapses between brain cells, and even more brain cells. All of us, I explain, have the capacity to rewire and rebuild our brains to become stronger—and one of the best ways to catalyze this process is through movement.

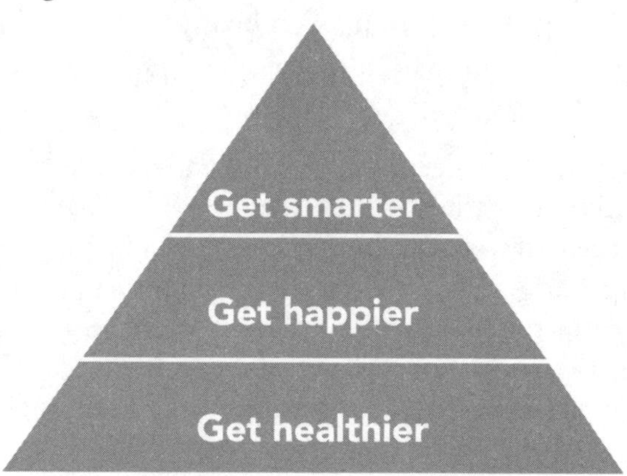

ACTION ITEM

MAKING THE CONNECTION

Have you ever had the experience of going for a walk or a run—and suddenly the solution you've been trying to uncover seems to reveal itself as if by magic? You've just experienced the power of contralateral movement, or crossing the right over left side of the body. These bilateral movements can actually facilitate more synapses between brain cells, connecting the left and the right side of the brain. Now, suddenly, you're using your entire brain and you're reaping the benefits of "whole brain thinking." For managers and leaders who are looking for innovation boosters, sell them on the *brain* benefits of movement!

ACTION ITEM

DEVISE A MULTI-DIMENSIONAL WELLNESS PLATFORM

Begin the creative process. Based on your vision, it's time to begin brainstorming solutions. Partner up with your core action team and ask big questions like, "Did you know that . . . ?" or "Wouldn't it be cool if we . . . ?" in combination with practical questions such as "What would one tiny win look like?"

Identify key areas of well-being. Based on your earlier visioning work with the collage, and based on what you've learned about the multiple dimensions of well-being, what are the areas your organization should focus on?

Get practical. A mundane but important consideration is how you will make sure that you're offering programs across all of the dimensions. You might consider using a color-coded calendar to keep track.

FINAL THOUGHTS

Disney is a company that was founded on one individual's imagination. Their mission today is "to use our imagination to bring happiness to millions." *Your* mission is to use your imagination—and the imagination of others—to bring well-being and vitality to all employees within your organization. Allowing yourself and encouraging others to imagine what's possible and what *could be* is the kind of open-minded thinking needed to catalyze your wellness movement.

Step 3

Uncover the Hidden Factors

(The Culture Imperative)

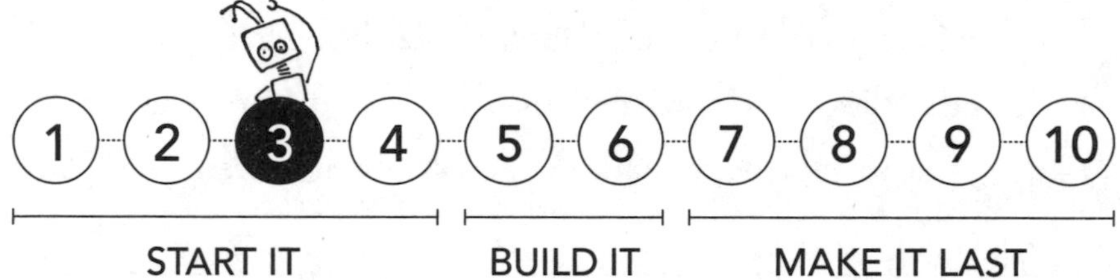

Two young fish are swimming. They encounter an older fish. As they cross paths, the older fish greets them, "Morning boys, how's the water?" The two younger fish keep swimming. A few minutes later one of the younger fish turns to the other and asks, "What the heck is water?"

This is the story that David Foster Wallace, philosopher and author of *Infinite Jest*, told to open his commencement speech at Kenyon College in 2005. It's also a great story to describe culture. Just like water, culture is something that surrounds us. It's so ubiquitous that we don't even see it, and yet it shapes our behaviors in ways that we could not possibly imagine.

While we will often say that we are creatures of habit, I would argue that we are more creatures of *culture*. Therefore, if we really want to start changing behaviors, we need to shift our focus from changing a few behaviors, a few people at a time, to changing many behaviors, entire cultures at a time.

In venturing into this vast territory of culture, your task is to first *understand* your culture, or hidden factors, to devise a wellness strategy that fits the culture. Second, you need to ascertain the extent to which the larger, organizational culture is going to either boost or undermine your efforts. Without culture on your side, it is much more challenging—but not impossible—to build Workplace Wellness That Works. The research clearly shows that there is a high level of interdependence between wellness and engagement, and culture plays a strong role in shaping employee engagement. Workplace wellness is simply much more likely to thrive in cultures that foster employee engagement.

In this chapter, we will clarify:

1. What culture is and why it matters for an organization's bottom line,
2. Why you need to understand the culture first in launching any wellness initiative,
3. Why culture matters in relation to well-being in the workplace,
4. Examples of organizations that invest in culture, and
5. How to get a better understanding of your current workplace culture.

YOUR STEP 3 CHECKLIST

- ☐ Conduct a Maslow Meets Mallory Culture Audit to assess the organizational culture.
- ☐ Conduct qualitative assessments to uncover the stories behind the data.
- ☐ Identify bright spots in your organization's culture.
- ☐ Identify cultural challenges, or mismatches between well-being goals and cultural realities.
- ☐ Share results and suggest recommendations in the form of a report.
- ☐ Initiate a dialogue with leaders.

WHAT IS CULTURE AND WHY DOES IT MATTER?

What is this amorphous thing called "culture"? Culture is the people and the ethos of the organization. It's the way you feel when you walk into the organization. It's how employees work together and rally around a common purpose. It's the leaders and the vision they communicate. It's the intention behind every interaction. It's the collective sum of shared values of the organization, social norms, policies, rituals, philosophy, and programs. In a recent post on his blog, Chip Conley, Airbnb head of global hospitality and strategy and bestselling author, wrote, "More and more, I define culture as 'what happens when the boss is not around.'"[1] Culture is all of these things, and it is so omnipresent, it's almost impossible to measure.

Given all of these intangible factors, what makes for a great culture? Very simply, great cultures put humans first. This, in turn, fosters employee engagement, well-being, and top performance, which in turn stimulates a high-performing organization.

In their book *Firms of Endearment*, Rajendra Sisodia, David Wolf, and Jagdish Sheth contend that a great culture invites openness and transparent communication, is built on a clear sense of purpose, fosters alignment among multiple stakeholders, promotes learning and growth, nurtures employee autonomy and involvement, focuses on long-term sustainability, and stands for humanity and fairness.[2]

At the heart of a great culture is a highly engaged employee. While the 2011 Job Satisfaction and Engagement Survey, conducted by the Society for Human Resources, showed that 83 percent of employees in the United States are satisfied with their jobs,[3] having satisfied employees is not enough to produce a healthy culture. Satisfied employees *accept* their *job*; engaged employees *embrace* their *work*.

An engaged employee goes above and beyond—even when the boss isn't looking. An engaged employee is one who works with consistency and passion, collaborates well with others, spreads positive energy throughout the organization, and contributes great ideas. Studies show that these employees outperform their disengaged coworkers by 20 to 28 percent.[4] Companies with an engaged workforce do better—*much* better—by a measure of fivefold, according to Kenexa research. Having engaged, high-performing employees catalyzes a chain reaction: better service, increased customer satisfaction, higher sales, increased profits, and ultimately higher returns for shareholders.[5]

Unfortunately, the majority of our workforce is not engaged. According to Gallup, 70 percent of workers in the United States are disengaged, including 18 percent who are not just disengaged, they're *actively* disengaged.[6] This means that these employees are going out of their way to build a toxic environment, bringing other coworkers into their negative spiral, and driving away customers. These high levels of disengagement are costing organizations a lot of money—an estimated $450 to $550 billion per year in the United States.[7]

On the basis of culture alone, companies can literally succeed or fail. Bill Autlet, managing director of the Martin Trust Center for MIT Entrepreneurship and author of *Disciplined Entrepreneurship: 24 Steps to a Successful Startup*, attributed the failure of his first startup, Cambridge Decision Dynamics, to his disregard for the importance of culture. "I used to think that corporate culture didn't matter," he said in a recent post. "Discussion of vision, mission, and values was for people who couldn't build product or sell it!"

"And, then," he writes, "my first company failed."[8]

COMPANIES THAT INVEST IN CULTURE

A strong culture, as defined by Joel Peterson, chairman of JetBlue Airways, is "one that will attract and keep the best people collaborating, innovating, learning and interacting around priorities that lead to world-class performance."[9] Companies like LinkedIn, Patagonia, Southwest Airlines, Whole Foods Market, The Container Store, Costco, Google, IDEO, Eileen Fisher, UPS, REI, and Zappos prioritize culture and invest in it heavily.

Tony Hsieh, CEO of Zappos, believes that "For organizations, culture is destiny."[10] He and his team have gone to great lengths to create a happy workplace to better support a triple bottom line: employees, customers, and shareholders. They recognize that happy employees are more likely to be committed to their work, stay with the company, and provide great customer service. To promote happiness on the job, employees are encouraged to have fun at work and are given the leeway they need to provide excellent customer service. This kind of service has translated into unmatched customer loyalty, which in turn has led to legendary profits. In a ten-year span, Zappos went from being a company with zero profits to one that was sold for $1.2 billion.

Southwest Airlines has set a new standard for what's possible in the workplace. By investing in culture, the company has created transformative experiences for its employees, customers, and even for its shareholders. Like Zappos, Southwest has consistently outperformed its competitors—and has even redefined an industry, making air travel accessible to the everyday American consumer.[11]

IDEO is another example of a company that has demonstrated a long-term commitment to fostering a healthy workplace culture.

IDEO—A CULTURE OF PURPOSE, EXPERIMENTATION, AND RECIPROCITY

IDEO, a Palo Alto, California-based design consultancy with offices across the globe, is driven to positively and disproportionally impact the world through design. To achieve this goal, it is committed to building and nurturing a culture of purpose, experimentation, and reciprocity. According to Duane Bray, head of talent at IDEO, "It's about giving people the biggest playground"—namely, the world.

Everything at IDEO starts with understanding values and purpose, on an organizational level *and* on an individual level. The next step is to find the nexus between the two. How are you (as an individual employee) aligned with the larger, organizational purpose? "That is what determines how you (as an employee) show up every day and why you would choose IDEO as a place to work in the first place," says Duane.

To build this culture, IDEO started with identifying organizational values that are "reflective of the behaviors that trigger success." These seven values, captured in a short hardcover book called *The Little Book of IDEO*, serve as the basis for the social contract between organization and individual.

1. "Be optimistic"—"Believing that something is possible will somehow make it so."
2. "Collaborate"—"The most powerful asset we have in our arsenal is the word 'we.'"
3. "Embrace ambiguity"—"Get comfortable with uncomfortableness."

(continued)

(*continued*)

4. "Learn from failure"—"Ask for forgiveness, not permission."
5. "Make others successful"—"Going out of our way to help others is the secret sauce."
6. "Take ownership"—"The unwritten social contract here: Individual ownership supports collective responsibility. Own that."
7. "Talk less, do more"—"Nothing is a bigger buzz-kill than overintellectualizing. Design is about rolling up your sleeves and doing things."

After the release of *The Little Book of IDEO*, all of the employees across the global offices were asked to create their own interpretation of the values in the form of videos. IDEO then shared these videos both internally and outside the organization.

According to Duane, "We are a culture that encourages experimentation and bringing one's whole self to work." The company sets out to *create the conditions* for employees to engage in interactive experimentation and to engender a spirit of playfulness. For example, the Singapore office spoofed the slogan "Talk less, do more" by creating onesies with the slogan "Poo less, talk more" in celebration of the abundance of newborns in the office.

IDEO consistently "signals" employees that it really *is* okay to take care of yourself, that it's okay to play, and that it's okay to "complete your experience."

At IDEO, there's not a strict line between life at work and life outside of work. In fact, the company goes out of its way to bring the two together. David Kelley, founder of IDEO, had a vision of creating a company where all the employees were his best friends. IDEO nurtures this notion of friendship and camaraderie on a daily basis.

IDEO extends a wide latitude of permission to all of its employees. IDEO employees are given free rein to use the equipment to work on any project—even projects outside of IDEO. At IDEO, there are no set hours nor is there a traditional vacation accrual policy. "We believe at IDEO that to be your best you need to have time off. You need to have the time that you need *when* you need it," explains Duane. Before taking time off, IDEO employees make arrangements with their teammates ahead of time. IDEO fosters a community in which employees take ownership and feel embraced. That's the power of their social contract.

Source: Duane Bray, interview with author, December 2, 2014.

WHY YOU NEED TO UNDERSTAND THE CULTURE

Culture may be the defining competitive advantage when it comes to accelerating business performance. Without a doubt, culture is also the defining competitive advantage when it comes to curating an effective workplace wellness initiative. For starters, it's critical to clearly *understand* the culture of the organization you're working within. You should first ask, "Is this a culture in which wellness is likely to succeed?"

John Thiel, director of wealth management at Merrill Lynch, discovered the hard way that his was not. He enthusiastically launched a wellness initiative advocating well-being practices such as meditation, restorative naps, nutrition, and finding a higher, more "noble purpose" in one's work. Unfortunately, he didn't take into account how these practices would be perceived by a group of hard-charging financial advisors and stockbrokers. In a money-oriented, results-only culture, the well-intended wellness initiative came across as too "touchy feely"—and fueled a backlash.

Instead of prompting a positive change in lifestyle habits, Thiel's wellness initiative spurred a reactionary and voracious consumption of "meat, potatoes, and booze," as one employee described at a recent corporate event. Thiel simply didn't take into account the existing culture—and he is paying the price with a deluge of negative press, both internally and externally—not to mention a failed wellness initiative. "Will Merrill throw Thiel out with the wheatgrass bathwater?" asks a recent article.[12]

This story exemplifies why even a member of the executive team must take into account the existing culture before launching a wellness initiative. As David Hunnicutt, former CEO of the Wellness Council of America (WELCOA), emphasizes, "Assess culture first, health second."[13]

Every organization has a different culture and a different set of circumstances, and this is why, frustratingly, there is no "one size fits all" when it comes to workplace wellness. Jennifer Flynn, strategy consultant at Mayo Clinic, has worked with organizations for the past decade on developing strategies and techniques that can support and contribute to a healthy culture. She is now part of a large, multidisciplinary team at Mayo Clinic focused on nurturing a supportive culture within the organization. She explains that while Mayo Clinic initiatives such as the Healthy Living Program, Healthy Living online platform, and other campus-specific initiatives have performed extremely well, it is impossible to simply transport a replica of these programs and strategy to other organizations and expect the same results.

CULTURE SHAPES LEVEL OF ENGAGEMENT

The next step is to understand the extent to which your organization's culture is likely to support or erode your wellness movement, and this is primarily a factor of the level of employee engagement. As we've discussed, the heart of effective cultures is *engagement.* If employees are disengaged at work, it's unlikely they will engage with wellness, no matter how well the programs are conceived. Flynn asks, "How can we expect our employees to engage in their health if they are not engaged in their work?" The key piece, she says, is "perceived organizational support."[14] If employees do not feel supported by their organization, by their manager, or by their coworkers, they are less likely to trust and therefore engage with any wellness efforts on a meaningful level.

Rosie Ward, coauthor of *How to Build a Thriving Culture at Work*, explains the intersection between culture and well-being, and how this largely comes down to the leaders. "It's about [leaders] having a mindset of valuing employees, really understanding the importance of organizational culture and recognizing that well-being is a *piece* of the total employee experience."[15]

Sadly, many organizations conduct annual surveys to measure the impact of their employee wellness efforts, but they fail to make the connection between these wellness efforts and the culture of their organization. One organization wanted to find out why nonparticipating employees chose not to take part in the company's wellness offerings. Their annual employee wellness survey asked, "If you chose not to participate in the wellness program, why not?" Responses ranged from "coworkers took the fun out of it" to "this is a workplace of manipulative, conniving units run by a power group of insiders" to a particularly aggrieved comment, "I DO NOT WANT TO WORKOUT WITH EMPLOYEES AT WORK—ONLY WITH FAMILY AND FRIENDS." These comments are not just about the *wellness* program; they are indicative of an ineffective and unhealthy culture.

A Negative Culture Can Undermine Workplace Wellness

There has been a lot of discussion about building a "culture of health," which refers to more superficial changes such as modeling by senior leaders or modifications to the environment. While these elements are important, and we will discuss these elements in greater depth in Step 8: Design Nudges and Cues, culture, in the larger sense, goes much deeper. Culture, as defined by Edgar Schein, author and former professor of management at the Sloan School of Management, takes into account both the behaviors we see within an organization, as well as the values, and even the assumptions that lie beneath these behaviors.

Wellness efforts that run counter to the underlying culture have the potential to foster feelings of resentment. Sheryl Niehbur, organizational psychologist who has worked with organizations like 3M, explains: "I'm skeptical that employees who experience modifications in their work environment don't experience some element of cynicism if at the same time they feel a meta message of 60-hour work weeks as the norm, the more face time the better, and where promotions are viewed as a function of time as reflected in terms of hours worked as opposed to contribution made." Combine a negative culture with an ill-conceived wellness program and you've got a recipe for disaster. In response to a provocative NPR article "Is That Corporate Wellness Program Doing Your Heart Any Good?", one individual commented: "I work 12 hour nights in a factory. I am underpaid, on camera all night, get tracked going in or outdoors with a badge . . . and with a phoney [sic] 'wellness program' (which is [designed] to cut their long-term costs and increase productivity) they literally want my blood."[16,17]

Unfortunately, what I see far too often is a distinct mismatch between the culture and well-intended wellness efforts.

THE STORY OF A MISMATCH BETWEEN CULTURE AND WELLNESS

On paper, an organization we worked with had an award-winning worksite wellness program. Prompted by results from an annual health risk assessment indicating that many employees were at risk for mental health issues, the company's wellness manager and her team put mental health at the core of their wellness programming. This was a smart move. According to the National Institute of Mental Health, 11 million Americans are suffering from serious mental illness and one quarter of Americans are affected by one or more mental disorders. The costs associated with these conditions are astronomical, estimated to be in excess of \$300 billion per year.[18] And the number of days missed due to depression exceeds any other condition—including cancer—by nearly 40 percent![19]

Despite the good intentions behind these efforts to support mental well-being and reduce stress, the company failed to address some of the larger cultural factors in the workplace that were driving the stress in the first place.

Over the course of several focus groups, an issue that came up repeatedly was the fact that the employees were not allowed to choose the channel on the TV in their employee break room. The channel was set on CNN, per the decision of the facilities manager, and the employees were given no say in the matter.

Meanwhile, the research clearly shows that lack of autonomy is one of the key drivers of stress in the workplace. In fact, a recent Harvard study showed that contrary to popular belief, our stress levels go *down* as we move up in an organization. The reason? When we move up, we have a greater perceived sense of control, or autonomy.[20] When people feel like they don't have choices and the ability to do things on their own terms, they feel stressed.

So my question was, rather than spending all of these resources on building an award-winning mental health program, why not simply let employees choose the darn TV channel in the break room?

Mismatches like these can be terribly frustrating for any wellness leader, and they beg the question: How do we avoid these disconnects in the first place—and when they are already in place, what can we do about them? Moving a culture forward is no small task. There are, however, specific steps you can take to start to shift the culture to better support your movement.

First, you can assess the culture to better understand it (as we are about to address)—and then take measures to work within that existing container. Second, you can think about making the case for *culture*—in a similar fashion in which you made the case for wellness. Third, you can take more of a decentralized approach, and help individual *teams* to nurture their own sub-cultures. These diffused oases of engagement and well-being can start to gain momentum over time to eventually move up and across the organization. Fourth, you can look for "stealth" opportunities for embedding culture change efforts into other initiatives. Finally, a very simple, but useful step you can take is to clarify your "sphere of influence."

ACTION ITEM

IDENTIFY YOUR SPHERE OF INFLUENCE

Here's a useful activity to do with your core action team as a way to help highlight what you can do in addressing your organization's culture. This is also a great exercise for managers and even leaders, who are often feeling that there are forces beyond their control that are impacting their ability to lead.

Here's how you do it:

1. Draw two concentric circles and label the inside circle "within our control" and the outside circle "outside our control."

(*continued*)

(*continued*)

2. Begin with the outside circle. What are the factors, such as unions, that you don't have control over? Other things that might come up include lack of resources, arbitrary decisions by executives, or attitudes toward wellness.
3. Now, direct your attention to the inside circle. What are the factors that are within your control, or within your sphere of influence? Ideas that might come up include how you work together as a core action team, the programs you design, your personal attitudes, and your personal whys.
4. Finally, discuss how the inner circle can actually start to shift the outer circle.

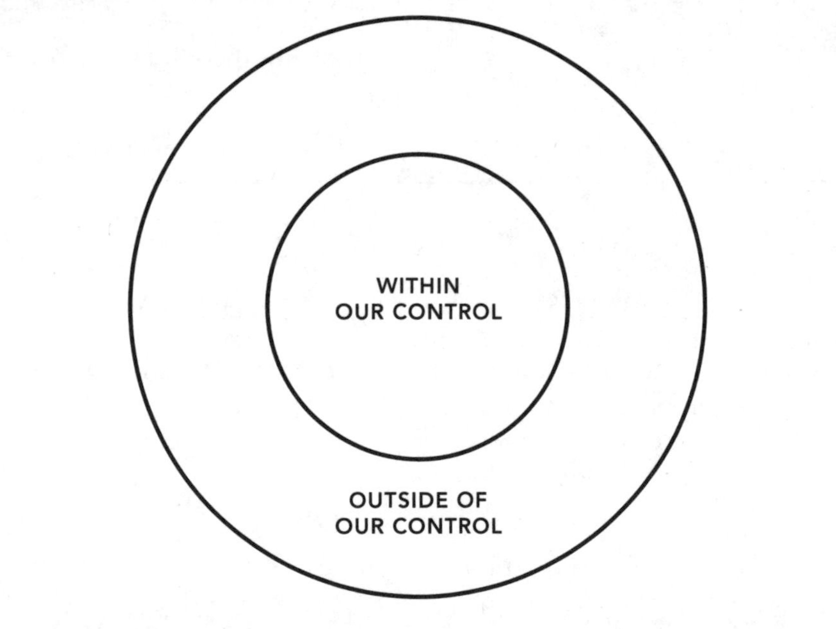

In contrast with a situation in which a negative culture undermines workplace wellness, Patagonia is a case in which a *vibrant* culture of well-being effectively negates the need for workplace wellness.

THE STORY OF PATAGONIA

Patagonia's legendary founder Yvon Chouinard once said, "The work can wait, but the weather can't."[21] This "Let My People Go Surfing" philosophy continues to shape the company culture: People regularly surf, train for marathons and ultramarathons, and hold meetings on the beach—during work time. Moving beyond physical well-being, employees even have the option to take a two-month sabbatical to work at a nonprofit of their choice.

I was interested in finding out more about Patagonia's wellness program. So I called up the corporate office and asked to speak with the wellness manager. The person who picked up the phone laughed and said, "Um, we don't have a wellness manager. We don't have a wellness program. But I guess you can talk with our leadership guy. He's probably the closest you're going to get to a wellness manager."

In other words, there is so much well-being embedded into the way work is done at Patagonia, there is no need for a stand-alone wellness program! Ultimately, isn't that our ultimate goal?

BEGINNING TO UNCOVER THE HIDDEN FACTORS: ASSESS

How do you assess engagement and culture? How do you assess whether the culture is serving as an accelerator or a barrier for overall employee engagement and, in turn, employee well-being? There are a few statistically valid assessment tools available, including the Denison Organizational Culture Survey and the Organizational Culture Assessment Instrument, developed by Cameron and Quinn. These tools have been tested with a large number of organizations. Probably the best-known assessment tool for employee engagement—which is a key indicator of culture—is the Gallup Q12 Employee Engagement Survey.

While useful, these tools are expensive. You may not have the luxury of having this kind of budget at your disposal and you may need to take a DIY approach to assess your workplace culture.

The techniques below are inexpensive ways to get a read on what's happening in your culture and get a better understanding of the hidden factors.

TAP INTO WHAT YOU ALREADY HAVE

Internal Data. In many cases, you'll find that you already have a lot of useful data that will help you to uncover the hidden factors. Engagement surveys, for example, are now standard practices in most organizations. Ask to see this aggregate data to get a picture of the extent to which the culture in your organization is likely to either sabotage or support your efforts to promote well-being. It's also useful to take a look at aggregate data on medical claims, absenteeism rates, turnover rates, productivity measures, number of employee referrals, and results from exit interviews.

External Data. In the age of transparency, there are a lot of external resources. Glassdoor (www.glassdoor.com) is a good one. This employee review website gives unadulterated, unfiltered commentaries on employee experiences—which is great material for you to pull from as you start to get a sense of your organization's culture.

DRAW SOME PRELIMINARY CONCLUSIONS

Identify the Bright Spots. Take a moment to notice any bright spots in your organization's current culture. Identifying these bright spots, or what's going right, is a great place for starting your movement. We'll discuss this more in Step 4: Start with What's Right.

ONE DEPARTMENT'S BRIGHT SPOTS

We worked with a department of a large health care provider to launch a yearlong culture change initiative, with a primary focus on improving teamwork, raising engagement levels, and decreasing rates of absenteeism. One of the first steps we took in this initiative was to identify bright spots. These bright spots were based on conversations with department leaders, results from a prior wellness initiative, other preexisting data, and observations.

The following is an excerpt from our report:

"The good news is that there are a number of bright spots that you can build on. These include improved patient access, increased phone call pick-up rate, a 10–15 percent improvement in patient satisfaction scores in the last quarter, good scores on quality metrics, strong participation rates in the previous wellness program, and overall, morale is better than it was two years ago. In addition, it is worth noting that there are still many employees who show up regularly, are actively engaged, work extremely well with others, and are high performers. In fact, it is a minority of the employees who are chronically absent."

Then Identify What's Missing. Once you've sifted through this initial data, you can begin to assess what's missing. What I often find is that the *human side* is missing. There are lots of numbers, but not enough explanation of the stories behind these numbers. The next section is focused on how you can start to get a more complete picture of your organization's culture through both quantitative and qualitative data.

GOING LOW-TECH

Marbles. This is a useful, totally low-tech method you can employ to assess the culture within a team—and a great idea that I got from my good friend, Rosie Ward. If you're trying to get a read across the entire organization, you'll probably need to have each team conduct the assessment and report results back to you.

Set out a jar and ask each employee to deposit a green, red, or yellow marble, depending on how the day went. If it was a great day, drop a green marble. If it was a terrible day, deposit a red marble. If it was somewhere in between, put a yellow marble in the jar. Run this test for two weeks, and then see what the configuration looks like. If you've got a lot of red marbles in the jar, then you know your team culture is in dire need of a tune-up.

Snow Day. Recently, an informal study on workplace culture in New England tracked the effort that employees made to get to work on a snow day as an indicator of culture. If you live in a colder climate, you can use snow days to get a measure of your organization's current culture. If a lot of employees are showing up on snow days, you probably have a pretty good culture and you can guess that those who are showing up are engaged. If there's barely a dusting of snow and nobody's showing up, chances are you've got a negative culture.

LEVERAGE MASLOW TO ASSESS THE CULTURE

Maslow Meets Mallory Culture Audit. In his book *Peak*, Chip Conley outlines "How Great Companies Get Their Mojo from Maslow." Inspired by his message, I developed what I call the Maslow Meets Mallory Culture Audit in order to go a little deeper into assessing the culture without spending huge amounts of money. It's a great tool with tons of useful exercises that almost anyone can easily use to size up the current culture. It's a great way to get a sense of what is—and what *could be.*

Just as we did in Step 2: Imagine What's Possible, we're going to leverage Abraham Maslow's hierarchy of needs, but now map it to an *organization's* hierarchy of needs. In working with leaders of organizations and teams in helping them to address the uncovered issues, I often suggest the image of "climbing a mountain," one camp at a time. First we need to reach Base Camp, before we can ascend to Camp 1, 2, 3, and so on up to the actual summit.

While Sir Edmund Hillary is given credit for being the first to successfully summit Mt. Everest in 1953, there's evidence to suggest that another climber, George Mallory, may have beaten Hillary—*by several decades.* Mallory and his climbing partner Andrew "Sandy" Irvine never made it back, and for many years it was assumed that they had not made it to the top—until 1999. Seventy-five years after Mallory's disappearance, mountaineer Conrad Anker and his team found his body, virtually intact. Mallory apparently had made a promise to his wife Ruth that he would place her photo on top of the mountain when he summited. When Anker searched Mallory's body, the photo was missing—giving evidence to suggest that Mallory may have placed the photo on the summit—and actually been the first to scale Mt. Everest.

Regardless of whether or not the story is true, it's inspiring, and I'm always a sucker for a good love story. With this great story in mind, you can use the Maslow Meets Mallory Culture Audit to gain a better understanding of your organization's culture.

This audit is based on the notion that organizations, like individuals, *can* become their "best selves." The roadmap to this cultural higher level begins with satisfying "lower order" needs for employees organization-wide, such as clarity of job responsibilities and adequate resources, before moving on to "higher order" needs, such as creating the conditions where employees feel inspired at work. These are the steps to designing what I call a "want to" culture as opposed to a "have to" culture.

Maslow Meets Mallory Culture Audit

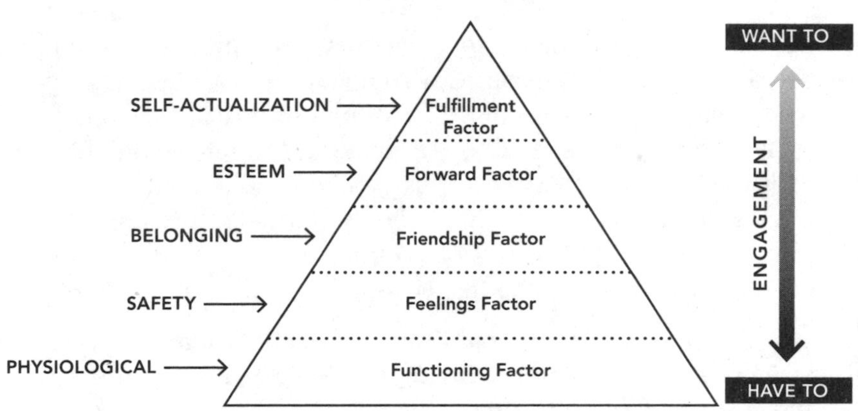

Level 1: Do people have what they need to do their job? This is what I call the "Functioning Factor."

Level 2: Do people feel appreciated and respected? This is what I call the "Feelings Factor."

Level 3: Do people feel connected to one another? This is what I call the "Friendship Factor."

Level 4: Do people feel like they have opportunities for growth? This is what I call the "Forward Factor."

Level 5: Do people feel like they are inspired and working toward their higher purpose? This is what I call the "Fulfillment Factor."

THE 5 "F" FACTORS

The Functioning Factor. At a minimum, employees are counting on having their basic needs met. Without these, it's nearly impossible to have a strong culture. Do employees know what is expected of them? Is the physical environment an inviting place to be? Are there effective systems in place to keep the workflow running smoothly? Do employees have what they need in the way of resources and materials to do their jobs? Do employees feel that they are physically safe? Are the basics of ethical behaviors being met, or are you seeing examples of immoral or even illegal activities?

AN UNDERRESOURCED MISSION

I often see employee needs not being met at this first Functioning Factor level in a nonprofit environment or academic setting. There may be a strong sense of mission but a lack of resources to sustain the employees. This is a recipe for burnout—and I have personally experienced what this is like. For several years, I worked in urban public high schools that were strapped for cash. At one school, we were required to pay for and bring our own personal reams of paper to make copies for students!

Therefore, I often would turn to friends working in well-resourced financial companies for bootleg copying. My friends and I would sneak into their offices at night, and the next day I'd return to my class with boxes full of reading material for my students. I even held a "Lemon Drops for Leadership" Benefit Event (your admission entitled you to a drink known as a "lemon drop" when you walked in the door) to raise money for a class project.

My experiences as an underresourced teacher are not unique. I, along with "millions of teachers across the country," according to a recent post on ABC News, dished out my "own hard-earned cash to pay for books, pens, pencils, and other basic supplies that have been provided in the past."[22] As reported by the National School Supply and Equipment Association, teachers spend an average of $300 or more of their own money every year on classroom supplies.[23] Not surprisingly, the burnout for teachers is high.

You can avoid this kind of burnout by making sure your employees have the basic tools to do their jobs.

The Feelings Factor. Maya Angelou said, "I've learned that people will forget what you said, people will forget what you did, but people will never forget how you made them feel." Feelings matter—especially in the workplace. The Feelings Factor is absolutely essential to the success of culture in any organization.

The Feelings Factor stems from employee perceptions of equality, encouragement, and respect. Is there trust in the workplace? Is there a culture of civility? Are people nice to each other? Do people, especially managers and leaders, pay attention to not just *what* they say, but *how* they say it? Is there a culture of compassion? Is there open and ongoing communication? Is there transparency and "plain talk" here—coming from all levels? Are there any toxic individuals who engage in abusive behaviors? Do people feel appreciated? According to an extensive study conducted by HealthStream Research, feeling appreciated is the number one reason an employee stays or goes.[24] Finally, is there a sense of fairness in the workplace? The hallmark of a toxic culture is one in which there is "blatant unfairness."[25]

For too long, many organizations have fooled themselves into thinking that employees can "check emotions at the door." This ignores one fundamental tenet: To be human is to be emotional. For any culture to flourish, an organization *must* pay attention to feelings. This was why Chip Conley dubbed himself the "chief emotions officer" when he was CEO of Joie de Vivre.

Hilton's chief human resources officer, Rob Webb, also understands the importance of the Feelings Factor, and pays special attention to empathy in the workplace. "Our job is to understand them [employees] and take an empathetic perspective on what is going on in their lives, managing them as individuals and having empathy to figure out their needs and wants," he says. "We can keep people engaged when we can make a place where people can catch their breath and really take time to care about each other."[26]

Paying attention to the Feelings Factor is not only good for morale—it's good for business. In *The Advantage*, consultant Patrick Lencioni clarifies that organizations need to be both "smart" and "healthy" to succeed. He notes that many executives view this kind of emotional stuff (which is vital to the health of an organization) as being "beneath them." Doug Conant, former CEO of Campbell's Soup, is a rare example of a business leader who embraced Lencioni's notion of "stooping to greatness."[27] Starting in 2001, Conant successfully led Campbell's through a massive turnaround, largely due to his persistent investment in the culture, especially in the area of building trust. Conant wrote more than 30,000 handwritten thank-you notes to more than 20,000 employees to start unraveling the pervasively negative culture.

In a blog post, Conant shared, "I let them know that I am personally paying attention and celebrating their accomplishments." Conant's efforts were handsomely rewarded. Under his leadership, Campbell's outperformed the S&P by fivefold. He remarked, "To win in the marketplace you must first win in the workplace."[28] Conant's efforts to generate positive feelings in the workplace generated real results.

According to a recent survey of more than 20,000 employees conducted by Tony Schwartz and the Energy Project, employees who feel respected by their boss report an 89 percent higher level of job satisfaction, are 55 percent more engaged, are 1.1 times less likely to leave the organization, and experience 56 percent higher levels of well-being compared with those who don't feel respected by their boss.[29] Unfortunately, as stated in this same survey, more than half (54 percent) of workers report that they *don't* feel respected by their boss.

As this survey reveals, the Feelings Factor often comes down to the manager. Many times, issues like trust, empathy, and respect amount to a team-by-team experience. The manager can make or break a worker's experience. The problem is that many managers consider the Feelings Factor to be outside the realm of their responsibilities. Truly incorporating the Feelings Factor into their management duties requires that they take a look at themselves. This is not easy to do, but it's not impossible.

THE STORY OF DR. SCOTT BUFFINGTON

Dr. Scott Buffington (not his actual name), orthopedic surgeon at the University of California at San Francisco Medical Center, like many surgeons, ignored the Feelings Factor. Ironically awarded for his outstanding patient care, he was brusque, demanding, sarcastic, belittling, and known for occasionally driving a staff member to tears. Looking back on this, Scott admits, "There are some surgeons who get irate and yell and scream and criticize. And I was one of them."

After repeated reports to the department chief, requests from staff to not work with him, and a recommendation from the medical committee, Scott finally decided to take action. He enrolled in a three-month intensive mindfulness-based stress reduction course and agreed to participate in a Faculty Assistance Program—which met on a biweekly basis for six months.

"It was a pretty significant commitment," he says. This commitment, however, led to noticeable changes in his behavior in the operating room. First, Scott began addressing every staff person by name. If he didn't know someone's name, he would ask. He began including everyone in the conversation—not just the favored inner circle. He even paid attention to the custodians who cleaned the operating room between operations, addressing each custodian by name and often giving them gift certificate cards that he regularly kept in his pocket. Scott also started a tradition of hosting a Friday night ping-pong social hour at his house with all of the staff, including the custodians.

Through his hard work and self-transformation, Scott changed his underlying assumptions about what it means to lead a team. Previously, he operated under the old paradigm that as "captain of the ship," he knew how to do every step better than everyone else—and everyone needed to defer to him.

Under the new paradigm, he recognized that employee empowerment was a better way. "If you empower everybody to care and to do their job, then first of all everybody works more efficiently, everybody feels respected, and everybody actually wants to perform at the highest level that they can," he explains. Now, he begins surgeries reminding his team, "You know what, guys? In the entire world this patient is so lucky to have come here because in the entire world there's no one who does what we're about to do better than what we're going to do." He notes, "It's always 'we'—not 'me'."

Under Scott's new style of leadership, the operating room became a productivity machine. The turnaround time between surgeries dropped to all-time lows. The supercharged custodial staff members, who regularly referred to Scott as "my man," did everything they could to clean and prepare the room in record time. Why? Because Scott was *nice* to them. He acknowledged them as feeling human beings, he included them, and he demonstrated a deep respect.

(*continued*)

(*continued*)

These changes caught the attention of the department chief, as well as the hospital. They wanted to know more about the magic behind the short turnaround time in Scott's operating room, and they wanted to know if he could train other surgeons, especially the cardiac surgeons. By paying attention to the Feelings Factor, Scott transformed his staff into a highly efficient, high-performing team.

Source: Scott Buffington, interview with author, December 7, 2014.

The Friendship Factor. The next level in Maslow's Hierarchy of Needs is the need for belonging. As you assess your organization's culture, it's critical to understand whether social connections and support are fostered in the workplace. Engaged workforces are generally *connected* workforces.

To assess the friendship factor, ask yourself: Is this workplace fun? Do individuals work well together? Do teams work well together? Do employees genuinely like their coworkers? Do employees have good friends and even a best friend at work? Gallup's research shows that employees who have a best friend at work are seven times more likely to be highly engaged compared with employees who don't.[30]

The Forward Factor. In looking at the Forward Factor, are there opportunities for learning and growth? Are employees promoted and given support to invest in their careers? Do employees feel like they're part of a winning team? Is the company growing? Do employees feel energized by getting to use their strengths every day? Do employees have the autonomy they need to achieve greatness? Are employees recognized for their great work? Do employees' opinions matter? Are there meaningful opportunities for employees to get involved in key decisions and help the organization to grow? Does management authentically listen to employee feedback?

The opportunity for employee growth is critical for a strong culture, and also for retention. Coauthors Beverly Kaye and Julie Winkle Giulioni, in *Help Them Grow or Watch Them Go*, advise managers about the perils of ignoring the "development imperative." "Every day," they warn, "employees who believe that their careers are not getting the attention they deserve make the decision to leave."[31] Or worse, they stay, but disengage.

The Fulfillment Factor. Finally, do employees feel inspired? Do employees feel like they're part of something larger? Do they feel a deep sense of purpose in what they do every day? Are they inspired to be their "best selves" at work?

A growing number of business leaders are embracing a commitment to a nobler cause and are building mission-driven organizations. Wellness can be a part of this conversation, which is something to keep in mind as you build your wellness "case" to get senior leaders, managers, and employees on board. The Fulfillment Factor is particularly important for retention and attraction. According to Josh Bersin, principal and founder of Bersin by Deloitte, "Our candidates today are not looking for a career, they are looking for an experience."[32]

ACTION ITEM

CONDUCT A MASLOW MEETS MALLORY CULTURE AUDIT

The Maslow Meets Mallory Culture Audit, inspired by George Mallory (and Chip Conley) and influenced by Abraham Maslow, is based on the notion that organizations like individuals have "lower order" needs, such as clarity of job duties, that must be satisfied before moving on to "higher order" needs, such as feeling inspired at work.

Using this framework, you can generate some simple prompts to build a simple survey. The anonymous responses from this survey can give you a read on your culture. After conducting this survey, you'll want to gather some qualitative data to tell the stories behind the data.

UNCOVERING THE STORIES BEHIND THE DATA

To really get a sense of your workplace culture, it's best to dig into the qualitative data: What are the *stories* that drive your organization?

Projective Questioning. Creative techniques like "projective questioning" can help uncover the stories of an organization. This technique uses indirect methods to get a deeper understanding of where employees are coming from. For example, instead of asking the question, "What would make this a better place to work?," ask the question, "You're the all-powerful king or queen of the universe. What would be the first thing you'd change here?"

Images. Another creative technique is to use images, rather than words. Over the course of an interview or focus group, I will often lay out a group of images (no more than 10) on a table and ask the individual or group to identify the image that best represents their day-to-day experience at work.

ACTION ITEM

GATHER THE STORIES BEHIND THE DATA

Below are sample questions and prompts you could use in your interviews and/or focus groups. You've already gathered data that can be quantified. The objective here is to uncover the *stories*.

- When you wake up in the morning and are getting ready to come into work, what's the first word that comes to mind?
- Tell me about a job that you've enjoyed most in your life.
- Tell me about a time in your life when you were happiest.
- Tell me about someone you have worked with or partnered with that you worked really well with. Examples: sports team, school, project outside of work.
- If your workplace were an image, which one would it be? Which one most accurately captures what it's like to work here? (Without thinking, which one comes the closest?)
- Tell me about your best day here ever.
- Tell me about your worst day here ever.
- What are you doing when you're not here?

- If you were king or queen of the universe, what's the one thing you would change here?

Tip: In follow-up to each question, avoid asking, "Why?" This question tends to encourage a more analytical response—and can even put participants on edge. It can feel like they have to "justify" their response. A better follow-up is the prompt, "Tell me more."

Words on a Paper? One of my favorite creative exercises to use in a focus group is to simply write out the company's core values on a posted flip chart sheet (without labeling them as such). Then I ask the question, "What are these?" If the participants don't know what they are, there is a good chance that the company's core values are just words on a piece of paper, and not an integral part of their day-to-day experience at work.

I've used this technique over and over again, and I never cease to be amazed at how often participants don't recognize their organization's core values. At a company like IDEO or Zappos, you can be sure that every employee knows the company's core values inside and out. Even customers at Zappos are familiar with them, as they're written on the packaging.

A follow-up activity is to prompt each participant to place a green, red, or yellow sticker dot beside each core value written on the flip chart. Green means that the company lives and breathes the core value. Red means that the value is just "words on a paper," and not in any way connected to their personal experience at work. Yellow is somewhere in between. This activity allows each employee to retain some anonymity and at the same time contribute a voice. The group composite will likely generate great follow-up discussion, and also provide good material for you in gathering the stories of the organization.

INITIATE A DIALOGUE WITH LEADERS

Your next step will be to synthesize, summarize, and evaluate the hidden factors in a report, including observations, themes, and recommendations. Then share these findings with decision makers, as well as your da Vinci team, which we'll discuss in Step 5: Take a da Vinci Approach to Change.

SAMPLE MASLOW MEETS MALLORY RECOMMENDATIONS

To give you a sense of what some of these initial recommendations might look like, the following is an excerpt from the report we provided for leaders of the medical department we worked with:

FUNCTIONING FACTOR:

- Clarify and reclarify job responsibilities.
- Assign reasonable workloads.
- Conduct an office environmental makeover.

FEELINGS FACTOR:

- Help people to ALWAYS feel included.
- Be real (transparent with information and authentic with emotions).
- Ask for feedback and ACT upon it.
- Build routines and rituals that foster trust.
- Encourage autonomy, and provide support when needed.
- Show appreciation every day (and mean it).

FRIENDSHIP FACTOR:

- Meet with staff regularly to collaboratively solve problems, build dreams, and exchange feedback (both ways).
- Make every meeting matter by PLANNING (assign roles, make sure there is a chair for everyone, create groups ahead of time) and DEBRIEFING among the Leadership Team (What went well? What would you change? Any other suggestions?).
- Foster a light-hearted climate (and actively discourage "doom and gloom").
- Actively promote on-the-job FUN.

FORWARD FACTOR:

- Work with each employee to create a career development plan and meet quarterly to ensure forward progress.
- Create a culture of learning (ask questions more often, encourage critical thinking, encourage inquiry, and demonstrate vulner-ability).
- Challenge people, and provide support when needed.
- Build on people's strengths.

FULFILLMENT FACTOR:

- Work with everyone in the department to identify departmental core values.
- Work with each employee to clarify his/her personal core values.
- Look for ways to draw the connection between departmental and personal core values.
- Help each employee to devise a personal project that is meaningful, and offers opportunities for creativity.

FINAL THOUGHTS

The next big step for you is to translate your newly acquired cultural insights into workable strategies for your wellness movement within your organization. It is likely that your wellness movement will also spark positive, "Let My People Go Surfing" shifts in the culture, as the two are tightly intertwined. Over the next three steps: Start with What's Right, Take a da Vinci Approach to Change, and Go Stealth, we'll talk about some specific ways that you can actually move your culture forward to better support your wellness movement.

STEP 4

Start with What's Right

(The Optimism Imperative)

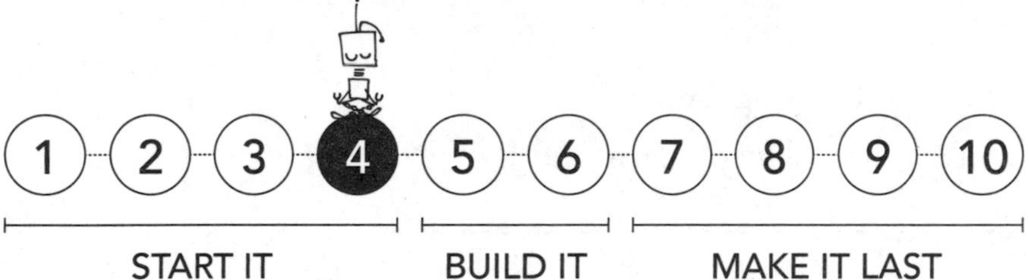

I was never a big fan of kickball or soccer or softball—all of the typical activities in my elementary school PE class. Hand-eye coordination or figuring out how to interface with the other players always eluded me. It goes without saying that I was never one of the kids running out of the classroom, excited for PE. Then one day, we did something different in my PE class: an obstacle course. Now, this was something that I was *great* at—and naturally, I wanted to do more of it. So I looked for avenues to do more of these obstacle course kinds of activities—and that's how I found my way into gymnastics.

I could have kept at those ball sports, chipping away at my lack of hand-eye coordination. Eventually, I *might* have become decent, but talk about a chore. Instead, I chose to follow my strengths. Within a short time, I was practicing gymnastics three hours a day, six days a week, and competing most weekends. I competed in national and even international competitions and eventually earned an athletic scholarship at Stanford University.

This was my personal experience with starting with what's right, as opposed to starting with what's wrong. It turns out there's a lot of research to show that my experience was not unique. All of us do better when we start with what's right. In this stcp, we'll explore the power of harnessing a "start with what's right" approach to foster a positive and optimistic mind-set—and why this foundation is so essential for the success of your wellness movement.

In this chapter, we'll discuss:

1. The strengths revolution,
2. How workplace wellness usually starts with "what's wrong,"
3. Why terror tactics don't work,
4. Turning around the negative vortex,
5. The happiness advantage,
6. The well-being advantage,
7. Identifying the bright spots, and
8. Reinventing the baseline.

YOUR STEP 4 CHECKLIST

- ☐ Employ activities and campaigns that start with what's right.
- ☐ Empower individuals to identify their well-being strengths, or bright spots.
- ☐ Identify the bright spots on an organizational level.
- ☐ Identify the key metrics to reinvent a baseline on current level of employee well-being.

THE STRENGTHS REVOLUTION

In 1999, Gallup came out with a remarkable idea. What if we forgo all of this talk about what's wrong with us? What if, instead, we start with what's *right* with us? *First, Break All the Rules*, cowritten by Marcus Buckingham and Curt Coffman, proposed the idea that a key to effective management is to focus on strengths. The coauthors encouraged managers to "focus on each person's strengths and manage around his weaknesses" in order to let each "become more of who they already are."[1]

Shortly thereafter, *Now, Discover Your Strengths*, cowritten by Buckingham and Don Clifton, spelled out this strengths-based approach for everyone. According to Buckingham, "We wrote this book to start a revolution, the strengths revolution."[2]

After a lifetime of being told to "focus on our weaknesses," suddenly, we were told that it's okay—in fact, it's *better*—if we focus on our strengths. Clearly, people were waiting for this revolution. Buckingham is now one of the highest paid speakers on the circuit, and more than seven million people around the world have taken the StrengthsFinder assessment.[3]

Companies like VMware Inc., Wayfair Inc., and Boston Consulting are adopting a strengths-based, "accentuate the positive" approach. Managers are encouraged to celebrate their team members' tiny triumphs, provide ongoing appreciation, and focus on what went right as opposed to dwelling on what went wrong during performance reviews.[4] At Facebook, 80 percent of employee reviews are dedicated toward discussing strengths, and the remaining 20 percent focus on how to manage around weaknesses.[5]

"Your strengths are those activities that make you feel strong," writes Marcus Buckingham in *Go Put Your Strengths to Work*. Conversely, weaknesses are those activities that make you feel depleted. Not only does it *feel* a whole lot better to start with what's right, Gallup has a mountain of research demonstrating that a strengths-based approach actually leads to better results.

Using one's strengths may be *the* critical factor for engagement and high performance. According to Gallup's findings, employees who are leveraging their strengths are six times more likely to be highly engaged in their work.[6] So a manager who wants to nurture high-performing teams should encourage each team member to know and apply their strengths every day.

This, of course, flies in the face of what we've been taught. We've been taught to "correct our weaknesses" rather than focus on our strengths, and unfortunately, traditional workplace wellness has followed suit. The classic model of wellness starts with what's wrong instead of what's *right*, and then focuses on correcting what's wrong over accentuating what's already right.

WORKPLACE WELLNESS USUALLY STARTS WITH WHAT'S WRONG

Wellness programs typically start with assessing risk factors, or what's wrong, gathered through two primary vehicles: health risk assessments

(HRAs) and biometric screenings. According to the National Business Group on Health and Towers Watson, 84 percent of U.S. organizations with employee wellness programs offer HRAs, and 76 percent provide biometric screenings.[7]

As we discussed earlier, the primary goals of HRAs and biometric screenings are to (1) provide baseline information for organizations and (2) feed information to individuals alerting them to areas that need improvement. Employees are encouraged to "know their numbers" with the hope that they will be motivated to take action to "reduce risk factors."

Sounds good in theory, but this approach is problematic on a number of levels. First, filling out an annual HRA is not particularly inspiring. Rather, it can feel like a mundane, check-the-box task. Worse, an HRA, and particularly a biometric screening, can feel threatening and even stigmatizing, especially when attached to an incentive or penalty.

Second, what matters is what people actually do, and the research overwhelmingly indicates that the mere act of self-reporting one's health behaviors and risk factors, or having them reported back after a screening, rarely translates into action. Just "knowing your numbers" does *not* inspire behavior change for most.[8]

Third, we're diverting a huge amount of resources and efforts toward measuring—and not enough toward doing. Biometric screenings, in particular, are not cheap. This means that there are fewer resources left for the actual programming that focuses on the *doing* part of wellness. Add on incentives (which are now averaging more than $600 per employee per year [PEPY]),[9] and even more resources are diverted away from the actual programming.

Fourth, the results from these assessments tell organizations what they already know: Most of us need to get more active, most of us need to eat better, and most of us are feeling stressed out. While the rationale for these assessments is to target those who are "at risk," the reality is that, with few exceptions, *all* of us need to practice more of these healthy behaviors. Instead of expending so many resources on pre-program assessments, it might be wise (and far more logical) to simply *assume* that the vast majority of employees stand to benefit from programs that will help them to get more active, eat better, and reduce stress.

Fifth, HRAs and biometric screenings only tell us part of the picture. Given the influence of other factors on our health and well-being, such as emotional, social, and career-related factors, we need to be conducting more *well-being* assessments. The good news is that the focus on well-being is gaining traction and, consequently, we're seeing a growing number of organizations now assessing and supporting multiple dimensions of well-being.

Finally, and perhaps the most damaging, is that this negative-first approach might be a primary contributor to low levels of engagement, the Achilles heel for most employers who are providing wellness services. According to the 2014 Willis Health and Productivity Survey, the number one commonly shared goal among employers is increasing employee participation and engagement: 70 percent of respondents reported this issue as their top priority in wellness.[10]

While long considered a best practice, a growing number of researchers, practitioners, and even employers are starting to question the use of these assessment tools, particularly the HRA. In a 2011 survey conducted by leading wellness vendor ShapeUp, 43 percent of surveyed employers reported that the HRA was "pretty useless" in terms of leading to any meaningful change in behaviors, and now are considering doing away with the practice altogether.[11]

While establishing a baseline is essential, there are other ways to gather data. At a minimum, I would argue that HRAs and/or biometric screenings be *preceded* by activities that foster a positive spirit and provide opportunities for employees to identify and begin leveraging their strengths *first*. In other words, let's start with what's right.

TERROR TACTICS DON'T WORK

The medical model, which is the primary inspiration behind the classic model of workplace wellness, is good at diagnosing problems, but not so good at motivating positive change. Rather, it's good at spawning fear, which for most of us is *not* motivating.

We repeatedly see examples of well-intended attempts to scare people into making a change. Cigarette labels are a great example. You would think that graphic warning labels on cigarette packages would effectively shock smokers into not smoking. According to Stanford psychologist Kelly McGonigal, author of *Willpower Instinct*, these graphic labels may actually backfire. While the labels may serve as a deterrent to those who are already nonsmokers, they seem to have the *opposite* effect on current smokers. A smoker is likely to look at the image and think, "Wow! That stresses me out! I need a cigarette!" Ironically, this stress response, she explains, tends to generate a "what the hell effect"—and can actually *perpetuate* the behavior.[12]

A heart attack would certainly be enough to frighten anyone into changing lifestyle habits—or so one would think. Surprisingly, that's not the case. Typically, only 25 percent of eligible patients who have either suffered a heart attack or have undergone cardiac surgery elect to enroll in follow-up, prevention programs. Out of those who do enroll, over *90 percent* drop out within a year![13] Dean Ornish, cardiologist, clinical professor of medicine at the University of California at San Francisco, and founder and president of the Preventative Medicine Research Institute, believes that the negative "make these lifestyle changes—or else you will die" approach is what's turning people away.

Therefore, he and his team have developed a different way: one that capitalizes on employing a *positive* approach, or starting with what's right. The "Dr. Dean Ornish Program for Reversing Heart Disease" encourages the same lifestyle changes that these other programs do: healthy diet, moderate exercise, and stress management. But, their programs replace fear mongering with optimism and hope. Instead of threatening patients with a "do this or else" mantra, Ornish and his team encourage patients to "embrace life," "love your life," and "get living."[14] They also use strategic messaging, such as "food is neither bad nor good," to eliminate judgmental overtones. They've even added a fourth component to the mix to reinforce a hope-based, optimistic approach: love and support.

The difference between these two approaches is nothing short of astounding. The typical approach results in one-year compliance rates of only 10 percent; Ornish's approach, on the other hand, results in one-year compliance rates of *85 to 90 percent*.[15] One study showed that after three years, a stunning 77 *percent* of Ornish's patients were still practicing healthy habits and in doing so, warding off costly follow-up bypass surgeries or angioplasty procedures. These success rates represent a cost savings of almost $30,000 per patient.[16]

These examples of "undoing heart disease" by emphasizing the positive are inspiring and informative, and can be applied toward workplace wellness. It's time to change the guilt-driven, negative, feel-badly-about-yourself approach to wellness, by starting with what's right.

FLIPPING AROUND THE NEGATIVE VORTEX

"We've gotten into this negative vortex," says Vic Strecher, professor of health behavior and health education at the University of Michigan and author of *On Purpose*, "where we continue building tools and products that focus on risks." Health risk assessments and biometric screenings, along with the explosion of "quantified self" products, like Fitbits, FuelBands, and pedometers, he asserts, give us knowledge, but not necessarily wisdom. We know more, he explains, but we're not necessarily *doing* anything differently.[17]

What if we flipped the negative vortex? If we go back to Gallup's research on engagement and work performance, we know that a focus on weaknesses depletes and de-motivates. Conversely, a focus on strengths does just the opposite: It motivates and *accelerates* performance. Relating this to workplace wellness, the natural question to consider is: Are our initial assessments (which are focused on flagging problems) motivating employees, or are these assessments doing just the opposite? Perhaps it's worth considering a health *strengths* assessment in lieu of, or at least *before*, a health risk assessment.

Whatever you do *first* sets the tone. Therefore instead of kicking off your wellness movement with a "what's wrong with you?" campaign—namely HRAs and biometric screenings—launch your wellness movement with a "what's right with you?" campaign! Borrowing from Jonathan Haidt, psychologist, motivate the elephant first; direct the rider second.

Consider doing what Patty de Vries does: Start with what's right and wrap all of your wellness efforts into a positive framework.

THE STORY OF PATTY DE VRIES

As wellness manager of HealthySteps, a joint wellness program between Stanford Health Care and Lucile Packard Children's Hospital, Patty de Vries always starts with the positive—and her impressive results show that this approach is paying off.

When she and her team took charge of the annual health fair, they bumped up the attendance from 1,500 to 4,000—in just

(*continued*)

(continued)

one year. Before she and her team came on, the wellness program had 32 wellness champions, or on-the-ground advocates for wellness. Fast forward two years later and Patty and her team built up a network of 1,075 wellness champions. This year, 52 percent of eligible employees voluntarily participated in biometric screenings—a significant increase from previous years.

Patty has the golden touch when it comes to engagement and delivering on results. What's her secret? Starting with what's *right* to create positive experiences from the outset.

"You can come into a situation with fear or with love," she explains. "I approach each with love, and the programs succeed because of it." Might sound hokey to the skeptic, but it *works.* Patty is a force who leads with her heart. Everything that Patty touches turns into a *movement.* She's what I like to call the Oprah Winfrey of workplace wellness.

The key to her success is employing intentional, and often unconventional, practices to build an atmosphere of trust and happiness. One of these unusual practices is kicking off every employee meeting with highlights from Don Miguel Ruiz's book *The Four Agreements*: "(1) Be impeccable with your word; (2) don't take anything personally; (3) don't make assumptions; and (4) always do your best."

Another unusual approach she takes is providing team development sessions that integrate wellness activities, such as gratitude, visualization, and breathing exercises, into the programming.

Only *after* these optimism-enhancing activities does Patty explicitly talk about wellness. She begins with telling employees, "You're perfect where you are. But, if you have wellness goals and want to make changes, we're here to help. My role," she persuasively explains, "is to make your world a little happier and at the same time help you earn your wellness dollars."

Because she's built a foundation of trust, safety, and goodwill, employees feel that Patty, and even their employer, really care about them as people, not just about their biometrics or health status. This is the power of starting with what's right!

Source: Patty de Vries, interview with author, November 15, 2014.

THE HAPPINESS ADVANTAGE

Starting in the 90s, Martin Seligman and his colleagues at the University of Pennsylvania began researching the science behind applying a strengths-based approach in psychology. Twenty years later, they're now directing these findings toward health, calling it "positive health." Just as Maslow reframed psychology in more positive terms, Seligman and his team are helping to reshape our views on health by changing the question from "how can we reduce suffering?" to "how can we experience optimal well-being and become lastingly happier?"[18]

Beyond making us feel good, a positive outlook and happiness lead to a litany of tangible benefits. For starters, they're really good for our health. Cheerful people, according to a Harvard study, are less likely to develop coronary heart disease than noncheerful people—with the same physical risk factors.[19] Men who are optimistic are three times less likely to develop high blood pressure compared with their more pessimistic counterparts, according to another study.[20] There's even research showing that a positive outlook can help protect against the common cold.[21]

In addition to better health, happiness helps us be more successful in all aspects of our life: our work, our ability to be creative, our ability to form social connections, and our ability to experience greater levels of energy.[22] Employees who are happy at work are 12 percent more productive than their less happy peers.[23] Happiness gives us a competitive advantage in life, or "happiness advantage," an expression coined by Shaun Achor, Harvard psychologist and bestselling author.[24]

Generating an optimistic outlook may be *the* key to improving well-being and tackling the engagement conundrum in workplace wellness, according to Barbara Fredrickson, leading positive psychologist, at the University of North Carolina. "Positive emotions, especially when experienced with others," she explains, "light the path to lifestyle change. Positivity improves our health and also fundamentally changes the way the brain works. We are able to see the big picture, connect the dots, try something new and engage in systemic thinking to solve problems like obesity and unhealthy lifestyles." Her groundbreaking research, in collaboration with other researchers, demonstrates that a "daily diet of positivity" with practices such as "loving-kindness meditation," a form of meditation that focuses on well wishes for self and others, can increase our capacity for sustainable motivation and, remarkably, can lead to health improvements on a cellular level.[25]

ACTION ITEM

NAME THREE GOOD THINGS

The act of retelling our personal life stories in a *positive* light can make a big difference in our happiness and health. Research shows that a simple practice of naming three good things on a daily basis can be more effective and longer lasting than Prozac.[26] Bryan Sexton, associate professor of psychiatry and behavioral sciences at Duke University explains that, as humans, "We are hardwired to remember the negative." But the good news is that with practice, we can develop a more positive mindset—and in doing so, boost our health and well-being.

Here's how you can get started: At the end of each day, name and write down three good things that happened that day. According to Sexton, for maximum imprint on our brains, it's better to do this about a half hour before going to bed. Next, identify your role in causing these three good things to happen and identify the emotion you felt as a result of the experience. Finally, share these findings with others to enhance impact.

THE WELL-BEING ADVANTAGE

"Happiness is not the belief that we don't need to change; it is the realization that we can," writes Achor.[27] In addition to the fact that happiness and optimism are in and of themselves good for us, they also help to build "self-efficacy"—or the sense that it is within our capacity to achieve goals and make change.

Starting with what's right, coupled with looking at the multiple dimensions of well-being, creates more opportunities to identify ways that we are already in good health. Let's take a made-up example: John is overweight, smokes, eats junk food, and has high blood pressure. John is extremely unhealthy, according to the classic model perspective. But, what if John is also in love with his wife, connected with his children, and passionate about what he does? Now, this changes the picture. Moving beyond the limitations of the classic model, one might say that John is thriving in his social and career well-being.

Now, let's say I'm John's wellness coach, operating from the classic model. My conversation with John would likely start with a discussion about his risk factors. In other words, I'd likely start off with a focus on what's wrong—and potentially *not even see what he's doing right.*

Simply by widening the lens and leveraging what we might call the "well-being advantage," however, I would be more likely to acknowledge first what John is doing right, encourage him to do more of it, and *then* help him to address his challenges, using his well-being strengths. It's not to say that his unhealthy habits should be overlooked, it's simply a matter of timing. What is going to keep John engaged, not to mention inspired to get started in the first place? The research suggests that starting with what's right is more likely to result in a commitment over time. In essence, flip the negative vortex.

If our goal is to truly empower employees to build self-efficacy, stay engaged, and ultimately achieve a higher level of health, well-being, and vitality, we need to pay attention to and learn from organizations like Playworks that go to great lengths to promote wellness in a positive way, by starting with what's right.

THE STORY OF ONE ORGANIZATION THAT STARTS WITH WHAT'S RIGHT

Playworks, an Oakland, California-based nonprofit organization, believes in the power of play to bring out the best in every kid. Their mission is to teach kids how to play, and how to do so safely and kindly. While one benefit is increased physical activity, the focus is not explicitly on physical health. It's about play. "Kids don't play because they want to be healthy. They play because they like it," says Elizabeth Cushing, president.

Playworks promotes play by bringing coaches on-site to elementary schools, teaching kids how to play games during recess. This year, the organization will serve 900 elementary schools around the country and more than 500,000 children. "Kids go back to class focused and more ready to learn," says Elizabeth. "It's not just about what happens on the playground; it's about how it makes them feel and the way they're engaged with school."

(*continued*)

(*continued*)

When I asked Elizabeth about her thoughts on workplace wellness, she responded, "My problem with wellness is that it implies that you're not well." In thinking about how to promote wellness with its employees, Playworks has taken a different tack. Elizabeth explains, "We're not going to say, 'Hey, you're not well! Take advantage of our wellness program.'" Rather, Playworks brings *play* to its employees—just like it does with kids. This avenue of *play* makes wellness far more accessible and, in Elizabeth's view, more compassionate.

Playworks now has 23 offices across the country. "One of the ways that we transfer culture [across these offices] is through recess," Elizabeth explains. While not mandated, every office is encouraged to hold recess at work. Employees are invited (but never pressured) to take part in recess with their colleagues. This is an opportunity for employees to renew, get some physical activity, and more importantly, interact with one another in a way that they wouldn't otherwise.

Elizabeth explains that the organization's low-pressure approach to play also extends to how they approach workplace wellness. Employees are asked, "Hey, how are you feeling? Want to come play, get to know each other a little bit?" Elizabeth describes how this informal interaction might serve as a portal to more traditional wellness offerings, such as smoking-cessation programs. "When something comes up," she says, "like you [the employee] want to admit that you smoke outside of the office, then we can say, 'Hey, did you know that there's a smoking-cessation program and it's free?' I just think that an employee's likelihood of taking advantage of a wellness program improves if they feel cared for in a way that's not judging and starting with what's wrong with them."

Says Elizabeth, "We find that when you want to modify behavior, it's better to do it through encouragement—and *play*." In other words, Playworks is placing its bets on starting with what's right to promote employee well-being.

Source: Elizabeth Cushing, interview with author, November 28, 2014.

IDENTIFY THE BRIGHT SPOTS—INDIVIDUAL

Just as Gallup has used the StrengthsFinder tool to help employees find ways that they are *already* doing good work, we can help people like John to find ways that they are *already* healthy. This is the well-being advantage. The following is an easy to do, low-tech way to help people self-assess their current level of well-being and vitality—starting with what's right.

ACTION ITEM

GREEN DOT • RED DOT

1. **Vitality wheel:** Each participant is given a blank vitality wheel that is drawn according to the well-being areas you identified earlier in Step 2: Imagine What's Possible. Each "slice" corresponds with an area of well-being. The sample vitality wheel below is organized around six areas of well-being: physical, emotional, social, community, financial, and career.

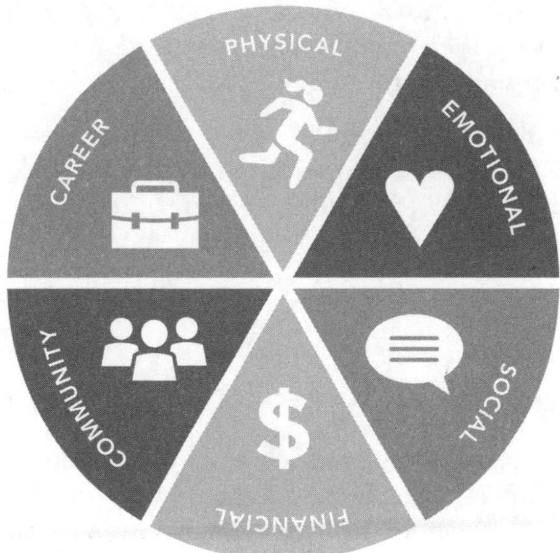

2. **Shade the vitality wheel:** Ask participants to shade in each slice according their level of well-being in that area. A higher

(*continued*)

(continued)

level of well-being is represented by more shading; a lower level of well-being is represented by less shading.

3. **Assess:** After shading in each slice, ask participants to rate themselves in each area, on a scale from 1–10 (10 = very high level of well-being, 1 = very low level of well-being).
4. **Green dot strength(s):** Now, ask participants to identify which area (or areas) they're doing well in right now ("green dot" strengths). Simply identifying these personal "bright spots" can help them to feel energized and more engaged.
5. **Red dot challenge(s):** Then, ask participants to identify which areas are more of a challenge ("red dot" challenges).
6. **Group inventory:** Now, help the participants to collaboratively build a group inventory on a posted group vitality wheel, using green and red sticker dots. Ask each participant to place a green dot in their area of strength and then a red dot on the area that's more challenging.
7. **Pair-share:** Following the group activity, ask each participant to turn to a partner and consider the following question: "How will I leverage my 'green dot' best practices to better address my 'red dot' challenge(s)?"

IDENTIFY THE BRIGHT SPOTS—ORGANIZATION

Let's not lose sight of the fact of what you're doing here is not just another program or initiative. This is a *movement*—and every movement needs energy to take hold. Just as individuals need to build self-efficacy, so do organizations. Let's look at an example of a company that started a movement by first taking stock of the bright spots.

THE STORY OF CHESAPEAKE ENERGY

Chesapeake Energy, an Oklahoma City-based energy company, is taking the leap. Amanda Parsons, employee health analyst, and Toni Parks-Payne, employee services director, are hitting the "refresh" button on Chesapeake's wellness offerings and leapfrogging from old school to new school. They've moved away from incentives to more of a focus on intrinsic motivators, asking employees to "Join the Movement."

To kick off this process, Chesapeake took stock of *what's right*. The truth is that there's actually a lot to celebrate. Chesapeake has already made inroads in providing multidimensional well-being offerings. Below is a summary of some of these bright spots:

- **Physical Well-Being:** Chesapeake's Oklahoma City corporate campus offers a fitness facility that is thriving with 75 percent of local employees as members. Outside the center, employees have access to an outdoor track, volleyball court, and field area. During lunch hour, it's common to see employees playing games such as ultimate frisbee. Also on the corporate campus, the on-site health clinic is heavily used. Here, employees have easy access to primary care physicians, nurses, a dermatologist, and an orthopedist, as well as a pharmacy. Employee Services also hosts activities to encourage healthy lifestyles, including free flu shots.
- **Emotional Well-Being:** In addition to a robust Employee Assistance Program that's in place (and utilized), Chesapeake offers an array of initiatives to support employee emotional well-being at work, including meditation and yoga workshops, and a flexible work schedule to encourage work-life balance.
- **Financial Well-Being:** Chesapeake Energy has a strong 401(k) program in place with a 100 percent match of an employee's contribution, up to 15 percent of an employee's salary. There's also a credit union at corporate headquarters that offers education and financial services to all employees, including those in the field.

(*continued*)

(*continued*)

- **Career Well-Being:** Chesapeake Energy has increased its efforts to promote from within in order to better support career advancement for employees. The company implemented a new talent management program in 2014 and also encourages career growth through its tuition reimbursement program.

Source: Amanda Parsons and Toni Parks-Payne, interview with author, December 19, 2014.

Feel inspired? Now, take a moment to identify the bright spots for your organization in terms of how it is already supporting employee well-being. Recall that you already uncovered your organization's cultural strengths in Step 3: Uncover the Hidden Factors. You may find that there is overlap.

ACTION STEP

IDENTIFY THE BRIGHT SPOTS

Ask the questions: What has your organization already done to create a strong company culture and enhance employee health and well-being? What are the bright spots that are worth noting and celebrating? What successes can you build on?

REINVENTING HOW WE ESTABLISH A BASELINE

Moving beyond, or perhaps reframing, HRAs and biometric screenings, calls for reinventing how we establish a baseline. The first step to assessing is getting to know your people—as *people*. Before you start launching well-being surveys and deciphering data, get on the ground, talk to people, and even shadow people. David Hunnicutt, former CEO of WELCOA, advises that you need to take at least a week to "wear the shoes that your typical employee wears."[28]

After you've walked in their shoes, you're ready to start identifying key metrics. Below are some more detailed metrics to help you get started.

ACTION ITEM

IDENTIFY KEY METRICS

In Step 2: Imagine What's Possible, you and your core action team identified the dimensions of well-being for your movement. How will you know if you're making progress in these multiple domains? Here are some metrics to consider:

- **Physical:** medical claims (and what kinds of medical claims are being filed), workers compensation and disability claims, absenteeism rates, energy audits, health plans and enrollment costs, fitness assessments
- **Emotional:** stress polls and energy audits, mental health-related claims, absenteeism rates, Employee Assistance Program usage rates, pharmaceutical usage
- **Career:** engagement survey results, turnover rates, employee referrals, number of employees taking advantage of professional development opportunities, rate of internal promotions
- **Financial:** number of employees contributing to retirement accounts and/or health savings accounts (if available), number of employees taking advantage of financial planning services (if available)
- **Social:** number of employees participating in company events, number of affinity groups, frequency of employee socializing, unused paid time off balances, internal social media usage rates, number of mentorship relationships

(continued)

(*continued*)

- **Community:** extent to which employees participate in community events, percentage of employees using volunteer benefit hours, amount that employees are contributing to charitable organizations
- **Creative:** allocation of time given to employees to engage in creative pursuits, extent to which bottom-up innovation is encouraged, frequency of creative expression on the job

FINAL THOUGHTS

If you want to help set people up for success, increase the likelihood that they will engage with their health and well-being, and build self-confidence, it is imperative that you focus on building a positive spirit *first* in your wellness movement. Your overriding goal should be to build goodwill, create emotional buy-in, and leverage the strengths, happiness, and well-being advantages. Remember that your movement is in its infancy—and it needs to be imbued with positive energy to grow and thrive.

SECTION II

BUILD IT (WORKPLACE WELLNESS THAT GROWS)

The next two steps focus on how to *build* a wellness movement in your organization.

Step 5: Take a da Vinci Approach to Change helps you implement an *interdisciplinary approach* so that you can start to integrate everything you've learned so far. This creative, silo-busting approach will help you break down barriers that stand in the way of a workplace wellness program that truly engages the entire organization.

Step 6: Go Stealth leverages the interdisciplinary da Vinci approach and helps you infuse well-being and vitality throughout the organization, even in unlikely places. This chapter pinpoints unusual points of entry for your wellness programs, creating a petri dish of wellness that goes viral and spreads throughout the organization.

Step 5

Take a da Vinci Approach to Change

(The Interdisciplinary Imperative)

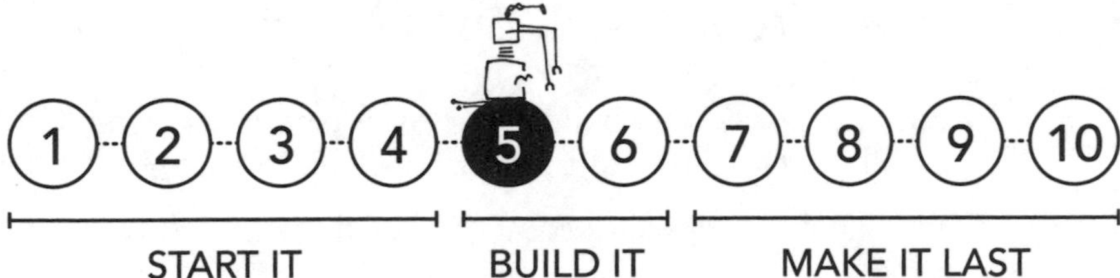

Leonardo da Vinci, best known for his beautiful rendering of Mona Lisa, was the embodiment of the "Renaissance man." As a painter, sculptor, inventor, architect, musician, mathematician, engineer, anatomist, geologist, cartographer, botanist, and writer, he united science with art, music with engineering, cartography with architecture, and sculpture with botany. Da Vinci's prolific contributions demonstrate the power of taking an interdisciplinary approach to work and life, and his contributions to our world celebrate the power of integration to make anything better.

Workplace wellness, on the other hand, has historically been compartmentalized and disconnected from other related efforts within the organization. I believe that the field is desperately in need of a good dose of da Vinci. Just as Ronald Reagan urged, "Mr. Gorbachev, tear down this wall!"—we need to do the same within our organizations: We need to tear down these siloes!

If we truly want to elevate workplace wellness to the next level and do a better job of meeting common goals, we *must* take a more interdisciplinary approach and seek cross-functional solutions among departments. Like da Vinci, your task will be to bring together unlikely partners to create a multifaceted and coordinated team that can work with you to build the movement. With this team in place, you'll then need to work together to develop and deliver da Vinci solutions.

In this chapter, we will explore:

1. What a da Vinci approach looks like in action,
2. Why it's better to take an interdisciplinary approach,
3. The people who need to be on your da Vinci team,
4. Steps to getting everyone involved, and
5. Brainstorming ideas for taking integrated action.

YOUR STEP 5 CHECKLIST

- ☐ Identify key players and build a case to help each understand why well-being is integral to their core objectives.
- ☐ Build your da Vinci team, composed of these key players.
- ☐ Collaborate with each of the da Vinci players to build integrated strategies.
- ☐ Start building the brand and marketing strategy for your well-being movement.
- ☐ Get people on all levels involved in the movement.
- ☐ Conduct a six-hat brainstorming session with the da Vinci team to generate ideas on getting the movement rolling.

DA VINCI IN ACTION

THE STORY OF MARIANNE JACKSON

Marianne Jackson, former chief human resources officer at Blue Shield, a not-for-profit health plan provider with more than 5,000 employees, was an unlikely leader for what has become an award-winning workplace wellness initiative: the Wellvolution Campaign at Blue Shield of California. With a background in human resources and organizational development, she did not fit the typical mold of a wellness leader. This qualification, however, turned out to be her greatest asset.

Early in her 10-year tenure at Blue Shield, while evaluating the annual renewal of benefits, she had what she describes as an awakening to the need to take action. "I was aghast. When I first saw our own premium increase, I blew a gasket!" Blue Shield's health care costs were increasing at a double-digit rate. She asked, "How can this be? We are in the business of health and wellness. And, what can we do about it?" From here, she took action.

"My premise," she explains, "was that the principles of *organizational* behavior were not part of the product design process with historical workplace wellness programs." In her view, the primary players at the table were people coming from the medical profession who were not fully grasping the *context* in which wellness would live—things like company culture, job responsibilities, and socioeconomic factors.

In true da Vinci fashion, Marianne assembled an initial, small, interdisciplinary team of players: herself, being the expert in organizational development; her vice president of human resources, who also happened to be a nurse practitioner and expert on the clinical side; and the director of benefits, who brought her expertise in the area of benefit design. In a living room in San Carlos, over coffee and dressed in casual attire, she says, "We white boarded; we brainstormed." Together they designed the framework for a next-generation wellness approach that would prove to be a positive disruption in Blue Shield's workforce wellness.

The team repeatedly asked the question, "How can we turn the tide?" Escalating costs, they knew, were not due to waste and poor consumerism alone. The heart of the issue really was the actual health status of employees. Armed with this knowledge, they laid the groundwork for what became nothing short of a movement, which they called their "Wellvolution."

(*continued*)

(*continued*)

Their mission clearly called for wellness, but they decided that it had to be done differently. In fact, they spent the bulk of their initial brainstorming session establishing their "*we won't repeat that*" principles. They decided that if they were going to make a difference, they needed to start by truly understanding the needs of employees. For example, a single mom working in a call center, who was "dead tired" at the end of the day and needing to pick up her kids, would be unlikely to take part in an after-work exercise class. So the first element of their strategy was to "make it easy to live well." (This slogan continues to live on at the organization.)

Next, Marianne and her core team knew that they needed to recruit senior leaders to be more than passive supporters. With their active support, the team and the leaders could *model* a practice of wellness to the 5,000 employees at Blue Shield. To accomplish this meant having the leaders not just talk about it, but actually experience it. She approached the CEO, Bruce Bodaken, and made her request: "Just hear me out," she explained. "I'd like to use our annual leadership conference to immerse our leaders in wellness so that they can personally experience what it could really be like to make wellness part of our culture." In essence, she wanted to launch the movement with a big bang. As an expert in organizational development, she knew that the leaders needed to not only cognitively understand the benefits—they also needed to kinesthetically experience it.

Marianne and her team created a two-day, full immersion, off-site retreat for senior leaders that focused on wellness—*their* wellness, including mind, body, and spiritual wellness. This, Marianne was convinced, was what was needed to set the ball in motion.

Following this two-day kickoff event, Wellvolution was delivered to all employees at all sites. A suite of wellness programs, resources, and online communities was set loose. The Wellvolution team watched carefully for what was going to work and what wasn't. "Our design method relied on rapid prototyping to get the program right as quickly as possible and then keep adjusting it as we learned more," she explains.

Marianne shares that her favorite part of her experience was what she calls the "elevator confessions." These elevator experiences were a clear indication that Wellvolution was infiltrating the culture. Nearly every time she stepped into the elevator, employees would see her and begin sharing their stories. "Look!" one might say. "I'm in my workout attire. I'm going to a yoga class." Or another might hide a bag of fast food behind their back. Most important, employees would share over and over again the difference that Wellvolution was making in their lives—and how this was also impacting their coworkers, friends, and family. This was a culture winner!

Thanks to this revolutionary program, or *movement*, Blue Shield has successfully increased wellness participation rates from only one in five employees at the outset in 2008 to today's rate of four out of five. Almost 50 percent of smokers have stopped smoking, bringing it down to one of the lowest rates in the country. Thirty-three percent of employees are physically active, and inactivity levels have fallen by about 50 percent. Based on sales in the company cafeteria, 75 percent of employees have increased their intake of fruits and vegetables.

These wellness changes add up to big wins for both employees and the larger organization. Since the start of the program in 2008, there has been a 27 percent increase in the number of employees who have improved their health status from "at risk" to "healthy." High blood pressure levels have dropped from 25 percent to today's rate of 10 percent. Employees are saving $3 million annually on health insurance premiums and are earning an aggregate total of 2,500 "health days"—days off that are dedicated to renewal and well-being.

Meanwhile, the company is accruing bottom line results: The company is experiencing a 20 percent decrease in disability costs for those four out of five employees who are participating (compared with a 60 percent increase in disability costs for nonparticipants), along with lower medical claims for those employees who are participating.[1,2]

Source: Marianne Jackson, interview with author, November 11, 2014.

WHY A DA VINCI APPROACH IS BETTER

Workplace wellness lives in some form in most organizations today. According to the 2014 Kaiser Family Foundation Report, 98 percent of large employers and 73 percent of smaller organizations that offer health benefits also provide some type of wellness offering.[3] But, as we've discussed, simply *having* wellness is not enough. Often, workplace wellness amounts to little more than disjointed screenings, campaigns, and weight loss challenges.

The da Vinci approach promises a much more powerful wellness effect with synergy and integration, across multiple channels and departments. The more you can coordinate your efforts with others coming from different disciplines, the more you can ensure greater impact in your organization, just as da Vinci would have done.

Below is a graphic depicting what your da Vinci team might look like.

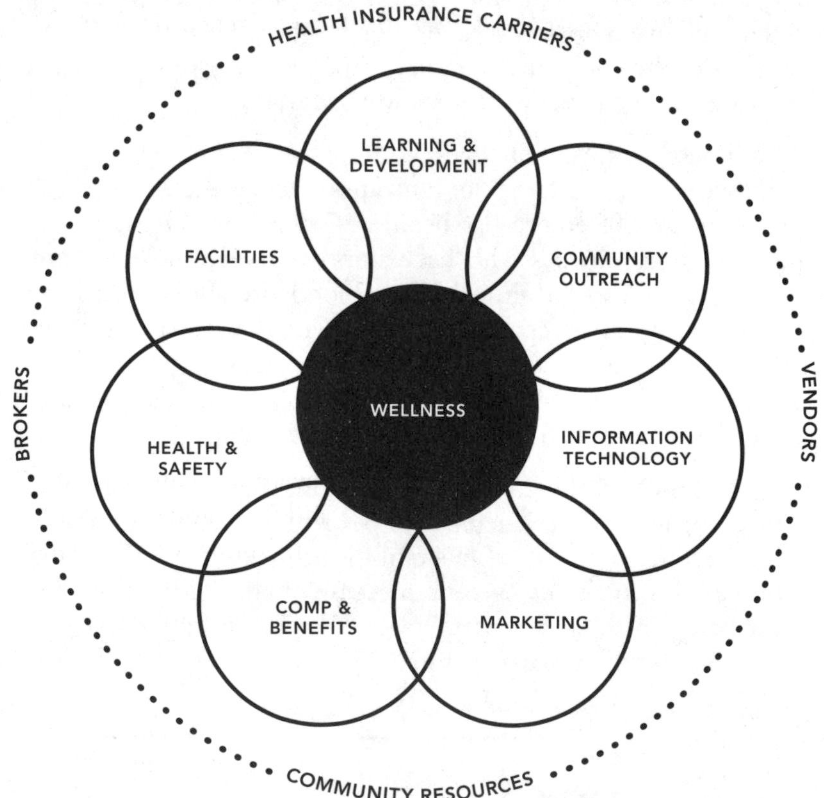

Da Vinci in Action at Brocade

Taking a da Vinci approach is baked into Brocade's wellness strategy. Brocade, a global technology company, launched a da Vinci-style "WellFit" council, composed of a cross-functional group of approximately 10 people, to build and implement the strategy for WellFit. The council was formed in anticipation of Brocade's new corporate headquarters that they were building from the ground up in San Jose, California.

The WellFit council consists of representatives from Brocade's corporate benefits, corporate affairs, facilities, internal communications teams, and wellness champions from around the world. This is a bona fide da Vinci team.

WellFit is housed under corporate affairs to ensure that the strategy is closely integrated with other Brocade initiatives, including their "B-Involved" community outreach program.

Under this program, employees are given 40 hours of paid time off to volunteer with local nonprofit organizations and schools. Past projects include volunteering at community gardens or riding in a bike event to raise funds for a children's hospital. These are great examples of how da Vinci in action can fuel well-being in multiple domains: community, social, and physical well-being.

Brocade also encourages employees to give back to the community by providing matching funds for employee donations. Many Brocade employees have made the connection between community, financial, and physical well-being, by participating in the American Heart Association's annual Heart Walk. Brocade also supports diversity and inclusion efforts. For example, Brocade offers awareness campaigns on women's health, along with additional learning and development opportunities for women. Largely due to its da Vinci approach, the WellFit council has successfully engaged employees across the many departments of the organization.

Source: Jacqueline Szeto, interview with author, November 11, 2014.

BUILDING YOUR INTERNAL DA VINCI TEAM

Who are the key players that need to be on your da Vinci team in order to expand upon your core action team? The following are the ones that are typically included in any discussion about workplace wellness.

Human Resources. In most cases, wellness is housed under human resources, so you will definitely need HR on your side. But remember, this is a movement, not just another program. You'll need to make sure your movement is viewed as *more* than just an HR initiative.

Compensation and Benefits. Especially post-Affordable Care Act, compensation and benefits are key players in the wellness game. According to Debbie Smolensky, health and wellness director at National Financial Partners, there are six ways that compensation and benefits intersects with wellness. First, you'll need to work together with compensation and benefits on the plan design such that the design helps facilitate rather than hinder any employee's participation in wellness. Second, if you're planning on including incentives in the mix, you'll need to work with the compensation and benefits team on planning for and administering the incentives. Third, you need to coordinate with compensation and benefits on eligibility. Fourth, you'll need to analyze the wellness program's impact on premium charges, especially if you are using incentives. Fifth, this group will be one of your key partners in empowering employees to become better health consumers.

Improving consumerism is a critical first step in addressing health care costs. Workplace wellness programs can serve as a first stop in helping employees to identify "centers of excellence," or health care providers that are cost-effective and provide high quality services. Clearly, the more you integrate centers of excellence into your plan design, the more likely your plan will positively impact rates of prevention, outcomes, and, ultimately, overall costs. Compensation and benefits can also be a valuable partner in evaluating high deductible health plan options, which can encourage more thoughtful consumption of health care services.

Legal and compliance considerations must be thoroughly integrated into your plan design in order to ensure that your program is in full compliance with all of the regulations, especially Health Insurance Portability and Accountability Act (HIPAA), Genetic Information Non-Discrimination Act (GINA), Americans with Disabilities Act (ADA), and Age Discrimination in Employment Act (ADEA). To make sure that these legal requirements are met, you will need to work extensively with compensation and benefits, along with someone from your legal and compliance team.

Facilities. After you've thought through all the financial and legal considerations for your program, you'll need to develop an ongoing close partnership with facilities managers for events such as health fairs, on-site fitness classes, lunch 'n' learns, or other seminars and workshops. Obviously, you'll need to work very closely with them for any big-ticket items such as building or renovating a fitness center or improving the stairwells.

You'll also need to work with facilities on more mundane but equally important items like obtaining permission for new wellness signage or posters or to create special communication devices. For example, Patty de Vries, wellness manager for HealthySteps, a joint wellness program between Stanford Health Care and Lucile Packard Children's Hospital, likes to create life-sized stand ups of different people in the organization (such as the CEO) to add fun and a sense of novelty. So before you prop up a mannequin dressed like the CEO in your cafeteria, get the go ahead from your facilities manager (and for that matter, the CEO).

Information Technology (IT). The IT department can be a real friend as you grow your wellness movement. As the percentage of tech-savvy millennials in the workforce continues to grow, and more and more creative technology solutions are developed for wellness programs, you'll need to partner with IT to employ technology-based solutions like gamification, social media platforms, and mobile apps. In addition, you'll need your IT partners to lend a helping hand for any events that require audio, visual, or other tech support.

Marketing. The smart people in marketing can be indispensable in branding your movement in a way that will *move and inspire* people. Visa has branded its wellness program "VisaCares"; and Chesapeake Energy, as we have discussed, is now calling its program "Join the Movement." Building a brand and leveraging multiple channels to publicize programs will be critical to the success of your wellness movement.

Creating an overall brand architecture with an evocative name can be a powerful way to communicate the *connections* between wellness and other core business objectives. As we discussed earlier, Schindler has adopted the term "Odyssey" for a series of initiatives that are linking well-being with core business objectives. "Leadership Odyssey," the original workshop, links leadership with well-being; "Safety Odyssey" links safety with health and well-being; and an upcoming initiative, "HR Odyssey," will link HR with well-being.

Building a brand and leveraging marketing channels to publicize programs will be critical to the success of your wellness movement. To increase impact, make sure that you use multiple avenues—high touch and high tech that encourage both top-down and bottom-up communications. As much as possible, personalize the communication you send out. Leverage mobile technology and social media to enhance communication. You can also use blogs and external websites.

To encourage bottom-up communication, which is essential for engagement and a sense of ownership, you and your da Vinci team will need to devise ongoing opportunities for employees to give feedback—through focus groups, town hall-style gatherings, smaller meetings between managers and employees, management "office hours," suggestion boxes, social media platforms, or even group e-mails. Employees' needs, values, perceptions, and opinions should shape the movement.

ACTION ITEM

BUILD YOUR BRAND

In collaboration with your internal marketing team, you're going to want to think about building a brand for your wellness movement. Your marketing team will have a lot of ideas, but here are some additional ones to help you get started:

- Pull out the collage you and your core action team generated during Step 2: Imagine What's Possible. Hang it up and see if it sparks any ideas.
- Without thinking too much about it, now choose some adjectives generated by the collage you've already created.
- Come up with the story for your movement. The most powerful brands are generated by a story. The Juice Shop, a San Francisco-based company that sells cold-pressed juices, orients all of its marketing around the story that sparked the business. One of the three brothers who started the

company, Charlie, returned home from a surfing trip in Central America with an inexplicable and painful condition. After multiple unsuccessful surgeries and a series of misdiagnoses, he looked for alternative solutions. Eventually, guided by a holistic practitioner, Charlie detoxed through juicing, which led to a miraculous recovery. His story then inspired the three brothers to start their company. Now, the story lives on in all of the company's marketing collateral and is the foundation to the company's brand.

- Be authentic instead of trying to "sound smart." There's lots of jargon in workplace wellness. Avoid this language and choose simple language. This is what will move people—and build trust.
- Be passionate. Your goal is to build bottom-up evangelism. A brand that conveys passion will help spark this.
- If you want more ideas, you can go to www.prestobox.com and click through the "Brand Genie," which will generate a brand for you at no cost.

WELLVOLUTION—MORE THAN A NAME

Marianne Jackson wanted a fresh brand for their "out-of-the-box" wellness program. Blue Shield's marketing team came up with the name "Wellvolution." It was perfect. It held real meaning behind what they were doing and elevated their initiative from just another program to a real movement. The name itself added magic to the movement. "It acknowledged that there was an evolution, or perhaps even a revolution. And it was about wellness. I thought it was brilliant," says Marianne. Over time, the name became an icon of their culture, she explains.

(*continued*)

(*continued*)

"Wellvolution became a verb, a noun, an adjective. 'I Wellvolutionized this,' 'I did Wellvolution today,' 'I feel Wellvolution.'"

The name and brand is what created the buzz behind the wellness program and has also been a strong contributor to the program's staying power.

Source: Marianne Jackson, interview with author, November 11, 2014.

BUILDING YOUR EXTERNAL DA VINCI TEAM

Health Insurance Carriers. Every carrier now has something to offer in the way of wellness—some are better than others. What I often see is that these wellness benefits are not well communicated and are usually underutilized. Some "low hanging fruit" you could capitalize on are the services and products already available through your organization's existing health plan(s) that simply need to be uncovered.

According to the Willis Health and Productivity Survey Report 2014, the most commonly provided services include wellness communications and resources, health risk assessments, biometric screenings, disease management programs, employee portals, employee assistance programs, and nurse lines.[4] Other offerings include digital coaching, health education presentations and workshops, exercise and weight loss challenges using social media, mindfulness classes, fitness classes, on-site diet counseling, incentive tracking, and depression screening. Major insurers also offer additional wellness consulting, which has seen rapid growth across all markets.

Again, though, the real issue is the actual uptake on these services. According to Dana Miller, wellness manager at Aetna, "The level of participation in these programs often ties directly to communication, implementation, and incentive strategies."[5] In other words, the success of these programs is, in large part, determined by the da Vinci factor.

Brokers. A growing number of brokers are increasing their emphasis on workplace wellness, like Presidio Benefits Group, a San Francisco-based brokerage and benefits consulting firm that specializes in working with midsized companies. Presidio Benefits is playing a leadership role in promoting employee health and well-being by helping their clients get the right health plans in place, as well as establishing the right match between their clients, health care funding alternatives, and third-party wellness vendors. Matthew Coan, principal of Presidio Benefits Group, says, "A wellness program's effectiveness is either going to be limited by or buoyed by the funding structure of the insurance program."[6]

In addition to making sure that a wellness-friendly plan is in place, the firm provides additional support for wellness. It sponsors speaker series events once or twice a year that include the country's leaders in wellness. Presidio Benefits Group also conducted a benchmarking survey to get a snapshot of the northern California organizational wellness landscape and then made these results available to their clients and to the public.

THE STORY OF DEL GRANDE DEALER GROUP

Del Grande Dealer Group, or DGDG, a San Francisco Bay Area-based auto dealership, was shaken to the core when one of their most senior employees passed away due to health-related complications. Galvanized by this tragedy, senior management decided they had to take action, and they turned to their Bay Area-based benefits broker, KBI Benefits, for guidance.

"We're not wellness experts," said Mike Radakovich, president of KBI, but "we decided to focus on what we could do rather than what we couldn't do, and then reassess." The first step Mike and his team took was to contact DGDG's health insurance carrier to enlist their support. "This required some hammering in getting them to actually deliver on bringing in their experts to provide some meaningful guidance," says Mike. Taking a da Vinci (and bulldog) approach, KBI collaborated with the insurance carrier and with leaders at DGDG to put together a solid wellness plan, which included forming a wellness committee. With senior management buy-in already in place, the committee included the dealership's owners as well as representation from all 14 locations that included salespeople, administrators, mechanics, and store managers.

The DGDG wellness committee kicked off the wellness initiative with a health fair, which featured more than 40 vendors,

(continued)

(*continued*)

along with music, DJs, food, and door prizes—from little knick-knacks to iPads. "We wanted to get people involved, we wanted to make it fun, and we wanted to build some awareness on things you can do at work, after work, and with your family," explains Mike.

The wellness initiative continued with a four-week physical activity contest. The wellness committee created a team for each store, which created a buzz and a competitive "store against store" atmosphere. This friendly, competitive spirit definitely in step with the existing company culture. In an effort to keep it simple and inclusive, the committee allowed any kind of physical activity to be included. The committee provided a basic app to make it easy for each team to track their activities. A wellness champion at each location rallied people to sign up and get involved, resulting in a 50 percent participation rate.

The wellness committee is rolling out the next phase of the initiative, including a speaker series on wellness topics. The speaker topics will be based on feedback from employee surveys to further increase engagement.

Though straightforward and not fancy, the wellness initiative has been highly effective. According to Mike, "The keys were getting ownership buy-in, matching the company culture with the actual activities, and then getting representation from the different parts of the company, ranging from entry-level employee to senior management, then making it informative and enjoyable, competitive, and, most importantly, conveying a message that we're concerned about you as a person. This is not because your employer says you should do it."

The power of the wellness initiative stems from the partnership between DGDG, the insurance carrier, and KBI. In fact, this partnership split all costs for the initiative. KBI understands the long-term value of investing in workplace wellness for clients like DGDG. "It enhances our credibility and partnership with our client. We're acting as a wellness consultant and actively investing in the health and productivity of their employees, which enhances the foundation of our relationship." Truly, a da Vinci team can benefit everyone.

Source: Mike Radakovich, interview with author, January 4, 2015.

Third-Party Vendors. Workplace wellness is growing—and there are a lot of vendors out there who can help you. According to the Willis Health and Productivity Survey Report 2014, 44 percent of organizations are now turning to a third-party vendor for wellness. This is certainly likely to increase. In scoping out vendors, you'll naturally want to make sure that you find vendors that offer services and products that not only meet your needs but also match the flavor of your organization's culture. There is a whole range of services and products out on the market, including the following:

Screenings: health risk assessments, well-being assessments, biometric screenings

Worksite: on-site fitness facility, on-site fitness classes, on-site clinic

Lifestyle and disease management: speaking and workshops, health and wellness coaching, challenges, apps and tracking devices, online tools, engagement and gamification platforms, disease management services, employee assistance programs

Health consumer support: price and transparency tools, health decision support, advocacy

Overall strategy: consulting, data mining

The majority of services and products are still largely focused on traditional wellness. This is changing—*rapidly*. Mindfulness is exploding, well-being assessments in lieu of health risk assessments are on the uptick, quality of life topics like financial well-being are entering into the mix, and products that build social networks are in high demand.

Community Resources. Finally, there are plenty of long-standing community resources that are willing and able to help. The American Heart Association provides a multitude of free resources, such as "My Life Check," an online heart-health assessment tool, along with guidance on becoming a "Fit-Friendly" worksite. Many of the branches send out volunteers into the workplace to speak about topics related to health and wellness.

The American Heart Association has even engaged leading executives in a CEO Roundtable. In a recent statement, Nancy Brown, CEO of the American Heart Association noted, "With the American Heart Association CEO Roundtable, we're starting a movement to transform the culture of the workplace to meaningfully engage employees to take simple steps that can dramatically reduce their risk of heart-related death and illness."[7]

The Wellness Council of America (WELCOA), is also a great resource—including lots of free downloads to help kick-start your wellness movement. You can find them at www.welcoa.org.

THE UNEXPECTED PLAYERS ON YOUR DA VINCI TEAM

"Whenever you increase the collaboration and cooperation among the siloed parts of an organization, you'll see great benefits," says Dr. L. Casey Chosewood, director for Total Worker Health™ at the National Institute for Occupational Safety and Health (NIOSH). "You will improve communication, better manage change, and be more successful when introducing new programs."[8] In other words, taking a da Vinci approach is critical to the success of any organization-wide effort—especially for workplace wellness.

Since your goal is to start and to build a movement that will last, you need to think outside of the box when recruiting members for your da Vinci team. Below are some key folks to consider, who are often left *out* of the wellness conversation, but could prove to be terrific contributors.

Safety. Tina Turner croons, "What's love got to do with it?" And we might ask the question, "What's safety got to do with it (health and wellness)?" Or, conversely, "What's health and wellness got to do with it (safety)?" Everything. In case we forgot, "Congress passed a law that was called the Occupational Safety **and** Health Act, not the Occupational Safety **or** Health Act," says Wesley Alles, director of the Health Improvement Program at Stanford University. "Whether we are talking about safety versus disease, it is the same lifestyle, the same risk factors at work."[9]

Oddly, health and safety have historically been separated. Fortunately, that's changing. Beginning in 2011, the U.S. government finally stepped up to the plate, teaming up with key research centers to launch Total Worker Health™, a strategy that integrates safety and health protection with health promotion. "The connection between workplace risks and personal risks is indisputable," says Dr. Chosewood. He believes that making that connection is absolutely critical. "Poor health habits, financial difficulties, tobacco use, poor diet, alcohol and drug abuse, stress on and off the job, and lack of regular physical activity all affect job performance, increase risks for injury/illness at work, and diminish wellness."[10]

There are some standout organizations that have been uniting safety and wellness for a long time. Dow Chemical has been integrating health with safety for over 20 years—with a goal to "drive to zero injuries and zero adverse events."[11] The San Francisco-based utilities company Pacific Gas and Electric's "Fit for Duty" program combines safety with wellness. Lincoln Industries, a smaller organization with 620 employees and five sites, has also taken steps to integrate health and safety. As a result of these efforts, work-related injuries at Lincoln Industries have dropped way below the industry average at a rate of 2.54 in comparison with the industry average of 4.9.[12]

ACTION ITEMS

- Change underlying assumptions by helping decision makers, managers, and employees to make the connection between safety and workplace wellness.
- Get representation from safety on your da Vinci team.
- Work collaboratively with your safety representative to devise a strategy that integrates wellness at work with efforts to reduce work-related illnesses and injuries.

Learning and Development/Organizational Development. Towers Watson and the National Business Group on Health are now moving a step beyond Total Worker Health™, advocating a three-pronged integration, dubbed a "health and productivity" strategy that integrates wellness programs, occupational health and safety programs, and employee benefits programs. The goal is to *simultaneously* increase employee health, improve employee safety, and enhance employee productivity.

Building on this integrative health and productivity strategy, you can partner with learning and development to greatly enhance the impact of your wellness movement. The crucial meeting point between workplace wellness and learning and development centers on employee engagement, which is a shared goal of both. Integrating the two can reinforce the desired outcomes on each end.

Gallup's research shows that employees who are engaged in their work are 28 percent more likely to participate in a company workplace wellness program.[13] Conversely, employees who have a high level of well-being are more likely to be engaged in their work. Companies are starting to make the connection, and therefore more are looking for holistic engagement solutions in which engagement and well-being are simultaneously addressed.

In Step 6: Go Stealth, we'll talk more about the generous "stealth" opportunities that come from integrating workplace wellness with learning and development programs.

ACTION ITEMS

- Change underlying assumptions by helping decision makers, managers, and employees make the connection between learning and development and workplace wellness.
- Get representation from learning and development on your da Vinci team.
- Work collaboratively with this representative to do the following:
  - conduct an audit to identify wellness activities that are already in current learning and development programming;
  - integrate well-being into learning and development, organizational development, and talent management initiatives; and
  - develop programming to help employees see and experience the connection between learning and development objectives and wellness objectives.

Community Outreach. Community outreach programs, also called employee volunteer programs or corporate social responsibility programs, are a great way to inspire and engage employees, enhance their well-being, and at the same time improve the surrounding community. The growing interest in community outreach offers yet another great opportunity for expanding on your da Vinci strategy. In Step 6: Go Stealth, we'll discuss how you can also tap into these programs to create "stealth" opportunities for wellness.

ACTION ITEMS

- Change underlying assumptions by helping leaders, managers, and employees to see the connection between community outreach and workplace wellness.
- Get representation from community outreach on your da Vinci team.
- Work collaboratively with this community outreach representative to do the following:
  - seek out ways to integrate multiple forms of well-being, such as social, physical, and emotional, into current community outreach initiatives;
  - make these connections explicit to participating employees; and
  - work with leaders to create policies that support employee engagement in community outreach.

RECRUITING LEADERS ONTO THE DA VINCI TEAM

Senior Leaders. Senior leaders set the tone for any workplace wellness initiative, and they must be on board for the movement to take hold on a broader scale. In some cases you'll get their sign-off at the beginning. In other cases, it might take longer. You may need to start the movement—and gather enough key influencers along the way to later sway the senior management team.

It's ideal for the success of your wellness movement that you have at least one senior leader on your da Vinci team. Senior leaders are critical players in promoting wellness and in helping you start the cultural evolution to more readily support your wellness movement. Some of the key ways that senior leaders can help to positively influence your movement are (1) modeling wellness; (2) speaking about the importance of health and wellness; (3) actively supporting wellness activities and programs; (4) supporting the da Vinci Team; and (5) taking part in the actual planning.

Just as Marianne Jackson did with the executive team at Blue Shield of California, encouraging senior leaders to actually experience the new wellness program through a kick-off retreat or workshop can serve as a great way to get them on board. Follow-up executive coaching can help to *keep* them on board.

A GREAT IDEA!

Kara Ekert, vice president of human resources at L'Oreal suggested the novel idea of having senior leaders deliver lunch 'n' learns (instead of relying on internal wellness personnel or bringing in outside speakers). What a great way to start a movement! If any of your senior leaders are up for it, train them on how to deliver a lunch 'n' learn.

Managers. While senior leaders set the tone, managers effectively give permission—or lack thereof—to their team members. One manager once confided in me, "I don't go to the fitness classes because I don't want my team to feel like I'm intruding." The opposite is true. The reality is that every time she actively participates, she cues her team that it's okay to take part in wellness.

TIP: I WANT TO SEE MY BOSS IN SPANDEX

It's one thing to get management support; it's another thing to get managers actively *participating* in wellness activities—Spandex and all. The latter is what really makes the difference!

According to Gallup's research, managers alone are 70 percent responsible for the overall level of participation in wellness. "Managers," the Gallup authors write, "are uniquely positioned to ensure that each of their employees knows about the company's wellness program, to encourage team members to take part, and to create accountability for results."[14] Gallup's research also shows that managers who invest in their personal well-being increase the likelihood that their employees will do the same. When a manager has a high level of well-being, their employees are 15 percent more likely to also have a high level of well-being.[15]

Tess Roering is an example of a manager who has taken her responsibility as a wellness leader to heart by investing in her personal well-being and by actively encouraging her team members to join her.

THE STORY OF TESS ROERING

Tess Roering, former vice president of marketing at Athleta, a woman's activewear company that is a subsidiary of Gap, understands how important the manager is in promoting employee well-being—and this starts with building a supportive culture within her team. She builds this culture through relatively simple techniques and regular practices. Every time she shares good news with her team, she always uses the pronoun "you," as in, "*You* did a great job on the last marketing campaign." Every time Tess shares bad news, she always uses the pronoun "we," as in, "*We* need to work together to bring up our productivity levels."

"Great managers understand that they need to manage down and manage up," she explains. In other words, great managers *can* create a subculture of well-being and engagement within their teams. Tess takes intentional steps to build this subculture of engagement and well-being by facilitating activities such as taking the StrengthsFinder assessment. At Athleta, she debriefed the assessment activity with her team over several months, beginning every staff meeting by asking a team member to share their results and insights with the group.

Tess also takes intentional measures to foster well-being within her team. Being active, Tess explains, is part of the brand at Athleta, and therefore physical activity *should* be part of the culture. Making it a regular practice, though, "requires a mind shift. It's less about saying, 'You *have* to do this,' and more about *showing* that it's okay to do it." This mind shift, she believes,

(*continued*)

(*continued*)

largely comes down to the manager—what he or she actually *does* and not what he or she says.

This meant that Tess would often save her workout time for the *middle* of the day and would announce it to her team. "Hey, guys! I'm going for a run!" Or she might participate in an on-site fitness class. "Hey guys, I'm going to Pilates at noon. Do you want to join me?" The influence of her enthusiasm and direct participation was invigorating for all of her team.

Even with a company whose brand is all about fitness and health, it was still easy to get into the trap of just working and not taking breaks to renew. "Managers don't recognize how much people mirror their actions," she says. "If you're someone who works through lunch or stays late, everyone else is going to do the same."

Now, in her new role as chief marketing officer for Core-Power Yoga, a fast-growing company whose tagline is "Live an extraordinary life," Tess stays committed to investing in her health and fitness—for herself and for her team. Tess is keenly aware that her team is looking to her to signal that "Yes, it's not only okay to do so, it's great to do so."

Source: Tess Roering, interview with author, December 15, 2014.

To encourage managers to embrace wellness to the extent that Tess does, look for ways to create wellness *experiences* for managers. You might consider a retreat for managers, as we discussed with senior leaders.

ACTION ITEMS

- Work with managers to address any underlying assumptions about their role as promoters of well-being.
- Train them on the top things they can do:
  - **Embody**—Managers need to start with investing in their own well-being. Well-being can spread like a virus, and

it's much more than just supporting wellness. Managers need to jump into the game, just like Tess does, and actually participate in the activities.

- **Engage**—All managers need to provide the right mix of support and challenge, using simple tricks like, "*You* are doing a great job on x, and *we* need to work on improving y."
- **Enable**—All managers effectively give permission to their team members to participate (or not) in well-being activities.

CREATING THE ENGINE FOR YOUR MOVEMENT

"The best programs involve different stakeholders early and involve them in the planning," says Jessica Grossmeier, leading health management research expert.[16] It is absolutely critical to your movement that you build in a sense of ownership at all levels.

Beyond senior leaders and managers, it's essential that you get employees involved—and ensure that their voices are heard. At JetBlue, for example, employees are regularly asked to provide input on the wellness offerings, and programs are added or deleted accordingly.

Creating a sense of ownership at all levels will help you and your da Vinci Team to create programs that are more likely to engage—and will help to evolve the culture at the same time. Below are three key employee groups you'll need to tap into and organize. Ideally, you'll bring in at least one player from each group to be a part of your da Vinci team.

Cultural Ambassadors—Your Keepers of Culture. In Step 3, we discussed the importance of uncovering the hidden factors, that is, the cultural factors, that have the potential to make or break your wellness movement. A great way to start to evolve the culture in your favor is by building a network of cultural ambassadors.

This is exactly what Chip Conley, author of *Emotional Equations*, did in his role as CEO at Joie de Vivre. He and his team organized a network of cultural ambassadors and even lead cultural ambassadors at each of the sites. They knew that these representatives were critical in building a strong culture across a dispersed workforce.

Action Items

- Identify informal leaders within the organization and appoint them as cultural ambassadors. These are the people who are agents of change who will be able to influence their coworkers.
- Give lots of love to your cultural ambassadors and empower them to feel like leaders of the movement. Give them meaningful opportunities to contribute their ideas and lead.
- Provide ongoing training and encouragement for cultural ambassadors.
- Create effective communication systems for cultural ambassadors to support one another.
- Work with senior leaders and managers to allow cultural ambassadors time on the job to meet the responsibilities of their role. You want to avoid leaving them feeling as if another responsibility has been "dumped" on them.
- Encourage cultural ambassadors to work closely with the wellness ambassadors.
- Make sure that you have representation from cultural ambassadors on your da Vinci team.

Wellness Ambassadors—Your Advocates for Well-Being. Early in his career, Paul Terry, leader in workplace health promotion, began building social networks while working in Zimbabwe to stem the rising tide of AIDS and HIV. Now, as chief science officer at StayWell, one of the world's largest wellness vendors, he continues to tap into the power of social networks to effect change. In his recent article titled "Tapping Passion: The Untold Talents of Wellness Champions, Ambassadors and Peer Educators," Terry shares his conviction that the real potential for promoting health and wellness lies in peer-to-peer, social connections, *not* through support from the experts.[17]

Your wellness ambassadors, also called champions, advocates, or coordinators, are the people who go beyond embracing wellness on a personal level: They're committed to sharing this passion with their coworkers. These are your key people to give input and provide ideas, help shape the movement, and also help to spread the word and expand the movement by promoting the programs and encouraging their peers to get involved. In collaboration with the cultural ambassadors, they will also play a key role in evolving the culture.

ACTION ITEMS

- Give lots of love to your wellness ambassadors and empower them to feel like leaders of the movement. Offer them meaningful ways to contribute their ideas.
- Work with each wellness ambassador, helping each to identify his or her "why." This is a critical piece to helping each to be an effective agent of change.
- Help all wellness ambassadors view wellness beyond themselves and look at what it means to *others.*
- Clarify expectations on what's involved in this role.
- Provide ongoing training and support for wellness ambassadors.
- Create effective communication systems for wellness ambassadors to support one another.
- Work with senior leaders and managers to allow wellness ambassadors time on the job to meet the responsibilities of their role. You want to avoid leaving them feeling as if another responsibility has been "dumped" on them.
- Encourage wellness ambassadors to work closely with the cultural ambassadors.
- Make sure that you have representation from wellness ambassadors on your da Vinci team.

Challengers—Your Reality Check. Finally, you want to make sure you've got voices on your da Vinci team that will challenge your ideas. You need challengers to provide a good dose of reality. If you want your movement to succeed, you must seek out and then *listen* to these voices. John Thiel, director of wealth management at Merrill

Lynch, could have benefited from a group of challengers before launching what is now reported as a failed wellness initiative.

Gather a cross-section of the organization—and make it a point to find your likely-to-be *resisters*. Engage them in a meaningful conversation. Find out why they're not interested in or perhaps even strongly opposed to wellness. Find out what would make the movement more appealing to them and to others like them.

Unions. If your organization is unionized, you will definitely need to bring union members into the conversation. Keep in mind that often the resistance from unions stems from concerns about invasion of privacy, resulting from the practice of HRAs and/or biometric screenings—another reason to reconsider the use of these standard practices.

Family members. Last, but definitely not least, you need family members to be part of the movement. Increasingly, organizations are making efforts to bring in family members. The research clearly shows that the most successful programs are ones in which employees and their families are collectively invested in health and well-being. In addition, bringing in family members is not only important from a reinforcement perspective, it also can serve as a great motivator.

GENERATING IDEAS YOU NEED TO BUILD A PLAN

You've got your da Vinci team in place. Now it's time to generate some ideas for your integrated well-being movement! Below is a short description of how to get started, applying an innovative brainstorming technique called Six Hats Thinking®, developed by Edward de Bono, a leader in conceptual thinking.[18]

ACTION ITEM

SIX-HAT BRAINSTORM SESSION

Too often, brainstorming sessions break down because the different players find themselves offering ideas and then defending them against others who disagree with the idea. The goal of the Six Hats Thinking® technique is to foster a generative discussion that *builds* on ideas, as opposed to a discussion that is sidetracked by participants defending their positions.

To accomplish this goal, de Bono suggests that the group "wear" a specified hat, and only one at a time. You'll need someone (likely you) to serve as the facilitator.

Below are the six different hats, each one calling for a different way of thinking.

- **White Hat: Facts.** The white hat is neutral and objective. When wearing the white hat, the thinker should imitate a computer and avoid interpretations or opinions.

  Sample White Hat Prompt: *Looking at the facts, or what exists today, what do we know about our current workplace wellness challenges?*

- **Yellow Hat: Logical and Positive.** The yellow hat is sunny, optimistic, and eternally hopeful. It probes and explores for value and benefit. Yellow hat thinking is constructive and positive.

  Sample Yellow Hat Prompt: *Assuming a best-case scenario, what types of wellness programs could make a difference in our organization?*

- **Black Hat: Logical and Negative.** The black hat is cautious and careful. It points out the weaknesses in an idea. It considers risks, dangers, obstacles, and potential problems. Although very useful, the black hat can often be overused to the detriment of the other hats.

  Sample Black Hat Prompt: *Knowing what we know about our organizational culture, what potential pitfalls should we be aware of in terms of implementing new wellness initiatives?*

- **Red Hat: Emotions and Feelings.** The red hat is about emotions. Wearing the red hat allows the thinker to say "this is how I feel about the matter." The thinker should never try to justify the feelings or find a logical basis for them.

  Sample Red Hat Prompt: *How do we* feel *about workplace wellness in general? How do we* feel *about the wellness initiatives we're proposing for our organization?*

(*continued*)

(*continued*)

- **Green Hat: Creative.** The green hat is all about growth—in the form of ideas and pure creativity. It searches for alternatives and seeks to move forward from one idea to the next. This hat is the fodder for dreams and visions.

  Sample Green Hat Prompt: *Thinking totally out of the box, what are some audacious, never-tried-before wellness ideas that we could consider?*

- **Blue Hat: The Plan.** The blue hat pulls it all together. It processes the information from the other hats and creates summaries and conclusions.

  Sample Blue Hat Prompt: *Given what we've learned from the white hat, yellow hat, black hat, red hat, and green hat, what should our next steps be for implementing a Workplace Wellness That Works program?*

FINAL THOUGHTS

The evidence is clear: Integrated action is equal to *more* than the sum of its parts. According to the authors of the 2013/2014 Staying@Work Survey Report, "The value of integrating all of these areas cannot be overstated."[19] In other words, we can continue to pursue each objective *separately*—greater well-being, increased levels of safety, increased productivity, higher levels of engagement. But if we want to create higher impact and greater value, then we must take a more integrated, da Vinci approach.

Now that you've pulled together your da Vinci team, you're ready to begin collaborating and scheming with them to continue building the movement. Let's now talk about how you can move the needle by "going stealth."

Step 6

Go Stealth

(The "Sneakiness" Imperative)

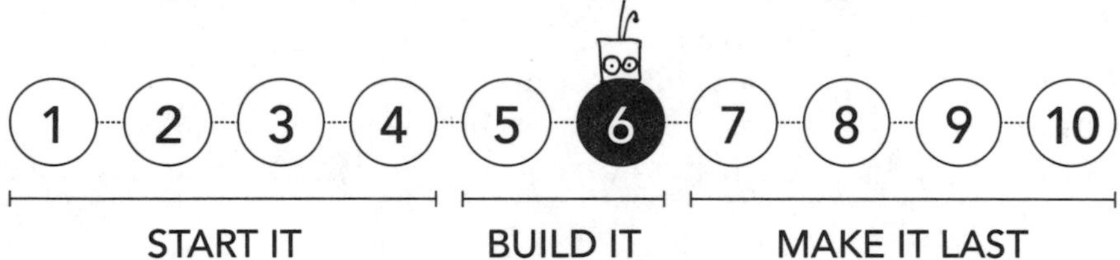

I often begin my talks and training workshops for workplace wellness practitioners with an image of Sisyphus pushing a rock up the hill. I ask, "How many of you feel like this when it comes to inspiring employee engagement and soliciting leader buy-in?" Invariably, people laugh.

Through the years, I've discovered that using a hard sell for wellness rarely works. Recently, however, I've discovered an ingenious way to address the engagement conundrum *and* get buy-in from decision makers: Go undercover and "sneak" wellness in, even leaving off "wellness" in the name of the program. This is what I call "going stealth." It is the equivalent of using a Trojan Horse to introduce wellness in your company, using other, more popular initiatives as cover.

In this chapter, we will discuss:

1. Why going stealth can open up new opportunities and additional resources,
2. A comparison of workplace wellness with the learning and development industry,
3. Research supporting the efficacy of going stealth, and
4. Top opportunities for going stealth.

YOUR STEP 6 CHECKLIST

- ☐ Clarify the top organizational priorities for your organization.
- ☐ Identify clever ways to embed well-being into key initiatives, based on top organizational priorities.
- ☐ Work with marketing to develop stealth language to rename wellness efforts.

THE DISCOVERY

I discovered the power of going stealth by accident. I now believe that this approach may be one of our greatest hopes, as an industry, to elevate workplace wellness to a higher level of perceived importance and more immediate relevancy.

THE POWER OF GOING STEALTH

I was invited to conduct a six-part wellness series for a medical department within a large health care organization. Following this initial engagement, I was then asked to conduct a much larger *work performance* initiative. This experience fundamentally altered how I now approach workplace wellness.

The goals of the work performance initiative were to help create the workplace conditions that would increase employee engagement and teamwork, and decrease absenteeism rates. The assumption was that these work performance issues called for a learning and development initiative—*not* a wellness initiative. Over the course of almost a year, I worked with department leaders, facilitating a series of leadership development workshops. I also worked with the entire department, leading team development workshops.

This initiative led to measurable differences in the department's culture: Employee engagement scores went up significantly and absenteeism rates went down. Based on results from a follow-up survey, along with feedback from the leadership team, there was also a qualitative shift in the department in terms of civility, trust, camaraderie, and personal investment at work.

To give you a flavor of the initiative (and also to give you ideas for your wellness movement), one of the activities we did was called "A Day in the Life Of." Each team was asked to document "A Day in the Life Of" from their team's perspective, using a disposable camera, and then assemble these images into a collage. We then came back together as a full department, bringing together the different teams—physicians, physical therapists, medical assistants, and reporters. Each team presented their team's "A Day in the Life Of," using their collage as a visual prop. One of the outcomes from this relatively simple exercise was that physicians got a much better sense of how many tasks medical assistants had to fulfill over the course of their workday, and they were genuinely surprised.

This was a pivotal turning point for the physicians and helped foster more empathy toward the medical assistants. Some of the physicians openly admitted, "I had no idea that you had so many responsibilities." Through the exercise, medical assistants also had the opportunity to share that they were often the primary targets of any frustrations a patient might be feeling, and in the process, spared the physicians from the venting.

Meanwhile, what was most eye opening for me was the yawning chasm between the resources devoted to the wellness initiative versus the learning and development initiative, even though both were addressing related needs. The learning and development initiative was allotted more money (by a factor of more than five) and more time (40 hours during work time, as opposed to 6 hours during lunch time) and elicited a much higher level of engagement in comparison with the wellness initiative. In the wellness initiative, the reception was, "Nice to have you." In the learning and development initiative, the reception was, "We *need* you."

(*continued*)

(continued)

As the designer of *both initiatives*, I knew that while the second initiative was labeled as a "learning and development" initiative, there were actually *more* well-being concepts used in that initiative than in the wellness initiative. In addition, many of the proposed solutions that emerged from the learning and development initiative actually addressed key components of well-being, including the following:

- **Physical well-being:** Stretches during the daily morning huddle
- **Emotional well-being:** Buddy system to help employees proactively manage stress
- **Social well-being:** More interactive activities built into staff meetings to foster a spirit of camaraderie; office hours program to allow time for employees to meet with their supervisors in a more relaxed setting
- **Career well-being:** Individualized career development plans, which included a plan for professional development opportunities
- **Creative well-being:** Personal projects, or special-interest projects to allow employees to explore an area of interest

Through this before-and-after experience, I recognized the power of going stealth by sneaking wellness into learning and development, and I realized that I no longer had to push the rock up the hill. In truth, these two fields are closely related, but learning and development gets the bulk of the attention in most organizations.

THE DIFFERENCE

I was so moved by this experience that I decided to find out more. I wanted to find out how much more organizations, across the board, were allocating toward learning and development (also known as training and development), in comparison with workplace wellness. I discovered that the difference is enormous. Often critics decry the expense of workplace wellness, but let's put this into perspective:

Workplace wellness is a $6 billion industry (and may be as high as $10 billion); learning and development is a *$164 billion* industry.[1]

In fact, the average large company (more than 10,000 employees) spends $17.4 million annually on learning and development, and the average small company (100–999 employees) spends $338,386 annually for training. This works out to an average spend of $976 per employee per year (PEPY)—across all-sized companies (small, medium, and large).[2]

In contrast, according to the most recent Willis Health and Productivity Report, 36 percent of participating organizations (of all sizes) have *no* defined budget dedicated to wellness. That's right, zero. Another 17 percent are spending $150 or more per employee per year—and 13 percent are spending $25 or less per employee per year. That leaves 34 percent who are spending somewhere between $26 and $149 per employee per year.[3] That's not a whole lot of money!

Industry	**Total $**	**$ PEPY***	**Hours PEPY during Company Time**	**Required?**	**C-Level Representation?**
Workplace Wellness	$6 billion	$169	Limited, if any	Optional	Few CWOs, CHOs, CMOs
Learning and Development	$164 billion	$1,208	32	Mandatory	CLO is standard

* PEPY = per employee per year.

Sources: RAND Workplace Wellness Programs Study Report, 2013 and 2014 ATD (formerly ASTD) State of the Industry Reports

Even in organizations that do provide wellness programs, employees are usually expected to take advantage of these wellness offerings on their *own time*, not company time. Companies like Dow Chemical that offer fitness classes throughout the day—and give employees permission to participate in these on company time—are few and far between. On the other hand, the average organization allocates 32 hours toward learning and development per employee per year *during company time*. More anecdotally, my sense is that many more organizations have executive representation in learning and development than in health and wellness. Chief learning officers are standard, while chief wellness officers, chief health officers, or chief medical officers are not. Companies that do have such executives, such as Cleveland Clinic, Johnson & Johnson, Safeway, and Dow Chemical, are the outliers.

There's obviously nothing wrong with not having a chief medical officer or with having to go to the gym on your own time after work, but with many companies struggling with how to crack the code on employee engagement in wellness (the Willis Report noted that 70 percent of organizations surveyed identified employee engagement in wellness as their top wellness goal[4]), perhaps there's a better way.

THE RESEARCH BEHIND GOING STEALTH

At Stanford University, researchers began looking for more creative and more effective ways to encourage people to adopt healthier behaviors. They knew that traditional methods, such as telling people to eat better and move more because it's "good for them," weren't working.

In their study, they examined two groups of students. One group was enrolled in coursework focused on the nutritional aspects of food. This group learned about healthy eating from the traditional approach: "Eat these foods because they're good for your health." The second group of students was enrolled in a course called "Food and Society," focused on food's connection to issues like the environment, labor rights, and human rights. The curriculum included books like Michael Pollan's *The Omnivore's Dilemma* and documentaries like *King Corn*. The students in the second group were encouraged to take on the role of being an agent of change. Their assignments included activities like writing an op-ed piece and creating a video to post on YouTube.

Both groups took the Food Frequency Questionnaire, a validated assessment tool to measure nutritional intake, before and after the respective courses. The researchers found that the students in the second group were much more likely to make improvements in their eating habits compared with the first group. The takeaway is that a stealth strategy likely produces better results in changing lifestyle habits, in comparison with an approach that explicitly focuses on the health benefits. Therefore, if you can find clever ways to "sneak" wellness into other initiatives, and incorporate broader missions into your wellness programming, you will probably get better engagement than with more narrow and traditional wellness-only programming.

This research also highlights what we've been discussing throughout the book: People want to connect with a higher purpose and they want to feel like they're part of a *movement*. If they do feel that way, then they're far more likely to make lasting change. According to the lead researcher of the Stanford study, Tom Robinson, professor of pediatrics and of medicine at the Stanford School of Medicine and director of the Center for Healthy Weight at Lucile Packard Children's Hospital, "When people get involved with social movements, it changes their behaviors more dramatically than what we've seen with more cognitive-based approaches." Applying a stealth strategy approach, he explains, helps to "tap into the deeper needs and desires of the participants—what we refer to as intrinsic motivators—while improving their health as a side effect."[5]

WHAT LEADERS ARE ACTUALLY FOCUSED ON

The key to applying a stealth approach is to tap into what is already deemed "important." According to the latest research from Bersin by Deloitte, a leading HR research group, the "Top Global Talent Priorities" for business leaders are as follows: (1) addressing gaps in leadership, (2) retention and engagement, (3) increasing skills for HR, (4) talent acquisition, and (5) learning and development to increase workforce capacity.[6] Notice that "wellness" didn't make the list. That's okay! In going stealth, you can easily embed wellness into any of these non-wellness, top-tiered objectives and "sneak" employees into better health and well-being. There's no need to keep pushing rocks up hills.

ACTION ITEM

CLARIFY TOP ORGANIZATIONAL PRIORITIES

Meet with your da Vinci team and discuss the five top global talent priorities. Do these match what your executive team is focused on? See if you can clarify the top five priorities for your organization—and then identify some key stealth opportunities.

STRESS IN THE WORKPLACE

Morgan Stanley employees recently produced a *Hunger Games*-inspired video as a spoof on their cutthroat culture. To say that many employees are experiencing stress on the job is an understatement. According to a recent study conducted by Joel Goh, Harvard Business School assistant professor, and Stanford Business School professors Jeffrey Pfeffer and Stefanos A. Zenios, stress in the workplace is responsible for an estimated $125–$190 billion annually in health care costs (which amounts to between 5 and 8 percent of the total annual health expenditure in the United States). Their research also revealed that up to 120,000 deaths per year may be due to an accumulation of stressors in the workplace, such as long hours, lack of job security, perceptions of unfairness in the workplace, and a perceived lack of control.[7]

Burnout, a close cousin of stress, is also on the rise. A survey conducted by Tony Schwartz and his team at The Energy Project with over 150,000 employees around the world, found that 74 percent of the workforce is "experiencing a personal energy crisis."[8] Slowly, organizational leaders are recognizing that stress and burnout are key issues that need to be addressed.

This extremely real and pressing issue of stress and burnout in the workplace also represents a potential stealth opportunity for you. In fact, Bersin by Deloitte's "Top Global Priorities" report shows that "the overwhelmed employee" is a top 10 priority. Fortunately, some leaders are taking action.

THE STORY OF A TECH START-UP THAT IS TAKING MEASURES TO PREVENT BURNOUT

Treehouse LLC, a technology start-up based in Portland, Oregon, is taking strides to address the issue of "the overwhelmed employee" by implementing a 32-hour workweek. Contrary to technology start-up norms, the office is closed on Fridays—and employees are encouraged to not work, but to stay at home, enjoy themselves, and recharge.

In a recent interview, Ryan Carson, founder and chief executive, shared how this practice of work-life balance is an invaluable recruiting device. "It makes recruiting and retention so much easier. When someone is considering Google or Facebook, we ask 'Well, are you going to work a four-day week there?' It's almost like our amazing ace up the sleeve. It's just something nobody can beat."[9]

According to one of Treehouse's investors, formerly on the executive team at Facebook, "The most forward-thinking and successful companies are realizing that giving employees more time to be creative and connected to other things besides their job creates a better and more productive employee. Ryan just had the courage to go and do that."[10]

Despite growing awareness of the disturbing trend of "the overwhelmed employee," research shows that there is a pervasive failure to act in most organizations. According to the National Business Group on Health and Towers Watson's 2013/2014 Staying@Work Report, the top wellness challenge identified by leaders is stress. Seventy-eight percent of leaders are reporting that this is their top concern, but only 15 percent of organizations are actually taking measures to address the issue.[11] Obviously, there is a massive disconnect between what leaders are saying is important and what they're actually *doing* about it. According to the authors of this report, this disconnect is likely a key contributor to the low levels of employee engagement in most workplace wellness programs.

By going stealth and by partnering with your friends in learning and development, you can influence your leaders to take action. My suggestion: Go stealth by referring to stress and burnout as an issue of "sustainable engagement" (a term suggested by Towers Watson). In fact, an ideal forum for promoting sustainable engagement, which combines employee engagement with well-being, is management training, *not* wellness. The former is standard fare for any organization; the latter is not.

THE COMPANY ADVOCATE CALLS FOR GOING STEALTH

A fast-growing mobile technology company decided to launch its first management-training program. In only three years, the company already had 12 offices throughout the United States, in

(*continued*)

(*continued*)

Asia, Europe, and Central America. While the human resources team had started a conversation with a coaching vendor to develop a group management-coaching program, they considered a proposal from my company, Motion Infusion. The task at hand was to persuade a conservative group of decision makers (who didn't buy into the idea of wellness) to go with a management-training program that had well-being embedded into it.

The conversation that follows is based on the actual e-mail thread that took place. In this, you will notice how my internal champion advocated going stealth.

Motion Infusion: Thank you very much for taking the time to talk with us yesterday. Attached is a brief summary and slide deck of what well-being integration looked like in the context of a recent leadership-training program we conducted. I think that this will help to illustrate what this could look like in the context of a management development program for Company X.

Champion: Awesome, thank you! My only concern is that the term "well-being" will not be well received by our HQ on the East Coast. When I show this to our HR, how about I change "well-being" to "sustainable engagement" or something like that? That term is a more ROI-linked term for our more conservative leadership team.

WHAT EMPLOYEES ARE ACTUALLY FOCUSED ON

Just as wellness or well-being is not top of mind for most leaders, the same, unfortunately, is generally true for employees. Most are not focused on health, wellness, or even well-being. However, leaders and employees alike are interested in performance improvement. One of the reasons why mindfulness has picked up so much steam in high-performing companies is that it has been positioned as a means to *increase* one's competitive edge—not diminish it. This is exactly the approach that Laura Young and her team are taking at Goldman Sachs.

Mindfulness At Goldman Sachs

In 2008 and 2009, with the financial crisis in full swing, employees at Goldman Sachs were experiencing almost unprecedented pressure. "We wanted to provide a positive solution for our employees," says Laura Young, vice president, Americas head of wellness at Goldman Sachs, "and we wanted to avoid using a term like 'stress management' that has a stigma attached to it. So we decided to call it 'resilience.'" At Goldman Sachs, resilience is defined as "a state of health, energy, readiness, flexibility, and having the capacity to adapt with confidence."

Employees wanted something beyond the traditional three lifestyle interventions—diet, exercise, and sleep—so Laura and her team piloted a single session on mindfulness in the corporate auditorium. It was a very quick demonstration. "We didn't expect that people would pay attention, but they did!" In fact, employees wanted more. This developed into a two-session program that now is offered on a quarterly basis, with more than 500 people signing up every time.

This enthusiastic response is not accidental. Laura knew that a hard-driving, Type A workforce would need to be shown the benefits of the practice—in language that made sense to them. "People were afraid that mindfulness would make them lose their competitive edge," she says. So she and her team set out to demonstrate the connection between mindfulness and increased productivity and performance. They also carefully designed the program to include the science behind the practice so that it would not be dismissed as a "new age" solution. Because of the success of mindfulness trainings, resilience offerings at the firm have expanded to include individual coaching sessions as well as customized department and division-specific programs.

This wave of mindfulness at Goldman Sachs is really part of a larger movement that's happening across many organizations, including many in the field of banking and finance. The

(*continued*)

(*continued*)

key selling point in most cases, as in the case of Goldman Sachs, is to demonstrate the increased capacity to perform and sharpen one's competitive advantage, as opposed to *wellness* benefits alone.

Source: Laura Young, interview with author, December 18, 2014.

GOING STEALTH STARTS WITH RENAMING

Finding clever ways to sneak wellness into other initiatives to increase impact means being creative and different, not traditional. Whatever you do, don't call it "wellness" or even "well-being." Call it "sustainable engagement" or "energy management" or even "leadership and resilience." Or, following the example of Laura Young and her team at Goldman Sachs, recast well-being programs as opportunities to sharpen one's competitive edge. Think about repositioning yourself as a human performance improvement leader, rather than a wellness specialist. This renaming and repositioning will increase the likelihood of getting senior leader buy-in and employee engagement. The following are some additional ideas of terms to use—and terms *not* to use:

Do Call It . . .	Don't Call It . . .
Energy	Health
Mindfulness	Stress management
Emotional intelligence	Mental health
Sustainable engagement	Wellness
Mindful leadership	Health intervention
Human performance improvement	Risk reduction

THE MASTER SPIN DOCTORS

Perhaps one of the best spins on "better health" has come from Jim Loehr and Tony Schwartz. In their original book, *The Power of Full*

Engagement, they proposed the novel idea of "managing your energy, not your time."[12] Unlike health, which is abstract and far off in the future, energy matters right now—and it ties in nicely with the concept of human performance improvement. As we know, the promise of better health is not necessarily going to win over decision makers (beyond a low-cost, check-the-box wellness program), but the promise of an energized workforce often does. In all candor, I can understand why many decision makers are more keenly interested in phrases like "energy management" and "human performance improvement" than in "improved health" or "reduced risk factors," and the Stanford research shows that they are not alone.

Both Loehr and Schwartz are masters at *speaking the language of business leaders*. The Human Performance Institute, cofounded by Dr. Loehr and Dr. Jack Groeppel (and later acquired by Johnson & Johnson) uses fabulous terms like "Corporate Athlete®" and "Human Energy Pyramid." The Energy Project, founded by Schwartz, uses phrases like "Discover a Better Way of Working," and "We energize people and transform organizations."[13]

The programs are marketed as performance training programs; they are *not* positioned as wellness programs. While a typical wellness program is hard pressed to get more than an hour at a time, these programs demand (this is the difference between "Nice to have you" and "We *need* you"!) one to two days, often off-site, *during* work time. While the packaging is different, the intended result is the same: improved health and well-being. By going stealth and focusing more on the *performance* benefits, Loehr, Schwartz, and their teams have been singularly successful in promoting the message of well-being.

ACTION ITEM

WHAT'S *YOUR* SPIN?

It's time to team up with your marketing partners and figure out language that's going to resonate for the people you're trying to

(*continued*)

(*continued*)

reach—leaders, managers, employees, even family members. It's not just a matter of deluging people with information; it's essential that you come up with language that is going to move people in *your* organization. Be sure to check in with your challengers to get some honest feedback on whatever you come up with!

TOP OPPORTUNITIES FOR GOING STEALTH

In a sense, the key to going stealth is to "give up the fight" in having to prove the value of wellness to either leaders or employees. Rather, the idea is to address what is already deemed important and stealthily bake in wellness. You may even discover that your organization is already investing in programs that incorporate well-being concepts. The more you can connect with other departments, with the help of your da Vinci team, the more you can create alignment between your well-being efforts and theirs.

You will also discover that there are many ways you can embed wellness into existing organizational initiatives. Here are some suggestions, but you and your da Vinci team can certainly brainstorm additional ideas!

- Staff meetings
- Leadership development
- Management trainings
- Team development initiatives
- Organizational development (which includes culture change initiatives)
- Safety trainings
- Onboarding
- Innovation initiatives
- Community outreach

Let's talk about a few of these in greater depth.

Staff meetings. Turn the mundane, often dreaded, staff meeting into an extraordinary event. Instead of just delivering information, use meetings as opportunities to enhance well-being and build a healthier, more vibrant culture. Consider following the lead of The Container Store, a company that has been listed on Fortune's "100 Best" List for over 15 years. The company employs twice-daily store "huddles" to share information, have fun, build meaningful skills, and promote a team spirit.

Leadership development. Leadership development programs receive a lot of support in many organizations—and also serve as a perfect avenue for going stealth. Leadership development is likely to be one of your most powerful levers in promoting wellness and in reshaping the culture to better *support* well-being. You'll definitely need to collaborate with your learning and development or organizational development partners to reconfigure leadership-training programs accordingly.

In Step 1: Shift Your Mind-Set from Expert to Agent of Change, we discussed an example of an organic, bottom-up movement that's being driven by agents of change at Schindler Elevator Corporation. Let's take another look at this company and discuss the success of their "Leadership Odyssey." One of the reasons this movement has been so powerful is that, from the outset, it's operated as a *stealth* wellness initiative—launched into one sector (organization development) and now infusing its way into other sectors of the organization.

The Magic behind Leadership Odyssey

Leadership Odyssey at Schindler Elevator Corporation is a unique leadership-development series that has generated a wellness movement within the organization. The magic behind the program? Participating managers were able to personally *experience*

(*continued*)

(*continued*)

well-being and then reflect on how this shift connects to becoming a better leader. Armed with the mantra, "It's the right thing to do, it's the smart thing to do, and it starts with you," each participant committed to make change in his or her own life and then to bring that message back into the organization in order to build a "winning team." (Building "winning teams" is one of the company's explicit, core business strategies.)

This program is the embodiment of a stealth initiative: The workshop was viewed as a prestigious leadership-training program, *not* a wellness program. However, while wellness was not the focus, well-being was incorporated *into* the programming, as a way to shift the culture to one that supports sustainable growth, as opposed to constant firefighting.

According to Julie Shipley, manager of general training at Schindler, the program was designed to address energy, sustainability, good decision making, and qualities of great leadership—all key facets of the company's core business objectives. It was not a "wellness" conversation about "needing to eat more vegetables or drink more water and then, oh, maybe I'll be a better manager." Every aspect of the program was tied to Schindler's core business objectives, including:

- building winning teams,
- promoting safety and ensuring zero accidents, and
- building a culture that fosters engagement and renewal.

Confirming the conclusions of the Stanford research, Julie noted that this bigger picture approach drew people in. "It really helped managers to see how well-being affects performance on the job every day. They've taken it to heart—and now are taking measures to actively promote well-being with their teams." This integration with core business objectives—and the fact that so many of these managers were personally feeling the effects of burnout from continued firefighting—both contributed to what Julie characterizes as a "burning platform." This platform allowed for lengthy discussions about the need to shift the *culture* to support long-term objectives. Discussions about personal well-being were reframed in the context of needing to move the organization to the sustainability end of a survival-sustainability model.

After the leadership program, managers left with a sense of empowerment that they could create the conditions for their team members to be more engaged with their well-being. They also left with a better sense of purpose, that they were actually part of a movement. The impressive result is that this conversation about well-being *continues* at Schindler—far past the end of the program itself.

Mike Yurchuk, director of organization development, shared, "It's happening through word of mouth and modeling of well-being. Moreover, these managers are now much quicker to *recognize* signs when team members are experiencing burnout and they're now more proactive in addressing these issues from a place of understanding and compassion." That's the start of a real movement!

Source: Julie Shipley and Mike Yurchuk, interview with author, December 12, 2014.

Management trainings. Managers are perhaps the most vital link to ensuring employee engagement in the workplace—and to promoting employee well-being. While senior leaders set the tone for any workplace wellness initiative, managers are the ones who effectively give—or don't give—permission to employees to actually participate in these wellness offerings. As we have discussed, I have found that leveraging the term "sustainable engagement" is often a perfect way to help get managers on board, especially for those who are more wellness-averse.

In the Towers Watson 2012 Global Workforce Study, the authors uncovered three critical gaps in the way most organizations are approaching employee engagement. The first key gap, enablement, can be addressed by "enabling workers with internal support, resources, and tools."[14] The second gap—and the one that is particularly useful to you—is energy, and it can be addressed by "creating an environment that's energizing to work in because it promotes physical, emotional, and social well-being."[15] The language here makes a perfect connection between a traditional learning and development function—management training—with the work that you're doing—promoting well-being. It also spells out an avenue for going stealth—through management training.

Research shows that the more employee engagement and wellness are interlinked, the more wellness will become *normalized* and infused into the fabric of organizations. It is likely that we will see more companies embrace initiatives similar to the Leadership Odyssey. A recent study conducted by Virgin Pulse, an institute that is promoting well-being at work in collaboration with Human Capital Media Advisory Group, the research arm of *Workforce* magazine, highlighted a growing awareness of the connection between employee engagement and well-being. Out of 1,395 human resources management professionals surveyed worldwide, 83 percent of executives and 79 percent of managers reported that improved employee well-being was a top priority for the year 2015. Taking this a step further, 86 percent of the participating organizations agreed that well-being influences engagement.[16]

The County of Solano in California offers another great example of how going stealth can help empower managers to embrace wellness. The County dedicated a quarterly half-day manager's meeting toward a training we provided called "Investing in Well-Being to Promote Sustainable Engagement." Inspired by this session, managers are now taking steps to (1) address their personal well-being and (2) build more energizing work environments for their teams to better promote employee well-being.

Team development initiatives. At Eileen Fisher, a New York-based fashion company, Leslie Ritter, wellness leader, describes how she goes out to meet with team leaders to find out their key concerns—and then builds on these meetings to create tailored team development workshops.

BUILDING WELL-BEING—ONE TEAM AT A TIME

"The company is led by teams," Leslie explains. "I ask each of these teams, 'What are the issues here for you all? And how can we as a company better support you?" All of this feedback is invaluable—and is ongoing. "It's just constant communication," she says. Leveraging what they learn through this communication, Leslie and her team develop team-based workshops. "We approach the different team leaders and we offer these customized workshops to them. It's been highly successful."

Source: Leslie Ritter, interview with author, December 16, 2014.

Onboarding. While leadership development and management training are effective ways to get top-down participation in wellness and evolve the culture, another great way to build employee engagement is through the *onboarding* procedure for new hires.

Organizations like Zappos and IDEO are highly focused on their onboarding processes, recognizing how critical it is to get employees engaged from day one. Maggie Spicer, CEO of Whisk, who has helped organizations like Airbnb build their culture, explains, "Culture takes a lot of work, intention, stewardship, refinement, and pruning." In this time-intensive process, onboarding is a critical step, as it is every employee's "first moment of *experiencing* an organization."[17]

Let's take a look at Virgin America, another company with innovative practices for building employee engagement, tied with promoting employee well-being.

THE STORY OF VIRGIN AMERICA

Virgin America is taking the lead by incorporating wellness into its new-hires training workshops. This is part of an evolution that

(*continued*)

(*continued*)

started in 2009 when the company first launched its wellness movement called "BeFit" under the leadership of Robin Oxley, benefits and compensation analyst at the time, and now manager of benefits and wellness.

At the beginning, Robin turned to the American Heart Association to help her get started. Year one: 10 people participated in the annual American Heart Association's Heart Walk. By the next year, the wellness movement had begun to take hold: 100 people participated in the Heart Walk—and the number has consistently stayed between 100 and 150 (out of a pool of 400 employees at corporate headquarters).

This was only the beginning. BeFit is now in full swing with participation rates averaging 77 percent. They've got quarterly challenges, BeFit champions at every Virgin America station, and lots of walking—tracked through Fitbits and mobile apps and uploaded onto their engagement platform, Virgin Pulse.

What is one of the most essential keys to their success? Incorporating wellness into onboarding. Part of the new-hires training workshop is dedicated to talking about wellness, and every new employee receives a pedometer within a week of coming onboard. "Our culture is very fitness minded," Robin explains, "but it wasn't always this way." The beginning required some coaxing and helping people to see the benefits. Now that wellness is built into onboarding, "It's something that's ingrained into them; people join BeFit from the beginning." These onboarding sessions in combination with opportunities for ongoing engagement and interaction through Virgin Pulse has created a culture that is oriented around fitness and well-being at work. Says Robin, "People talk about it a lot; people are much more active at work, and we see evidence of well-being in every aspect of our culture."

Source: Robin Oxley, interview with author, January 10, 2015.

Community outreach initiatives. More and more companies are putting their efforts into giving back. According to the Committee Encouraging Corporate Philanthropy, 89 percent of companies in the United States now offer some type of employee volunteer program.[18] These programs offer a unique way to improve the culture (employees feel proud to work for a company that supports the community), boost employee engagement, and improve employee well-being, especially in the areas of community, social, and environmental well-being.

Community outreach is an integral part of the employee experience at Salesforce. From the outset, employees join in a volunteer activity as part of the new-hire training, and then are given *six* paid days off every year to volunteer with a local nonprofit organization. These activities are part of Salesforce's "1–1–1 Model" of integrated corporate philanthropy: 1 percent of Salesforce's equity, 1 percent of Salesforce's product, and 1 percent of employees' time are donated to the community. In the last 16 years, Salesforce has given $80 million in grants and delivered technology for free or discounted rates to more than 24,000 nonprofits. In addition, Salesforce employees have volunteered 840,000 hours in their local communities.[19] "Giving back has been a core value since the day Salesforce was founded," says Lynn Vojvodich, Salesforce chief marketing officer. "Our employees donate their time to everything from food drives and book sales to charity sports events, school fundraisers and computer literacy training. They follow their passion and make a difference."[20]

Community outreach offers a tremendous opportunity for you to stealthily build your wellness movement. Not only does it activate employees as agents of social change, it can also bring tangible health and well-being benefits by generating physical activity, career satisfaction, and social connections—without explicitly naming these as wellness benefits.

THE STORY OF #CLEANSTREETS

In 2012, Square, a San Francisco-based technology company, launched its #cleanstreets community outreach initiative in partnership with the San Francisco Department of Public Works. Ever since, every Friday between 11:30 AM and noon, Square employees have been cleaning up their neighborhood streets. The local government department provides the supplies and collects the trash at the end of the day—and Square employees volunteer their time. It's a win-win.

According to a spokesperson at Square, "We started #cleanstreets because we care about being good neighbors, and the growth and success of a community depend on those who support it. We believe that small actions can spur broader change in urban environments." The inspiration behind the initiative is the so-called broken windows theory, or the idea that small contributions, like picking up trash, can positively impact social norms in an urban environment.

While the focus of the initiative is on community outreach and is explicitly named as such, there's a whole lot of wellness packed into it—community, social, and physical well-being. "#cleanstreets is one of our community engagement efforts," the Square spokesperson says. "We want to be active and engaged participants in our neighborhood, and #cleanstreets is one way to do just that."

While exploring the neighborhood, employees have the opportunity to get involved in their community. They get to be part of something larger—collaborating with local government officials to support the Department of Public Works' Giant Sweep Initiative. The initiative also addresses social well-being. "It's also a great opportunity for employees to meet people outside of their team and create new relationships." It's even a way for employees to form connections with employees in *other* companies and organizations in the neighborhood. "We invite others to join us, and we've had participation from several companies in the area." Finally, on a physical level, Square employees are getting up from their desks, moving their bodies, and taking in fresh air.

As a way of deepening the impact—and also as a way of enhancing collegial connections—employees organize themselves into teams. Each team "owns" #cleanstreets each month. This lends itself nicely to friendly competitions between teams and at the same time drives up the collection of trash. "We've fostered healthy competition by announcing at our company all-hands where teams fall in terms of metrics." They're closely tracking these metrics of success: number of Square participating employees, number of non-Square participants, pounds of trash, and even a tally of unique items. On average, 75–100 employees collect up to 300 pounds of trash on a weekly basis.

Furthermore, this initiative is a great example of how small steps, quite literally, can make a big difference. "Local businesses are taking notice," according to the Square spokesperson. Recently, the initiative even attracted the attention of a homeless man in the neighborhood. Moved by what he saw, he offered to donate a dollar. "When we're in the neighborhood picking up trash, we are often stopped by people who want to know more about the program. We always invite everyone to join us."

#cleanstreets is one of many ways that Square employees are giving back to their community and at the same time bolstering their well-being.

Source: Square spokesperson, interview with author, November 2, 2014.

Rising tides of organizations are taking community outreach and corporate social responsibility to a whole new level, identifying themselves as "B Corps" or "firms of endearment" or part of the "conscious capitalism" movement. Chipper Bro, cultural ambassador at Patagonia, explains, "We are a B Corp, so it is our job to solve environmental and social problems." Everything at Patagonia—from operations to culture to employee well-being to product development—is connected to that purpose and is organized around a B Corp mentality of "using business as a force for good." This growing level of consciousness is perhaps our greatest opportunity for going stealth: embedding well-being into efforts to simply make the world a better place.[21]

ACTION ITEMS

- Rename and avoid traditional "wellness" terms.
- Consider the top priorities identified by Bersin by Deloitte and brainstorm ways to connect well-being with these.
- Identify your organization's top initiatives and find ways to embed well-being into these priorities. How do these key objectives connect to the multiple domains of well-being and with the F Factors of the Maslow Meets Mallory Culture Audit?
- Develop and deliver workshops for senior leaders, managers, and employees that stealthily integrate well-being.

FINAL THOUGHTS

Going stealth is much more than a sneaky way to infuse well-being into your organization. Because it involves a process of identifying shared goals and helping to create meaning around those goals, going stealth can actually be a much more effective way to work with company leaders, managers, and employees to collaboratively build an engaging wellness movement that goes beyond the traditional, failed approaches.

Now, let's talk about measures you can take to ensure that your wellness movement has lasting power.

Section III

MAKE IT LAST (WORKPLACE WELLNESS THAT WORKS)

The final set of steps focus on how to *sustain* a wellness movement in your organization—by giving employees the tools to engage with the movement.

Step 7: Create Meaning explores tangible ways to shift away from incentives and go deeper by connecting with our *intrinsic, human needs*. By creating alignment between the purpose of the individual and the purpose of the organization, your wellness movement will have the framework to last.

Step 8: Design Nudges and Cues discusses tangible ways to *change the environment* through nudges and cues that promote wellness throughout the organization. This chapter helps you continue to evolve the culture of the organization to authentically support and sustain individuals' efforts to integrate well-being into their daily activities.

Step 9: Launch and Iterate discusses the importance of fostering a *growth mind-set* to nurture ongoing support of wellness for individuals, teams, and for the organization as a whole. This chapter offers tips on how to experiment more, learn more, and devise wellness programs that actually work.

Step 10: Go Global goes beyond national borders and discusses how to grow the movement across the international branches of your organization. Even if you're a domestic organization, you can take a global outlook for unexpected answers. This chapter explores effective wellness movements that have gone global, such as Chade-Meng Tan's "Search Within Yourself," to help you discover wellness approaches that resonate for individuals and cultures of all nationalities.

Step 7

Create Meaning

(The Engagement Imperative)

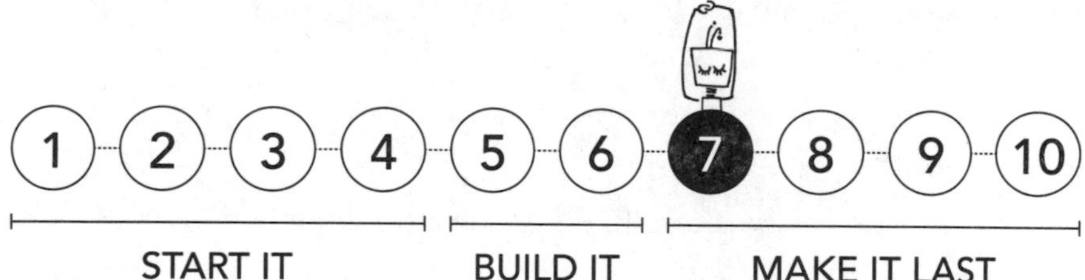

When I taught history in an urban high school, my students used to ask, "Why do I need to know this stuff about history?" For a long time, I fired back, "So you can get a good grade." Or, if I got really frustrated, "You need to pay attention or I'll send you to the principal's office."

Then, one day, I stopped. I turned the question around. "Well," I asked, "why do *you* think we're studying this?" Rather than simply giving the normal "do this—or else" response, I began to go deeper. By turning a one-way question into a collaborative quest for meaning, I discovered that my students started listening more and taking more ownership into looking at what history meant in their own lives.

My initial responses to my students, while understandable, focused on what the lesson in history would *get* them (or help them to avoid). My initial answers *sometimes* led to the desired short-term result, namely a student paying attention to what I thought was a brilliant history lecture. Usually, however, this didn't last. What I learned as a teacher is that grades and threats are only part of the motivation package. Encouraging long-lasting motivation has to stem from a place of inquiry and a search for meaning.

This brings us back to our original billion-dollar dilemma: How do we motivate employees to make healthy behavior changes? While many organizations have turned to short-term fixes like incentives and penalties, there is increasing evidence that change is only sustainable through intrinsic motivation. In this chapter, we'll discuss what intrinsic motivation is and how to build it into your wellness movement.

In this chapter, we'll discuss:

1. Short-term behavior change versus sustainable behavior change,
2. The distinction between extrinsic and intrinsic motivation,
3. Current trends in workplace wellness around the use of incentives and penalties,
4. Some potential pitfalls in having a strategy that overly relies on incentives,
5. How you can create the conditions for promoting intrinsic motivation, and
6. How to apply these findings toward taking action.

YOUR STEP 7 CHECKLIST

- ☐ Create your motivation plan.
- ☐ Devise activities and programs to support intrinsic motivators: competency, autonomy, relatedness, purpose, and play.

AWARENESS IS NOT ENOUGH

What we definitively know is that awareness is not enough—recall the billion-dollar dilemma. When it comes to health and wellness, most of us know what to do; we just have a hard time translating that knowledge into action. Michael O'Donnell, founder and editor-in-chief of the *American Journal of Health Promotion*, estimates that awareness only accounts for 5 percent of behavior change. Motivation, skills, and opportunities, the remaining three legs of his AMSO model, a framework for developing behavior change programs, are the critical elements that factor into behavior change. In this chapter, we're going to zero in on the motivation piece. Unlocking the keys to motivation has perhaps generated the greatest amount of controversy in the field of workplace wellness. So let's dive in!

MOVING BEYOND AWARENESS TO INCENTIVES

In an effort to motivate people to change behaviors, we have moved beyond building awareness to using incentives. According to behavioral economists David Asch and Kevin Volpp, "The implicit argument is that if we pay people for health-promoting behaviors, they will engage in them. It works to a certain extent, but typically not as much as program sponsors would like."[1]

Incentives will never serve as a motivation panacea. They may lead to a jump in participation rates at the beginning, but in most cases, adding more incentives results in only incremental (but disappointing) differences, and in some cases, it can even diminish or extinguish intrinsic motivation. In one study, post-cardiac patients were incentivized through free medication in an effort to increase the rates of compliance (actually taking the medication). The result? Compliance only increased by five percentage points, from 39 percent to 44 percent.[2]

The use of incentives can be frustrating and expensive. In an effort to mitigate these costs, some employers are actually transferring incentive costs to employees through reduced deductions in other areas. Not a nice tactic. Nor is it effective. According to Asch and Volpp, "Money has its limits as a carrot, yet an enormous industry in wellness is devoted to this highly transactional approach of delivering points, badges, miles, or dollars to encourage good behavior."

So if incentives, by and large, don't work, how do we create meaningful behavior change when it comes to wellness? Let's take a closer look.

BEHAVIOR CHANGE: EASY TO START, HARD TO SUSTAIN

Behavior change is *the* mantra for any worksite wellness program and the key selling point for any wellness vendor. Examples of behavior-change solutions include campaigns, team challenges, health coaching, gamification platforms, weight loss competitions, and, of course, incentives.

"Behavior change is easy! The real issue is *sustaining* the behavior," says Michelle Segar, author of *No Sweat: How the Simple Science of Motivation Can Bring You a Lifetime of Fitness* and director of the Sport, Health, and Activity Research and Policy Center (SHARP) at the University of Michigan. In her view, the lack of sustainability largely comes down to motivation and how to *stay* motivated over time. Segar has spent her career looking into motivation, primarily behind exercise, but we can apply her findings toward workplace wellness.

Lasting motivation, she proposes, starts with finding the "right why"—a why that is personally meaningful to each individual. Just as you established your personal why in Step 1: Shift Your Mind-Set from Expert to Agent of Change, your task will be to empower employees to do the same.

Segar suggests that too often in workplace wellness, we've made the mistake of selling "better health" as the why behind healthy habits. This is problematic, as health is not motivating for most (as we discussed in Step 2: Imagine What's Possible) and perversely can end up being translated into what Segar terms the "wrong why." "The assumption that health, changes in biometrics, and changes in health status are going to motivate people to stick with a health behavior is just plain wrong," she explains.

Launched by the wrong why (which might be "better health" or "lose weight"), we start to lose steam; the wrong why degenerates into a "should," which leads to feeling guilty, and that puts us even further off track. We are now stuck in what Segar calls the "vicious cycle of failure."

The right why, on the other hand, is more likely to keep us on track—and lead us into a "sustainable cycle of success." The right why is what's actually compelling and is different for each of us. It could be the energy we feel, or that we get to spend time with friends, or that we'll be around for our grandkids.

Like the behavioral economists, Segar contends that motivation and our resulting behaviors are largely a factor of our emotions—*not* our rational thinking. Therefore, a why that is based on our emotions, rather than logic, is much more likely to be the right why. According to Segar, "The nature of the why—right or wrong—is what shapes our perception of the habit we're trying to adopt either as a chore (stems from the wrong why) or as a gift (stems from the right why)."

Segar's research shows that if we're doing something for the wrong why, no matter how much we "should" do it, we're unlikely to keep at it. So how do we get to the bottom of these right whys?[3]

ACTION ITEM
FIND OUT WHAT EMPLOYEES VALUE

If we want to help employees start tapping into the right whys, we need to do a better job of uncovering these. A simple place to start is to keep a pulse on what employees value. A survey is one way to do this. Another way is to get out there and simply ask. You can organize focus groups or you can even go around and have one-on-one conversations. Try asking something like, "What's something we could offer here that would be meaningful to you? What's something that would feel like it had real value for you?" Seems like a pretty basic thing to do, but surprisingly not done enough. The programs need to be relevant to the organization—*and* to the employees!

WHAT IS YOUR WHY?

"Life is why," reads the American Heart Association's new tagline. For some, though, even life itself has become a chore rather than a gift. This is what Sergeant Kevin Briggs became deeply acquainted with during his 17 years of patrolling the Golden Gate Bridge. His job was to "create meaning" between the jumper and him—and to do it *fast*.

For some, meaning came from a newfound connection they felt with Sergeant Briggs. One jumper, when asked why he climbed back to safety, responded, "Kevin wouldn't give up."[4]

In his best attempt to save each person, Sergeant Briggs would try to find the hook, the one thing that the jumper cared enough about to compel him or her to reconsider. To do so, Sergeant Briggs engaged each person in a conversation, trying to extract any piece of information that could possibly lead him to this hook: "Are you married? Do you have children? What do you love to do?"

In one case, Sergeant Briggs found out that the jumper had children. With this new shred of information, Sergeant Briggs knew he had a chance. He asked the jumper if he knew about the research indicating that children of parents who commit suicide are far more likely to commit suicide themselves. This information caught the jumper's attention and brought him back. In the nick of time, Sergeant Briggs was able to tune into what this person cared about most—his children.

Just like Sergeant Briggs, a big part of your work will be working with your da Vinci team to create the conditions in which people are empowered to find their right whys—and this begins by getting a better understanding of what's really behind human motivation.

MOTIVATION COMES IN TWO FLAVORS

Motivation, one might say, comes in two flavors: extrinsic and intrinsic. Extrinsic motivation is doing something in order to get a reward or to avoid a penalty. Both come from the outside. Examples include grades and money. "I'll study harder so I can get an A." "I'll show up on time so that my paycheck doesn't get docked." Extrinsic motivation often is connected with things that we "have" to do.

Intrinsic motivation stems from real meaning and enjoyment from the activity itself. "I'll work on this math problem because I enjoy figuring out puzzles." "I'll pitch in on this project because I enjoy working with the group." Being truly intrinsically motivated, fully engaged and "in the zone," is what psychologist Mihaly Csikszentmihalyi defines as a "flow" experience. Intrinsic motivation is connected with things that we actually want to do and can lead to a lifelong commitment.

Mikaela Shiffrin, gold medalist in the 2014 Winter Olympics, explains, "I do this [ski racing] because I love it. I get this adrenaline rush from just going down the course and feeling like I made a really great turn, and I'm going to do it again and again and again. That feeling can't be replaced, and that's the feeling I'm striving to get every time I go out there."[5] That's intrinsic motivation—love of the activity itself, and nothing short of a flow experience. Shiffrin demonstrates her *intrinsic* motivation to ski and compete rather than just a focus on the prize, or *extrinsic* motivation.

TIP: GET REAL ABOUT MOTIVATION

Motivation is probably the toughest part of any workplace wellness program. There are two types of motivation: extrinsic and intrinsic. Extrinsic motivation may trigger short-term wins, but intrinsic motivation is much more likely to lead to long-lasting results.

PARTICIPATION VERSUS ENGAGEMENT

To start this conversation, we need to tease apart two terms that are often used interchangeably: participation and engagement. Participation means showing up, but engagement is much deeper. Engagement is the *intention* behind the participation. Are people showing up to just collect on a reward, for example, or are they showing up because they actually want to be there? Authentic engagement is when we are fully invested in an activity and when the activity itself energizes us. What the research overwhelmingly suggests is that engagement is a critical factor in influencing lasting behavior change. People who are highly engaged are more likely to stay in the game, more likely to continue trying and, ultimately, more likely to achieve positive outcomes. In contrast, people who are disengaged—or just checking the box—are more likely to get distracted and give up.[6]

THEORETICAL UNDERPINNINGS OF EXTRINSIC AND INTRINSIC MOTIVATION

Extrinsic motivation is based on behaviorist theories. A behaviorist approach calls for increasing "adaptive"—or good—behaviors through reinforcement and decreasing "maladaptive"—or bad—behaviors through absence of reward or punishment. Great idea if you're working with dogs; not so great if you're working with people!

Behaviorist theory got its start with Ivan Pavlov, the architect of what I call the "good dog/bad dog" thinking, also known as the "Pavlovian response." His research in the late 1890s, largely based on research he conducted with dogs, led to his conclusion that we, as humans, can be conditioned into adopting certain behaviors.

Behaviorism was taken to a whole new level in the 1930s with Burrhus F. Skinner's "if-then" theory. His research showed that more rewards create stronger associations in our brains, which lead to an increased likelihood of engaging in the desired activity. Conversely, more punishments strengthen associations to *not* do a certain activity, leading to a reduced likelihood of engaging in the activity.

Twenty years later, Jerome Bruner, educational psychologist and a leading crusader against behaviorist thinking, argued that the brain is not just an "information processor." Rather, he proposed that the brain is a "creator of meaning." This laid the foundation for an alternative to behaviorism: a theory called "constructivism." Constructivism, largely applied in the classroom, is based on the notion that real learning happens when teacher and student, together, co-create new meaning and understanding. If we apply this concept toward workplace wellness, real change can happen when coworkers *collaboratively create meaning*—the heart of intrinsic motivation.

The self-determination theory, originally proposed by Edward L. Deci and Richard M. Ryan in the 1970s, is the most broadly cited framework for understanding intrinsic motivation. Their research clarifies, first and foremost, that motivating others is an impossible task. Rather, each of us naturally has an enduring sense of volition, despite external forces. It's called *free will.*

Therefore, as leader of a wellness movement, your task is to create the conditions in which employees are more likely to motivate *themselves.* This process begins with tapping into three fundamental, psychological needs: autonomy (wanting to do things on one's own terms), competency (wanting to feel a sense of mastery), and relatedness (wanting to be socially connected). We'll break down each of these components momentarily.

For now, let's further explore the course that most organizations are taking.

MORE CARROTS AND EVEN MORE STICKS

Is there a disconnect "between what science knows and what business does?," Daniel Pink asks in *Drive.*[7] "Business as usual" in the world of workplace wellness is to add more incentives and penalties. According to a recent survey by the National Business Group on Health, 74 percent of employers that offer wellness intended to use incentives in 2014, up from 57 percent in 2009, with an increase in average payment from $430 in 2010 to a record-breaking $693 per employee per year in 2014.[8] Almost a quarter of employers who have wellness incentives in place now use penalties, which is double the rate it was two years ago. It's expected to double again this year to 46 percent.[9]

There is a spectrum of carrots and sticks used to promote wellness. On the extreme stick side, a few companies base hiring and firing decisions on health-related activities, specifically smoking. Companies like Scott's Miracle Gro offer smoking cessation to employees who smoke, usually for a year, and then mandate being tobacco-free at the end of the year or risk termination. A less extreme measure, used by many employers such as Whole Foods, is to place a surcharge on the health plan for smokers. On the other side of the spectrum, carrots used in wellness programs range from gift cards, discounts, raffle tickets, and merchandise, to more significant benefits such as reductions in health care premiums and contributions to health savings accounts.

Carrots and sticks are usually used to encourage employees to *participate* in some type of wellness activity such as a health risk assessment, biometric screening, weight management program, physical activity, or tobacco-cessation program. They're also used to encourage employees to *meet* actual health outcomes or behaviors, such as weight loss or reduced blood pressure or tobacco use. According to a Kaiser Family Foundation 2014 report, only 8 percent of large employers with wellness programs use incentives and penalties based on health achievements.[10] However, especially in the wake of the Affordable Care Act, this number is likely to increase.

The Affordable Care Act enables employers to increase incentives from 20 percent of total cost of coverage to 30 percent, and in the case of tobacco-related programming, up to 50 percent. The law establishes parameters around when incentives are permissible and also requires that employees provide alternative options for employees who are unable to participate in wellness programs due to medical limitations.

As of March 2015, a new bill is up for consideration, called the Preserving Employee Wellness Programs Act. The goals of this bill are to keep these incentives intact, permit spouses to participate and provide up to 180 days for employees to request alternative wellness options.

MONEY CAN GET PEOPLE IN THE DOOR—BUT IT WON'T KEEP THEM THERE

Much debate in the wellness field has focused on whether incentives lead to sustainable behavior change. The rationale behind incentives is that they get people in the door and may provide a "jolt" for those who are on the fence. Undoubtedly, research has shown that incentives increase participation in immediate and one-time activities, like taking a health risk assessment, participating in a screening, or getting a flu shot. But what happens *afterward*? We cannot fool ourselves into thinking that these one-time events necessarily translate into lifelong habits (which is really the ultimate goal).

Researchers at the University of Oxford reviewed 17 different studies to assess whether or not incentives led to any long-term changes in rates of smoking cessation. "None of the studies demonstrated significantly higher quit rates for the incentives group than for the control group beyond the six-month assessment," the researchers concluded. "There was no clear evidence that participants who committed their own money to the program did better than those who did not, or that different types of incentives were more or less effective."[11] What we have learned from the field of management is that money is simply not as motivating as one might think. An attractive paycheck or bonus draws people to a job—but it doesn't necessarily keep them there. Research has shown that other needs become more important, such as opportunities for career growth and feeling recognized. HealthStream Research conducted a study with more than 200,000 participants and found that the number one factor that plays into employee engagement and retention is the manager's ability to provide purposeful recognition.[12]

In an effort to stem costs associated with turnover, companies have typically implemented extrinsic solutions such as perks and bonuses. But research has shown that these solutions don't bear out the hoped-for results. Lack of appreciation, it turns out, especially from their immediate supervisor, is the number one reason why people leave a job—not money.

TIP: IF YOU DO USE INCENTIVES, PROCEED WITH CAUTION

The trend is definitely more carrots and more sticks. The problem is that sustainable change must be intrinsically based, and research has shown that the use of incentives and penalties may undermine intrinsic motivation.

ARE SOME FORMS OF INCENTIVES BETTER THAN OTHERS?

Some organizations like Lincoln Industries are experimenting with unusual incentives.

THE STORY OF LINCOLN INDUSTRIES

Lincoln Industries, a medium-sized manufacturing company with 620 employees at five different sites, builds all of its efforts on a core belief that "wellness and healthy lifestyles are important to our success." The purpose of wellness at Lincoln Industries is to help employees to "become the best versions of themselves." To make this happen, Lincoln Industries provides the following unique programs:

- **Fuel for Performance:** Health coaching with a focus on sleep, healthy eating, and physical activity
- **HealthyU:** Free, on-site medical center for employees and their families
- **HealthyU Fit:** On-site fitness facility
- **Platinum Wellness:** Experience-based incentives

While incentives are usually in the form of reduced health care premiums, prizes and raffles, or contribution to a health savings account, Lincoln Industries has decided to design their incentives differently. They've created *experience-based* incentives. Employees who achieve certain health outcomes are invited to participate in the annual "Platinum Mountain Climb," an all-expenses paid trip up a 14,000-foot mountain in Colorado. In their view, this unique offering is the key reason behind why smoking rates have dropped from 42 percent (in 2004) to less than 13 percent today.[13]

SHOULD INCENTIVES BE USED AT ALL?

The real question revolves around whether or not we should use incentives at all. Alfie Kohn, author of *Punished by Rewards*, is one of the leading voices against the use of any incentives—ever. Incentives and penalties, he argues, foster short-term compliance and undermine long-term intrinsic motivation.

Some companies like Dow Chemical are taking these voices seriously and have committed to never using incentives to encourage participation or outcomes. Dow has successfully inspired more than 85 percent of its employees to participate in its wellness programs on an annual basis—all on a completely volunteer basis. Goldman Sachs for the most part, also eschews incentives, other than a $250 reimbursement given to employees who exercise 50 or more times in a six-month period.

Some companies that have traditionally employed incentives are starting to move *away* from the practice. Johnson & Johnson experimented with an incentive program geared toward obese and overweight workers (beyond the $500 incentive that's already in place for employees who participate in an HRA and health coaching). Due to lack of interest, the additional incentive program was scrapped—and now the company is focusing more on recognition-based campaigns in lieu of financial incentives.[14]

Incentives and penalties certainly can catalyze a short-term activity that does not require creative thinking. But, again, we return to our earlier question: *What happens next?* Are the participants more likely to take the next step, as in actually participating in the subsequent programs? Or are they less likely to do so? And what about the following year? Evidence clearly shows that participants will need something more than an incentive or a penalty to keep them engaged over the long haul.

A MINEFIELD OF UNINTENDED CONSEQUENCES

Ultimately, intrinsic motivation always trumps extrinsic motivation. Research has borne this out over and over again. The question is, do extrinsic motivators create unintended and undesirable consequences? There is a lot of evidence to suggest that they do.

Here are some potential downsides to using incentives and penalties.

Punitive Overtones. Incentives, particularly penalties, can feel punitive. In a heavily commented NPR article on the efficacy of wellness program, one reader expressed his frustrations: "My employer charges us if we don't meet certain health requirements and they add it to our insurance premium. I meet every single requirement, except for the waist circumference. So, that's an extra $30 a paycheck. . . . If you don't participate fully, you get charged an extra $30 a paycheck. . . . It's not a wellness benefit program, it's a penalty program."[15]

In addition to anecdotal evidence, a mounting body of research indicates that incentives and penalties can lead to resentment. A recent employee survey conducted by the National Business Group on Health found that the majority of employees polled resent having participation and outcomes tied to rewards.[16] According to another survey, conducted by the Kaiser Family Foundation, 62 percent of workers polled feel that participation-based incentives are inappropriate, and 74 percent disagree with the use of outcomes-based incentives.[17]

Penalties have sparked a number of lawsuits, including a recent one filed by the Equal Employment Opportunity Commission (EEOC) against Honeywell International Inc. EEOC argued that the use of penalties attached to biometric screenings violated both GINA and ADA. Although Honeywell prevailed in this case, there are still a number of other lawsuits that are pending—and the number is likely to increase.

Perhaps the most well-publicized story about incentives and penalties gone awry is the story of Penn State. Here, organizers opted for stiff penalties—up to $1,200 a year—for employees who chose not to take a health risk assessment and submit to a biometric screening. Ultimately, the faculty rebelled, the news went viral, the program folded, and the reputation of the university suffered.[18]

Oversimplification. While incentives and penalties may be useful in encouraging people to perform simple, one-time tasks, making a lifestyle change demands a more enduring solution. Making a lifestyle change is definitely not a one-time, check-the-box activity. Tying incentives with participation or outcomes tends to oversimplify the task at hand and can potentially lead to negative effects in the future.

Too Much Focus on the Reward. Putting a spotlight on the reward, and taking it off of the activity itself, can be particularly dangerous. "Biggest Loser" contests, fashioned after the popular TV show and now prevalent in workplaces, are perhaps one of the egregious examples of how rewards can lead to *reduced* health.

BIGGEST LOSER CONTESTS = A REALLY BAD IDEA

One of the most popular wellness offerings may be one of the worst for our health. Given that most of us need to lose weight, it would seem that these would be a really good idea. The problem is that weight loss in the short term is easy. It's maintaining the weight loss over time that's the hard part. Losing weight quickly only fosters the typical pattern we see almost every time: weight

(*continued*)

(continued)

loss, followed by weight gain. The research shows that 95 percent of dieters regain their weight—and the majority of these dieters gain back more than they originally lost.[19]

When we add incentives into the mix, we only intensify this terrible cycle. The wellness manager of a client we worked with complained of a phenomenon she noted during her company's regular "Biggest Loser" contests. Incentivized with weekly rewards, some of the participants would lose enough weight to win the reward one week, then *regain* the weight the following week, only to lose the weight again the week after in order to qualify once again for the weekly reward.

A better option to consider is a weight-*maintenance* challenge. Kaiser Permanente promotes a Healthy Holiday Challenge to encourage both employees and community members to maintain their weight during the holidays to avoid the typical 1–2 pound weight gain.[20]

Short Cuts and Cheating. There is a lot of evidence to suggest that adding rewards and punishments into the mix increases the likelihood of cheating. The focus shifts to the reward and, as human beings, we can't resist the temptation to "game" the system. I was at a party and overheard a friend sharing her secret to racking up steps on a pedometer: Put it on the dryer. (The pedometer picks up the motion of the dryer as "steps.") Every time I mention this story when I speak to a group of fellow workplace wellness professionals, they laugh. Why? Because they've seen similar antics at their workplace. During a recent talk, one of the audience members shared another common trick: Put your pedometer on your dog.

Undermining Intrinsic Motivation. Another well-documented effect is the so-called Sawyer Effect. In a nutshell, if you pay someone to do something, the activity then feels like a job and becomes less interesting—and the net result is *diminished* intrinsic motivation. As Daniel Pink explains in *Drive*, study after study has demonstrated this phenomenon, making it "one of the most robust findings in social science—and also one of the most ignored."[21]

SO NOW WHAT?

Clearly, the use of incentives and penalties has some problems. As the leader of your wellness movement, what can you do? In addition to addressing the culture (which we discussed in Step 3: Uncover the Hidden Factors) and building a culture and environment of well-being (which we will explore further in Step 8: Design Nudges and Cues), I suggest you incorporate the following philosophies to blend the powerful potion of intrinsic motivation into your wellness mix.

Make It Enjoyable Right Now. We all know that our health matters, but most of us have more pressing and immediate concerns, such as picking up our kids from day care or meeting a deadline at work. As the leader of a wellness movement, it would behoove you to focus less on the long-term benefits, such as health, and more on the short-term benefits, like immediately increased energy through exercise.

Segar's research has repeatedly shown that focusing on "here-and-now" benefits of exercise is much more effective than focusing on longer-term results of exercise like weight loss or increased physical fitness. Ironically, those who focus on these short-term benefits are more likely to reap the long-term benefits. Segar's research demonstrated that women who exercised for "energy" as opposed to "managing weight" were 34 percent more likely to keep exercising over time.[22]

It's Ultimately about Meaning. Tapping into a real sense of meaning is the key to creating wellness programs that endure. In a recent article in *Time* magazine, journalist Eric Barker writes, "Your mind may *require* meaning. Studies show that it's the key factor underlying happiness and motivation."[23]

When employees feel a sense of meaning, they are much more likely to:

- Participate because they *want* to, not because they have to,
- Be passionate about what they're doing,
- Ask big questions,
- Share what they've learned and what they're doing with others, and
- Start their own wellness movements.

Let's look at tangible measures you can take to create conditions in which employees are more likely to experience intrinsic motivation.

KEYS TO LASTING MOTIVATION

Fostering intrinsic motivation means tapping into what research has demonstrated are universal needs, part and parcel of being human. These deep human needs are compelling and create meaning. They are more likely to tap into the right whys and will help generate a collaborative creation of meaning. First, we all have a need to feel **competency**. One of the best ways to increase feelings of competence is by beginning with and then leveraging our strengths. Second, we all need to feel **autonomy**. All of us have a need to feel in charge of our own destiny—and to be given the tools to change on our own terms. Third, we all need to feel **relatedness**. Connecting with others helps to increase both accountability and enjoyment. Fourth, we all yearn for a sense of **purpose**. Tapping into our deepest sense of purpose is critical for sustaining a change. Finally, we all have a need for **play**. Yep, we really do like to have fun—and if you want to get people to authentically engage, you have to make it fun and enjoyable.

TIP: ALL WE NEED IS LOVE . . .

. . . and competency, autonomy, relatedness, purpose, and play. If we want to intrinsically motivate people, we need to tap into these universal human needs—with an emphasis on emotions over logic!

COMPETENCY

Building a sense of competency through your wellness movement will be critical for lasting impact. The following are some keys to building a sense of competency, or mastery.

A great way to foster a sense of competency is to ask people about their experiences and tap into their knowledge. People love to share their stories. Make sure you ask lots of open-ended questions to really draw out personal reflections. The more people share their expertise, the more meaningful the program will become for them. This is where it is so important to remember that you should play the role of agent of change—not the role of medical expert! It's much more empowering to others when you facilitate a conversation, rather than inundating people with information.

TIP: STOP TELLING ME WHAT, SHOW ME HOW!

Let's face it: wellness is not rocket science. We all know *what* to do, but not necessarily *how* to do it. In addition to motivation, building skills is an important component to making a change.

Learning new skills can be very motivating, as human beings are naturally curious. Acquiring new skills is also essential for addressing the "how" element of making change. For example, improving eating habits calls for cooking and meal-planning skills.

The key here is that these skills need to be actually meaningful—and that means, don't give them the same old stuff. "SMART" goals, while useful, are often overused. Consider updated goal-setting techniques, such as creating "tiny habits," a method developed by B. J. Fogg, director of the Persuasive Tech Lab at Stanford University.

Also, pay attention to trends, such as the mindfulness wave that is sweeping the country. At Goldman Sachs, more than 500 people sign up every quarter for their mindfulness program, according to Laura Young, vice president, Americas head of wellness. Below are some fun activities you can experiment with to foster a sense of competency.

ACTION ITEMS

FOSTER COMPETENCY

1. **Identify your keystone habit.** Charles Duhigg, author of *The Power of Habit*, suggests that we each need to identify our foundational, or "keystone" habit. Ask participants: What's the one change that will effectively create a chain reaction or domino effect on all of your other habits that play into your health and well-being?
2. **Identify tiny habits.** Now, encourage participants to break down their identified keystone habit into "tiny habits," as recommended by B. J. Fogg. If your goal is to exercise regularly, a tiny habit you might start with would be walking around the block.

(*continued*)

(*continued*)

3. **Set positive goals.** When we set avoidance goals like "I'm not going to smoke" or "I'm not going to eat sugar," our brain tends to fixate on what we've just declared we won't do. We can increase our chances for success if we focus on what we are going to do. This is why, for example, a first step in any evidence-based tobacco cessation program is to identify the activity that is going to replace the activity of using tobacco.
4. **Develop habits of mind.** Our brain, which can be our greatest challenge, can also be our greatest source of hope. We can build "habits of mind," or fundamental ways of thinking, in terms of how we approach learning and making change. This is a term popularized by Ted Sizer, a leader of educational reform, founder of the Essential Schools Movement, former professor at Brown University, and past mentor of mine. The idea is to focus less on content delivery and more on empowering people to build habits of mind that will serve them well on their journeys of well-being. Sizer's "essential" habits of mind that are relevant for our purposes include critical thinking, creativity, imagination, commitment, empathy, communication, and analysis. Instilling these habits of mind is useful for keeping people engaged over time—and empowered to make lasting change.
5. **Develop mindfulness skills.** Mindfulness is not just a trend; it can serve as an essential skill in building habits that promote health and well-being. Even when you indulge and "give into" a bad habit, pay attention—without judgment. This mental process of noticing is a first step in breaking any form of addiction, according to Stanford psychologist Kelly McGonigal.
6. **Keep track.** Just monitoring your progress increases your chances for success. In the era of the quantified self, there are zillions of mobile apps out there to help you—and a lot of organizations are leveraging these apps in their efforts to engage employees in their health and well-being. If you're old school, pen and paper will work just fine.

AUTONOMY

Former Yale Professor William Deresiewicz, author of *Excellent Sheep*, poses the question: Are we teaching kids to be "really excellent sheep"? In other words, are we simply teaching our kids to jump through hoops, but not actually engage with—and make meaning—of their education and their lives? We might ask the same question in relation to workplace wellness. Are we simply encouraging employees to be "really excellent sheep" that jump through hoops, but never make meaning of wellness on their own terms? Researchers like Deci and Kohn would argue that the industry's use of incentives fosters a sheep mentality, which undermines engagement, not to mention sense of well-being.[24]

To foster intrinsic motivation, Deci advocates "autonomy support." In layman terms, autonomy support means that individuals feel as if they are in charge of their own destinies but still feel supported. This means that any wellness program should have a facilitative, coaching tone rather than a controlling one. Sarah Stein Greenberg, executive director of Stanford's renowned Hasso Plattner School of Design, shares the story of Becca, a student at Stanford who described her experience of coming back to school after taking a year off. "This year is the first year I feel like I've taken control of my academic education in a meaningful way. I no longer have incentives to get good grades, but my grades are better than they have ever been."

The transition we see here in Becca is that she now is taking ownership of her education. Similarly, your goal is to empower employees to take ownership of their health and well-being—and this is only possible when you tap into people's innate need for autonomy.

ACTION ITEM

FOSTER AUTONOMY

The following are ways to foster a sense of autonomy in your wellness programs:

1. **Provide multiple points of entry.** One way that you can foster a greater sense of autonomy is by creating programs

(*continued*)

(*continued*)

that incorporate multiple intelligence styles. Each of us has our own unique way of engaging with the world, making sense of information, and ultimately making change. For starters, some of us are more visual, others are more auditory, and yet others are more kinesthetic. If you want to go even deeper, you can leverage the "five entry points of entry," proposed by Howard Gardner, educational psychologist at Harvard University who developed the multiple intelligences theory.

a. **Narrative:** Use storytelling to deliver content.

b. **Logical-quantitative:** Use data and analysis to inform.

c. **Foundational:** Ask big, philosophical questions.

d. **Aesthetic:** Emphasize sensory and aesthetic experiences.

e. **Experimental:** Facilitate hands-on activities.[25]

2. **Be provocative.** Too many well-meaning wellness programs provide only *answers*—without giving people the chance to consider any *questions.* If we want to empower people to *do* and to become agents of change in their own lives, we need to encourage them to ask questions—deep questions—and become critical thinkers.

3. **Customize the wellness brand.** At the American Heart Association, employees are encouraged to create their *own* version of the "Life is why" brand. "My Dad is why," "Building a healthier Bay Area is why," or even "The future of my son is why" are examples of some of these individualized brands. You can launch a similar program within your own organization by encouraging employees to create and post their own versions of your organization's wellness brand.

RELATEDNESS

Antanas Mockus, mayor of Bogotá, Colombia, during the mid-1990s and early 2000s, took highly unorthodox measures to combat endemic corruption and lawlessness, employing a creative mix of "mimes, superhero capes, and relentless positivity"[26] to address intractable issues like jaywalking.

While the standard, extrinsically oriented approach would call for stiffer penalties, Mockus decided to do something very different: Hire mimes. Whenever a jaywalker would step out on to the crosswalk, so would a mime—mimicking the offender and instigating uproarious laughter among onlookers. The stunt worked. Fatalities related to traffic violations like jaywalking dropped by 50 percent.[27] What Mockus ingeniously did was to tap into the human need for "relatedness," or being in connection with others. This factor is one of the most powerful ways to promote intrinsic motivation.

"Make 2015 an 'ussie' not a 'selfie,'" reads an ad for It's Just Lunch dating service. When it comes to promoting health and well-being, two is definitely better than one—and more than two is even better. We are social beings, hardwired to be connected to one another. As we discussed in Step 5: Take a da Vinci Approach to Change, building peer-to-peer social networks, through mechanisms such as cultural and wellness ambassador networks, may be *the* most important factor in engagement and long-term success.

Recall how Marianne Jackson, former senior vice president of human relations at Blue Shield of California, spoke about the phenomenon of "elevator confessions"—or impromptu conversations that happened almost every time she took the elevator. Employees wanted to share with her the successes, and even setbacks, that they were experiencing in their wellness efforts.

Leslie Ritter, wellness leader at Eileen Fisher, also seeks to build wellness in the organization "one conversation at a time," as she describes it. These conversations are what enable her to understand what's truly happening with employees, managers, and teams, helping her to better create meaningful wellness solutions. Sheri Snow, general manager of wellness at American Cast Iron Pipe Company, largely attributes the success of the company's wellness program to her team's extensive efforts to actually meet employees in the field. She believes these continual, face-to-face interactions have been pivotal.

Laura Young of Goldman Sachs adheres to the same approach. "Our wellness program is successful because we meet people where they are. Each individual is unique, with specific needs and circumstances."[28]

While health coaching, or one-to-one counseling, has been a mainstay in many wellness programs, the field is increasingly moving away from targeting the individual toward activating *groups*. Without a doubt, there is a growing sensitivity to the need for the "we" in "wellness," as Joel Bennett, president of Organizational Wellness & Learning Systems and author of *Raw Coping Power*, characterizes it.

Even virtual connections can promote intrinsic motivation. A recent Stanford study looked at the effects of being physically apart, yet *feeling* like you're part of a group. In this study, two groups of students were given a challenging puzzle to solve. Individuals in the first group were prompted to feel as if they were part of a team, whereas participants in the second group were made to feel as if they were on their own. The results showed that the first group was more engaged, less likely to get tired, did a better job at actually solving the puzzle, and kept at the task 48 to 64 percent longer than the individuals in the second group. According to Gregory Walton, lead researcher of the study, "The results showed that simply feeling like you're part of a team of people working on a task makes people more motivated as they take on challenges."[29]

To promote this sense of virtual cohesion, many employers, across all industries are turning to social media platforms and gamification to promote social unity; engage employees around common, meaningful goals; and build excitement around wellness.

Peer pressure, as long as it maintains a positive and supportive spirit, can be a great way to support intrinsic motivation. Wellness challenges, such as walking or active commute challenges, can encourage friendly competition across teams and even global offices.

In some cases, employers take it a step further to competitions across organizations. Every year, Stanford University takes part in a one-week, Pac-12 Fitness Challenge, in which faculty and staff try to outstep faculty and staff at other Pac-12 universities. According to Eric Stein, senior associate athletics director and head of Stanford's BeWell@Stanford initiative, over 2,800 Stanford faculty and staff participated in the 2014 event.[30]

In a recent interview, actor John Travolta credited his children for his motivation to work out at 3 AM. "They [my children] still want me to play with them at the level of a much younger man. So in order to stay healthy for them, that's what I do."[31] Building initiatives around connection to one's family can be one of the most powerful ways to build intrinsic motivation. Companies like Skanska and Schindler

Elevator Corporation connect safety with family to encourage employees to comply with safety procedures, using novel techniques to cement this connection. At one Skanska construction site in California's Bay Area, workers tacked pictures of their family members on to their helmets. This easy-to-do practice led to award-winning safety adherence.

According to Jeff Coles, former president of Schindler Canada, "We tell our team, 'There's nothing more important than coming home safely to your family.'" Under Jeff's leadership, Schindler Canada made this mantra even more real.

THE STORY OF DYLAN

At the age of 16, Dylan Angus lost his father, Ross Angus, a highly respected and highly skilled elevator technician at Schindler Canada, due to an accident on the job. Three years afterward, Dylan joined with Jeff Coles and his team in creating a video as a tribute to Ross. Dylan and Jeff jointly appear in the video, speaking side by side. One week after the release of the video, Dylan then came on site, partnering with Jeff and his team to run safety walks. Instead of the words just coming from the boss, now they were also coming from Dylan. "Hey, guys," Dylan told technicians and maintenance workers, "it's real. Don't count on your experience. My dad had 30 years. Experience doesn't matter. I lost my dad. Had he followed the steps on the six-inch rule, he'd be here still."

The difference was night and day, according to Jeff. Why? Because now Jeff and his team were tapping into one of the deepest intrinsic motivators: the need for human connection. The conversation transitioned from one of just compliance to one about being able to be with one's family. Says Jeff, "I've done hundreds of safety walks during my time with Schindler, and I've never seen people so engaged, listening, and attentive. It's really powerful."

Before Dylan got involved—and just six months after Ross's fatal accident—Jeff and his team conducted a technical compliance audit. Jeff assumed, "Of course, guys are going to do it right. We've just had this fatality. They have all of this training. They'll

(*continued*)

(*continued*)

do it right." Instead, all four workers who were tested failed, miserably. Not only that, each was defiant and lackadaisical. Jeff was shocked.

Now, let's fast forward to bringing Dylan onto the scene. "This time," Jeff explains, "every guy we went to see did it right—*exactly* right. And each guy was fully engaged in the conversation: eye contact, asking questions back—as opposed to 'yeah,' 'no,' 'I don't know.' In past times, you could always tell that each one wanted it to be over. In this one, they were each interested in learning more. 'Hey, what about this?' they'd ask. They were interested in engaging in a dialogue—which *never* happened before."

Jeff and his team continue to receive a mountain of positive feedback from the team with comments such as: "It really hit home for me"; "This really had an impact on me—and I'm going to really make sure I listen and follow these processes, because it makes a lot of sense." By tapping into the right why and creating real meaning, the level of engagement has done a "total 180," says Jeff.

Source: Jeff Coles, interview with author, December 14, 2014.

ACTION ITEMS

FOSTER RELATEDNESS

The following are ideas to foster more social connections:

1. **Group Work.** I love group work, especially in a workshop setting. A key to remember, though, is that you always need to give learners a clear call to action and provide specific directions. For example, ask that group members designate roles, such as presenter, timer, facilitator, and recorder. Clarify the time frame from the outset and provide time checks.

2. **Team Challenges.** This is a common program, and as long as it's not tied to weight, it can be a good one. Having team awards, rather than individual awards, can be more meaningful. Team walking challenges can be a great way to promote physical activity and social interactions at the same time.
3. **Affinity Groups.** Provide a forum for employees to form groups around common wellness interests.
4. **Social Media.** Social media can provide a great platform for employees to share goals and provide peer-to-peer support and encouragement. It can also provide a nice forum for employees to share their expertise in the form of blogs.
5. **Family Connections.** Bring it back home—and encourage employees to even bring their families on-site. The more you can help employees to connect their choices with their families, the more likely they'll be intrinsically engaged.
6. **Peer Coaching.** Rather than investing in expensive, and often underutilized, "expert" wellness coaching programs, try building *peer* coaching into your programs. By providing some tips on best practices in coaching, along with a structure on how to implement, you can empower employees to support one another in making lasting change. It's likely to be a less-threatening and ultimately more effective way to support lasting change.

PURPOSE

The fourth and perhaps the most important piece to this matrix of intrinsic motivation is a universal need for purpose. Vic Strecher, professor of health behavior and health education at the University of Michigan and author of *On Purpose*, built and sold a highly successful company, HealthMedia, that applies best practices in behavioral theories and modification techniques. With a reach of more than 40 million people, "This company not only developed health risk assessment tools; it added behavioral programming to it to help you change behavior," he says. Using these behavioral-based strategies led to a 20–30 percent success rate, he estimates. "That's not too bad if you consider that the price of our program was relatively low."

Now, he's building a new company that applies best practices in *finding one's purpose*—which started with meeting Jim Loehr, chairman and cofounder of the Human Performance Institute. "Jim's approach to thinking about behavior change was a focus on mission, or purpose, and a focus on energy management as opposed to time management." This, Strecher found, was the first program he had experienced that was directly helpful, and out of it he began developing purpose in his own life. Four years later, after tragically losing his daughter, he lost part of his purpose—"because a big part of my purpose was giving her a big life."

Despondent for months, Strecher then had an epiphany of his daughter telling him, "Dad, you really have to get over this." This event freed him to redefine his purpose, which became to treat each student *as if each one were his own daughter*. "That meant I needed more energy in my life." He started walking every day, meditating on a regular basis, eating better, sleeping more, and dedicating time toward creativity. All of these gave him the energy he needed to live with purpose, and now he's building a company that is dedicated to helping others to do the same. Purpose, he explains, "is a deeper motivator for me than messages from an HRA." He believes this is a relatively untapped opportunity in the field of workplace wellness that we should explore further.[32]

Identifying one's purpose and mission in life is energizing and motivating. It can even help us self-regulate and exercise our willpower. According to Kelly McGonigal, psychology researcher at Stanford University and author of *Willpower Instinct*, our wanting side can lead us astray, but staying connected to a higher purpose—and using mindfulness along the way—can help us stay on track.

Most hotels have recognized the power of purpose. Step into any hotel bathroom today, and you're likely to see a sign that gives you the option to reuse the towel—or not. There's no charge should you choose to get a new towel, but the sign reminds you that you can be a part of something larger, namely saving the environment. This is pure brilliance. The hotels offer no incentives and impose no penalties; they simply offer an opportunity to be a part of a larger sense of purpose.

If we really want to tap into this need for purpose, we need to be asking the question, "What do *you* care about most?" This is where we can achieve an entry point into helping people to make a change.

ACTION ITEMS

BUILD A SENSE OF PURPOSE

The following are ways to help employees to identify and connect with their deeper purpose:

1. **Time for Reflection.** In a world that is focused on doing, simply "being" and taking time to reflect is a good way to start tapping into one's higher sense of purpose. At Eileen Fisher, they do exactly that. Most meetings are kicked off with a moment to be silent and simply reflect.
2. **Journaling.** Journaling can be more free-form—or it can be more specific, like the "Name Three Good Things" activity we discussed in Step 2: Imagine What's Possible. This simple practice can encourage deeper reflection—and help people get closer to what matters most for them.
3. **Conversations about Life Purpose.** In building a career development plan, the more it aligns with an individual employee's life purpose, the better it is for the employee—and the better it is for the organization. Having the sense that we are meeting our higher purpose, or calling, is essential for career well-being.
4. **Connecting Purpose with Energy.** This is exactly what CEO Tony Schwartz and his team at The Energy Project do. They ask participants, "Do you have the physical, emotional, mental, and spiritual energy you need to accomplish your purpose?" This is an important question to ask—and a great way to frame wellness activities as avenues to better reaching one's purpose in life.

Arguably, incentives can undermine intrinsic motivation. However, in cases like American Cast Iron Pipe Company which has a wellness program that incorporates incentives, both the pervasive sense of autonomy and control (the company is employee-owned) and connection to a higher purpose are clearly playing a role in promoting intrinsic motivation.

AMERICAN CAST IRON PIPE COMPANY
A COMPANY THAT'S TAPPING INTO PURPOSE

American Cast Iron Pipe Company (AMERICAN), headquartered in Birmingham, Alabama, is a company that is steeped in a rich tradition of living by the Golden Rule. It's also a company whose wellness program recently won the highly coveted C. Everett Koop Award, arguably the most prestigious award in workplace wellness. Though seemingly unrelated, this achievement can be traced to the company's very beginnings.

Named by *Fortune* Magazine as "one of the 100 best companies to work for in America,"[33] AMERICAN is no ordinary company. Originally conceived by a forward-thinking businesswoman by the name of Charlotte Blair, AMERICAN was formally incorporated in 1905 under the leadership of its first president, John Eagan, who would later become the company's sole owner. At a time when Jim Crow laws were still in effect, Eagan decided to build a company that treated everyone with equal respect and equal dignity. Eagan lived by the Golden Rule, and he wanted his company to also live by the Golden Rule also. Eagan took a personal interest in his employees and would occasionally pay home visits. Before he died in 1924, he bequeathed ownership of the entire company in a trust to employees—a practice that was not legally recognized at the time. His widow testified in court on his behalf to ensure that his wishes were met. She won the case, and to this day, employees still share ownership of the company.

In addition to this commitment to social justice shaped by his strong Christian beliefs, Eagan was an advocate for healthy living. He spoke about fitness and the benefits of getting fresh air. More important, he *modeled* healthy living by walking to and from work most days. He took action to bring health to all of his employees, and as early as 1915, the company started providing on-site medical care for employees (now a 36,000-square-foot facility), along with dental care the following year.

The foundation that Eagan built has enabled an employee-focused wellness culture to flourish and grow at AMERICAN. In the early '90s, the company deepened its commitment to wellness by hiring Rebecca Kelly, a dietician. One year later, Rebecca hired Sheri Snow, and the two worked collaboratively to build what would become an award-winning program. This 20-year partnership began with exploring creative responses to the connection between costs and employee risk factors.

Together, they built a wellness strategy that now serves 7,500 people, including employees, dependents, and retirees. The strategy starts with the "WellBody Club," which includes a screening, health risk assessment, and a results-based incentive. Each participating employee is placed into a "club" based on health status and given an incentive accordingly. The incentives—up to $650 per employee—are structured so that employees are rewarded for both participation and outcomes. Sheri Snow now leads the company's wellness programs, and for eight years in a row, Sheri and her team have achieved their goal of an 80 percent participation rate.

Sheri and her team assess risk factors, share results with employees, and then guide employees toward programming and resources to build healthy habits. Some of the types of programs offered to employees include an on-site fitness facility and exercise classes, health coaching, tobacco cessation programming, a diabetes education program, and dietary counseling. In addition, the on-site medical clinic, now privately operated, continues to expand upon the services it offers: primary care, preventative testing, and dental and optometry services. The company also offers on-site physical therapy in the wellness facility.

Recently, the company completed an internal study spanning 2008–2012. The savings of both medical costs and productivity costs related to absenteeism resulted in a total savings of $361,783 for medical, as well as $316,404 for absenteeism. Savings from the decrease in health risk, medical costs, and absenteeism provided a 1:7.1 ROI. According to Ron Goetzel, senior scientist and director of the Institute for Health and Productivity Studies at Johns Hopkins Bloomberg School of Public Health, who oversaw the administration of the Koop award, "American Cast Iron Pipe Company's efforts demonstrate that, when done right, evidence-

(*continued*)

(*continued*)

based health promotion and disease prevention programs not only make workers healthier, but they can also produce a positive return-on-investment."[34]

On the surface, AMERICAN is an example of the classic behaviorist model that depends on extrinsic motivation. If we dig deeper, we see a larger sense of *purpose*, initiated by the founders of the company, that sustains the wellness programs. The ethos of living by the Golden Rule ensures that employees feel that their company deeply cares for them.

After learning he had high cholesterol, Leo Nabors, a blacksmith at AMERICAN, began working out. Before, he couldn't even get through 15 minutes of a workout; now he's teaching classes. "You get so much from working out that money can't buy," he says. "You can buy medicine, but not health."[35]

Nabors echoes the sentiment that money can't buy everything, but purpose and feeling socially bonded can. The fact that every employee has a vested interest in the company's success helps reinforce this foundation of trust. Most important, however, Sheri attributes the high level of engagement to her team's efforts to be "visible and mobile." They go out to where the employees are—in hard hats and hard shoes—and it's the power of these face-to-face connections that really makes the difference. By building an organization with a strong foundation of trust and doing the right thing, AMERICAN has created the ecosystem for a Workplace Wellness that Works.

Source: Sheri Snow, interview with author, December 8, 2014.

PLAY

Stuart Brown, author of *Play* and professor at University of California at Berkeley, has dedicated his life's research to the powerful effects of play. "We are built to play and built through play," he writes.[36] His research shows that play is the foundation of social relationships, happiness, and fulfillment, and is also essential for creativity, innovation, and productivity. Play is also the essential ingredient to moving workplace wellness from a "have to" activity to a "want to" activity.

Southwest Airlines, a company that is all about fun and creative expression at work, was the first in the airline industry to recognize the power of play. They realized that if they wanted passengers to pay attention, they'd be better off making it fun. Ride any Southwest flight, and you're likely to hear jokes and even rap songs when the safety announcement comes on. And what do passengers do? They *listen*—and if it's really good, they even clap!

Let's bring this back to wellness. In an initiative sponsored by Volkwagen and captured in a YouTube clip that's been replayed more than 21 million times, mischievous innovators replace the normal, boring stairs with "piano stairs." Walking up the stairs turns into a Tom Hanks scene from *Big*. The results were stunning: 66 percent more people chose the stairs over the escalator. According to a spokesperson from Volkswagen, "Fun can obviously change behavior for the better." This, he said, is what "we call the fun theory."[37]

ACTION ITEM

REPLACE BORING WITH FUN!

Playworks, a nonprofit organization that teaches kids how to play, is now bringing the same set of games to adults. How did that happen? Play, they believe, is for everyone—even for their board members (who also happen to be executives in big companies). The response they heard often from board members when playing these games: "Hey, my company spends money on team building, and this is a lot more fun than what they force us all to do. Would you do recess for my employees?"

Now, Playworks games are replacing traditional team-building events in corporations across the country. A long list of companies are signing up, including ABC, Chevron, Deloitte, Gap, Google, Kaiser Permanente, Hewlett Packard, PG&E, PriceWaterhouseCoopers, and Salesforce.com. Turns out you also can tune into these games. Playworks has the "PlayBook" online: playworks.org/playbook.

Source: Elizabeth Cushing, interview with author, November 28, 2014.

MOVING FORWARD

The classic model has "build incentives into your wellness plan" as a given. This does not have to be the case. As we've discussed, the research shows that incentives and penalties can take us off track. That said, there are examples of organizations such as AMERICAN and Cleveland Clinic that do have incentives and even penalties in place—and still have amazing wellness success. Some organizational cultures are more suited to incentives than others, and this is certainly something to keep in mind as you build the strategy for your wellness movement.

Whether you're using incentives or not, you'll still want to make sure that you build a wellness movement that taps into the five components of intrinsic motivation that we just studied: competency, autonomy, relatedness, purpose, and play.

ACTION ITEM

CREATE YOUR MOTIVATION PLAN

How are you going to tap into each of the big five intrinsic motivators? Think about how you can build on each of them—and then how you will infuse these intrinsically based programs throughout the organization, in an integrated da Vinci fashion.

FINAL THOUGHTS

Perhaps the biggest problem with a focus on extrinsic motivators is that it perpetuates the myth that behavior change is largely a matter of personal choice and just a matter of "getting" motivated enough and applying self-discipline. As we've discussed at length, culture and environment are what really sway our choices the most. This is a long, evolutionary process, which largely comes down to leadership. In the next chapter, we'll discuss what you can do in the meantime: Start implementing "nudges" and "cues" and continue evolving the culture.

Let's keep exploring.

Step 8

Design Nudges and Cues

(The "Make It Easy" and "Make It Normal" Imperative)

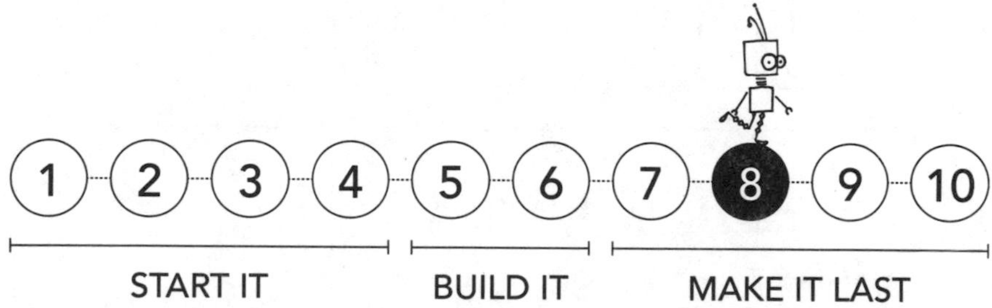

In the opening chapters of *Alice in Wonderland*, our heroine falls prey to the power of nudges. First, in response to the prompt "DRINK ME" and a view onto a garden that looks delightfully appealing—but through a door that's too small to enter—Alice drinks a magic potion and shrinks. She then comes across another prompt, "EAT ME." She, of course, obliges.

What We Can Learn from Alice

Alice does what most of us do: We eat or drink whatever is put in front of us, especially if there is some sort of temptation involved. This is the power of nudges. A nudge, as defined by *Nudge* authors Richard Thaler and Cass Sunstein, is "any aspect of the choice architecture that alters people's behavior in a predictable way without forbidding any options or significantly changing their economic incentives."[1] It is fair to say that Alice's behavior is predictably altered by these tiny little nudges. It is also fair to say that this is an all-too-human tendency that we all share. The good news is that you can leverage this tendency in the design of your wellness movement.

In the last chapter, we talked about how you can take steps to create the conditions in which employees are more likely to feel *motivated* to make a change. In this chapter, we'll discuss how to use the power of nudges and cues to help sidestep the motivation piece altogether and simply create an environment and culture that's more conducive to well-being.

In this chapter, we will discuss:

1. How you can now create the conditions in which employees are more likely to practice well-being habits at work,
2. Practical ways that you can design "nudges and cues" to support lasting change, and
3. Specific actions you can take to build a culture of health and well-being.

YOUR STEP 8 CHECKLIST

- ☐ Conduct nudges and cues audits.
- ☐ Implement nudges and cues to build a culture of health and well-being.

WHAT ARE NUDGES AND CUES?

Nudges are the *environmental* prompts that make the health and well-being choices the easier choices (and, conversely, the unhealthy choices the harder choices). Examples of nudges include signage, healthy options in the vending machines, desk equipment, and intentional office design such as stairway enhancement, second spaces, and reconfigured meeting spaces.

Cues, on the other hand, are *cultural* prompts. Cues make it normal—*or* abnormal—to engage in certain practices. Examples of cues include policies, organizational values, rituals, communication, encouragement, recognition, modeling (especially by senior leaders and managers), and core business practices. Cues give employees explicit permission to engage in certain activities and to make specific choices.

NUDGES AND CUES MAKE BEHAVIOR CHANGE EASIER

Both nudges and cues collectively contribute toward building what's often referred to as a "culture of health"—and what we'll refer to as a "culture of well-being." Research shows that employees in companies that manifest a culture of health are three times more likely to engage in their health and well-being, compared with companies that don't. Unfortunately, this same study also shows that only 26 percent of employees believe that their company has a strong culture of health in place.[2] By using nudges and cues, you can help close this gap to successfully build an environment and culture of well-being.

Applying a nudges and cues approach helps to take some of the pressure off the individual. Change then becomes less of an issue of individual willpower and more about an individual getting in sync with the surrounding environment and culture.

NUDGES AND CUES IN ACTION

Nudges and cues work best in concert. One of the best examples of the power of cues, and how these can follow on the coattails of nudges, is the reduction in smoking rates. Smoking in the '60s was the norm. In 1965, almost half (42.4 percent) of U.S. adults smoked.[3] It was normal to smoke in any public or private place, whether it was a hospital, a restaurant, a sidewalk, an airplane, or a house party. Today, in almost all public locations in the United States—and increasingly around the world—not only is it not allowed, it's considered abnormal. Today, only 18 percent of U.S. adults smoke.[4] While we need to keep making progress, it's worth noting that this change is a huge public health success story.

We would be mistaken to think that the massive reduction in smoking rates—which have fallen by more than half—is primarily due to individual motivation. On the contrary, the reduction in smoking rates is mostly due to changes in *policy*, such as outlawing smoking in public spaces and levying cigarette taxes (nudges), which both corresponded with changes in cultural norms (cues). My grandfather, for example, was a smoker who loved going to the movies. He attributed his quitting solely to the fact that, with changes in policy, he could no longer enjoy going to the movies without suffering a nicotine craving. So he quit!

According to the most recent Willis Health and Productivity Survey Report, almost half of employers (46 percent) have a written policy on tobacco use and almost half (45 percent) have designated smoking areas. Almost a third (31 percent) of workplaces are completely tobacco-free.[5] These policies are making a difference. A review of 19 studies on the impact of smoke-free policies concluded, "Because of the duration of time spent at work, workplaces are probably the most significant sites where smoking restrictions cause smokers to reduce their tobacco consumption."[6] Very simply, we have made it much, much harder to smoke (nudge factor), and in doing so, we have changed cultural norms (cue factor).

EARLY PIONEER OF NUDGES AND CUES

Jack Welch, former CEO of General Electric (GE), wanted to crystallize a cohesive vision for the company through increased employee interactions. To foster this, he used nudges and cues: He created a built environment in the company headquarters that would nudge people into engaging with one another more, and he established policies that would cue people into connecting more. He nudged employees into using the stairs more often by having a main, open stairwell built front and center. Why? Because stairways can serve as prime meeting points.

He ensured that the buildings were no more than three stories tall, to make it easy to use the stairs. He also nudged employees away from the elevators by installing the slowest elevators possible. He set the parking lots far away from the buildings to encourage employees to move more and, in doing so, to interact more. He cued employees into connecting more by encouraging employees to communicate face to face, rather than resort to e-mailing.

NUDGES AND CUES REINFORCE WELL-BEING ON A DAILY BASIS

While wellness challenges such as walking challenges, healthy eating challenges, and even mindfulness challenges are great, *daily practices* that are ongoing are even better. These are perhaps the most powerful way to cue employees into better health and well-being.

TIP: FOCUS MORE ON NUDGES AND CUES (AND LESS ON THE INDIVIDUAL)

Ultimately, optimizing the environment and the culture around people is probably the most powerful way to get people to change. By making it easier (and more normal) for people to make the healthy choices and harder (and less normal) for them to make the unhealthy ones, the healthy choice becomes the default. Every organization can create an oasis of wellness that nudges and cues employees toward greater well-being.

EXAMPLES OF REAL WORLD NUDGES

Imagine working, day in and day out, with patients and their families who are dealing with cancer and end-of-life issues at a center that is world-renowned for providing the best care for cancer. Stress at work is a given for employees at MD Anderson Cancer Center in Houston, Texas.

After a request from senior management in 2003 to find stress management solutions, one physician half-jokingly proposed the idea of a treadmill in his unit to "walk off stress." The idea took off and today MD Anderson is nudging employees to proactively reduce stress at work with pop-up "BeWell Stations," or mini-workout stations, strategically placed throughout the campus. Each one is equipped with a few items such as an elliptical machine, a strength chair, and an exercise guide. These stations are specifically designed to serve as stress relief tools *during* the work day.

Since 1998, the Centers for Disease Control and Prevention has been nudging employees in its Atlanta headquarters to take the stairs. Marketed as the "StairWELL to Better Health" campaign, the designers added music, upgraded the appearance of the stairwells with new paint and attractive artwork, and added motivational signage—all for under $16,000.[7] The organization landed on a quick and *easy* way to encourage more physical activity for everyone throughout the day.

Brocade, a global technology company, decided to harness the power of nudges when building their company headquarters. Employees were already requesting more wellness offerings, so the planners responded by incorporating wellness into the building's physical blueprint. To nudge employees into exercising more, the company built a fabulous, state-of-the-art fitness center on-site. To promote more movement throughout the day, they designed the stairs to be extra wide, brightly lit and attractively painted. To promote healthy eating, they stationed the cafeteria salad bar front and center. To promote physical activity and social connections, they created an all-glass wall in the cafeteria that looks out on an athletic field, allowing employees in the cafeteria to watch their coworkers enjoy a game of soccer or volleyball.

IDEO, a design and innovation consulting firm, decided to leverage the power of nudges to reduce employee soda consumption. Rather than removing the soda entirely, they simply moved the soda to the lower shelves out of eye level, and moved the water and sparkling water up to eye level. Soda consumption went down precipitously.

Google also takes advantage of the nudge factor in their cafeteria to prompt—one might even say to "trick"—employees into healthier eating. Like Brocade, they decided to place the salad bar at the front of the cafeteria. Google also offers smaller plates and posts signs touting the benefits of reduced caloric consumption. Like IDEO, Google makes it more difficult to access the junk food. The soda is placed behind opaque glass, and candies that used to be featured prominently are now tucked away.[8] Nudges like these are easy, relatively inexpensive, and can be implemented by almost any organization.

To nudge employees into renewal and well-being on the job, an increasing number of organizations like the Huffington Post are embracing the power of mini-siestas, installing nap rooms that are available to employees during work time. In her talks, Arianna Huffington describes walking by the nap room one day as *two* people were leaving the room. She laughed and joked, "Whatever it takes!"[9]

NINTENDO'S NUDGES

Nintendo's Redmond, Washington, headquarters is literally saturated with highly effective nudges and cues. First, the company purposefully created an environment that lives and breathes well-being, collaboration, playfulness, and a demonstrated commitment to sustainability. Recipient of a Gold Leadership in Energy and Environmental Design (LEED) rating, the company headquarters are filled with renewable sources, such as bamboo flooring, and energy-saving features, such as elevated floors to allow for a more efficient heating and cooling of the building, and a walkable roof that has 75,000 square feet of green vegetation. Designed to create a more pleasant working environment infused with natural light, the interior lighting dims and brightens according to the level of natural light outside. To spark playfulness and collaboration, there are Wii U kiosks available for employees to use, benches throughout the building in the shape of a d-pad or control pad, and zones that are playfully themed according to Nintendo gaming characters.

To nudge employees toward healthier eating, Nintendo offers a daily "Green Arrow" healthy option that is heavily subsidized, and other healthy options, such as the salad bar, in its on-site cafeteria. These nudges have actually catalyzed a Green Arrow movement, helping individuals to make huge changes in their lives.

Flip Morse, senior vice president of corporate resources, enthusiastically describes how one employee became a "Green Arrow guy," and in doing so, transformed his health and well-being. Flip tells the story of being approached by this employee at an event: "'I want you to know,' he told me, 'that I came to this company 5 years ago. I was 300 lbs, and it was the pricing in your café that drove me to eat healthy. Then I joined the biking team and started going to the on-site gym. In 5 years, I turned from that soft fat guy into a rock. I can't tell you what an impact this has had on my life. It's because of the culture of this company.'"

Another particularly unique nudge that Nintendo has in place is its specialized storage unit for bikes—and this is no ordinary storage facility. Keep in mind that the Pacific Northwest is wet, and the last thing any active bike commuter wants is

(*continued*)

(*continued*)

to put on wet attire at the end of a long day. Flip and the executive team cleverly came up with a solution: Build a storage unit that has a ventilation system, so cyclists can store their bikes—and hang up their wet biking clothes, which will be dried out and ready to go at the end of the day. This clever nudge makes biking to and from work that much more appealing, and therefore that much more likely to happen. The American Heart Association took note, awarding Nintendo a wellness innovation award for the design of this system. As evidenced by this award, Nintendo is meeting its wellness challenges by thinking about their specific cultural and employee needs. This is no "check the box" wellness program!

These nudges are particularly effective at reaching the people who are in the middle, Flip says. "I'd say we have three groups at the company: people like me who are health nuts committed to a healthy lifestyle, people who are never going to be health-conscious no matter what you do, and then there's the big population in the middle that can be swayed. That's whose behavior we're trying to affect."

Creating these kinds of conditions, which nudge and cue people to motivate themselves in making the healthier choice, is the hallmark of any effective wellness program. "You can lead a horse to water, but you can't make it drink. We've made it easier to make the healthy choices by offering the resources to get healthier," says Flip, "and we have leaders who model it."

Source: Flip Morse, interview with author, October 31, 2014.

SOME NUDGES REQUIRE AN INVESTMENT

Standing desks, another example of the nudge factor, have become a standard issue and even a status symbol in the technology industry. From start-ups like Asana to large companies like Google, AOL, Twitter, and Facebook, technology companies are nudging their employees to sit less by offering standing desks (without requiring a doctor's note). It's their belief—and there's a growing body of evidence to support this—that the investment is well worth the benefits in terms of increased productivity and enhanced motivation, not to mention better health.[10]

A pilot study conducted jointly by the Stanford University Center on Longevity and Blue Shield of California measured the impact of providing standing desks for employees working in a Blue Shield of California call center. Participants reported that the increased standing time (and reduced sitting time) helped them to be more productive and feel more energetic throughout the workday.[11]

There are organizations that are taking it a step further with treadmill desks, enabling employees to not only stand, but to actually move throughout the day. The Johnson County Communication Center in Olathe, Kansas, recently installed four treadmill desks for their call center workers—as a productivity-enhancement, stress-reduction, and even life-saving solution. "Are they worth the investment?" asks Tom Erikson, public information officer for Johnson County's Sheriff Office, in a recent interview. "All of the research led [us] to the conclusion that yes, they're well worth it. We have had dispatchers that have actually died in their chair here at work. We don't want that to ever happen again."[12]

Movement nudges are limited only to your imagination. You can do simple things like moving trashcans to central locations and away from desks so that people have to get up from their desks every time they throw something away. You could also bring in stationary bikes for the reception area. Gyms, volleyball courts, ping-pong tables, and playful props are additional ways to get people moving—and at the same time promote fun and innovation. The global venture capital firm ff Venture Capital has brought standing desks into its meeting rooms in order to generate a more robust sharing of ideas between employees. Google has taken it a step further with seven-person "conference bikes" for outdoor meetings around campus.

On-site clinics (definitely a considerable investment) make it that much easier for employees to get regular checkups, preventative screenings, and even appointments with specialized physicians, such as dermatologists. Goldman Sachs has an on-site clinic that is used by 80 percent of its employees and is greatly appreciated, according to Laura Young, vice president, Americas head of wellness. SAS, a software company based in Cary, North Carolina, is another company that has an on-site clinic, which is used by almost 75 percent of employees for their primary care.[13]

STORY OF CLARABRIDGE

Clarabridge, a global technology company, has incorporated well-being nudges into the design of its headquarters in Reston, Virginia. Inspired by progressive corporate sites in Silicon Valley and Washington, D.C., senior vice president of talent and culture Emily Markmann paid close attention to the architectural details that would foster enhanced well-being on the job. She felt one key item was having access to natural light, so she flipped around the standard office design and placed the executive offices in the center of the office space so that the employees had the direct access to the windows. In addition, the executive offices are glassed to allow the natural light to penetrate throughout. Instead of using tube lighting, she opted for the more pleasant LED lighting. To nudge collaboration and a sense of togetherness, she paid attention to the importance of sightline, meaning that employees can actually see one another and are not impeded by cubicle walls. Throughout the building, there are beautifully designed conference spaces to hold meetings, along with intimate booths to facilitate ad hoc discussions. There are even counter-height, long tables that have stools and enough space to accommodate up to 10 people—some sitting, some standing. To really get employees moving, there are a few treadmills peppered throughout the space, which are regularly used.

Says Emily: "Our new workspace promotes collaboration, transparency, mobility, and innovation. It represents the huge investment Clarabridge made in employee health and productivity and truly sets us apart as a top employer in the region."

In concert with these positive nudges, Emily has organized a Culture Club, a group of employees who work together to define and nurture the culture at Clarabridge. The members of this club even wear special Culture Club T-shirts. This group enhances the intersection between culture and well-being by organizing events such as walking challenges.

Clarabridge leaders regularly celebrate successes to promote employee recognition, through practices such as sending out e-mails that acknowledge individual successes. To increase impact, they then encourage employees to add their thoughts. The e-mail goes out and people can respond to it, elevating an individual success to an office-wide celebration. Recently, after hitting a company milestone of 5 billion processed documents, CEO Sid Banerjee held an impromptu, afternoon champagne toast for all employees in the corporate headquarters.

Source: Emily Markmann and Susan Ganeshan, interview with author, December 22, 2014.

Cues Are Important Cultural Prompts

Across Japan—from libraries and schools to construction sites to corporate offices—employees start the day with a series of exercises and stretches. The practice, called *asa taisou*, stems from a philosophy of continual improvement, or *kaizen*. There's even a national radio station called Rajio Taiso that broadcasts music you move to and accompanying exercise instructions.[14]

This ongoing practice, or cue, is simply a way of doing business—and has had a profound impact on employee health, well-being, safety, and productivity. At Honda, this morning practice has expanded into an intensive two-week fitness program for new hires. The program prepares them for the job, physically and mentally, ensuring more accuracy, greater productivity, and increased worker safety. Truly a win/win! Nissan has even brought the practice of morning calisthenics to its Smyrna, Tennessee, manufacturing plant.[15]

This practice of integrated stretches is also finding its way into United States-based companies. In some Chevron sites, fitness trainers infiltrate the workspace to lead employees in stretch breaks during the workday. At L.L. Bean, which has received multiple awards for its wellness programming, including the prestigious C. Everett Koop award, employees in the manufacturing plant engage in three five-minute stretch breaks every day. The company has measured a resulting 100 percent ROI in increased productivity. Fifteen minutes of stretch time translate into an added 30 minutes of productivity per day per employee.[16]

At LinkedIn, if you have a one-on-one meeting with Jeff Weiner, CEO, bring your walking shoes because it's likely you'll be taking a stroll on the nearby trail. In a recent blog post, he wrote, "I'll take walking 1:1s over office meetings any day."[17] Weiner has adopted walking meetings as a practice—and in doing so, has cued the entire company that walking meetings are the normal thing to do.

In a recent (walking) interview with a Bloomberg reporter, he explained that these walking meetings help free up conference room space—which can be a problem for fast-growing companies like LinkedIn. Another benefit? Employees get out of the office, get a fresh perspective, and get an opportunity to engage with colleagues in a way that they might not otherwise. Says Weiner, "People interact and connect differently when they're outside and they're walking together." In his view, this setting enables more direct communication that is free from the typical distractions—like checking one's phone.[18]

When practices such as walking meetings become a part of the company's perceived *normal behavior*, wellness has a much better chance to sustain itself over the long haul. The great news about practices like these is that they don't cost any money and anyone can do them, anywhere.

THE STORY OF SIOUX EMPIRE UNITED WAY

At Sioux Empire United Way, in Sioux Falls, South Dakota, every day, twice a day, coworkers get up from their desks and walk together for a mile. It is an office-wide event that happens every day, twice a day—at 10 AM and at 2:30 PM—rain, shine, snow, or ice. This story is one of my favorite examples of how *any* organization can infuse well-being and vitality into the workplace and can do it in a way that is effective, lasting, and intrinsically motivating. This program costs no money, requires no outside assistance or expertise, is completely homegrown, and has been ongoing for *more than 11 years*. This is nothing short of magnificent! I have begged and pleaded with organizations and teams to consider just standing up for a minute twice a day—and it's too much. And this all started as a *movement*—by one plucky woman—who also happened to be the CFO.

The wonderful thing about this workplace wellness practice is that it goes way beyond providing the obvious physical benefits. It builds social well-being and creates an incredible working community. Coworkers get to know each other on a personal level.

The good news is that this practice is really good for their bottoms (nice way to stay fit)—and for the organization's bottom line. This level of camaraderie is not just a "nice to have." It is one of the very best ways that this United Way office has fostered employee engagement and built an awesome organizational culture. Every day, coworkers contribute toward building an amazing culture—and at the same time, nurture their own personal well-being.

Source: Jay Powell and Cale Feller, interview with author, November 20, 2014.

THE RESEARCH BEHIND NUDGES AND CUES

From Bogotá to Detroit to Lisbon to San Francisco, communities are starting to experiment with nudges and cues. Enrique Peñalosa, former mayor of Bogotá, Colombia, dubbed the "Mayor of Happiness," used urban redesign to reorient the city from one of cars and few shared public spaces to an environment that invites walking and biking and people coming together in shared spaces. According to an article in the *Guardian*, "Peñalosa's first and most defining act as mayor was to declare war: not on crime or drugs or poverty, but on cars."[19]

In Detroit, Michigan, creative individuals are converting abandoned warehouses and underutilized public spaces into urban ski slopes.[20] The company Smart has taken the lead in leveraging the power of nudges by installing interactive "dancing traffic lights" in Lisbon, Portugal, that make it fun to wait before crossing the street, leading to a net result of 81 percent more people waiting at the red light.[21]

THE STORY OF A SAN FRANCISCO POP-UP FITNESS HUB

Jenn Pattee, "a relentless pursuer of playtime" and owner of Basic Training, is committed to making the world a better place by bringing fitness outdoors, making it fun, and designing spaces that nudge people to play. Recently, she joined forces with Douglas Burnham—a forward-thinking architect whose company Envelope A+D has designed spaces for companies like Facebook and Google—to convert a San Francisco parking lot into a Basic Training Pop-Up Fitness Hub. This is part of a larger, temporary-use project called "PROXY" that merges culture and commerce in Hayes Valley, a San Francisco neighborhood.

The mission of PROXY, Douglas explains, is to "activate vacant space and make it come alive." The space hosts an evolving collection of diversions that have included pop-up art galleries, a mural, and food and drink vendors. PROXY is even getting ready to house an outdoor movie theatre, feature a lecture series, and hold impromptu jazz performances. Adding a Basic Training Pop-Up Fitness Hub into the mix, well, seems kind of normal. "Having people working out, climbing poles, jumping boxes, swinging on monkey bars and coming together in a circle—these are all ways to activate movement and play. And, this fits in with our mission to get people to rethink what's normal in a city," says Douglas.

Jenn explains, "Douglas and I worked together to co-create a space where people would feel welcome and would not be able to resist play." Anybody can use it; it's open 24 hours a day, 7 days a week; and it's inviting individual acts of expression, a breakdown of social barriers, and an emerging set of new norms—or cues. "It's not unusual to see individuals recruiting others—maybe their date or their kids or their parents—to join them in experimenting with movement in this playful space."

Together, Douglas and Jenn's efforts demonstrate how a combination of nudges and cues is a great way for a city and its people to come alive.

Source: Jenn Pattee and Douglas Burnham, interview with author, November 20, 2014.

A growing body of research suggests that community-based nudges and cues like this pop-up fitness hub play heavily into rates of physical activity.[22] Positive nudges like accessible sidewalks, adequate lighting, parks,[23] biking paths,[24] and even aesthetics[25] can increase physical activity levels. On the other hand, negative nudges like a shortage of sidewalks, as well as perceived lack of safety, can decrease physical activity levels.[26]

Richard J. Jackson, professor and chair of the Department of Environmental Health Sciences at the School of Public Health at the University of California, Los Angeles, has been a leading voice in championing a nudge approach to change. He believes in the power of a "built environment." In his view, changing behaviors starts with creating the conditions where people can be healthy. "The *built environment*," he defines, "is everything we have made in order to live our lives. It is in our homes, places of business, public spaces, and parks and recreational areas—or lack thereof." He goes on to write, "If we are going to make changes, we ought to be creating spaces that work for our health, the economy, and the planet—places that are *of the heart*."[27]

Up to this point, most of the research has focused on the role of nudges and cues in the community. According to Ron Goetzel, researcher at Johns Hopkins, "To date, there has been a paucity of research on the effects of environmental and policy changes at the workplace and whether they can produce a substantial impact on outcomes such as improved worker health, reduced utilization of health care services, and improved productivity."[28] Nonetheless, this community-based research adequately demonstrates the effectiveness of nudges and cues, and provides lessons on how every organization can build its own oasis of well-being through intentional design and the shaping of a supportive culture.

Action Items You Can Use to Increase Everyday Movement at Work

The following are nudges and cues that are specific to activating more movement, but the concept of nudges and cues also can be applied toward other areas of well-being.

(*continued*)

(continued)

Nudges = Environmental prompts → it's easy to . . .

- **Signage:** Post signs to nudge people to move more, such as signs directing people away from the elevators and toward the stairs.
- **Stairway enhancement:** Make design changes to encourage increased stair use, through lighting, decorations, fun messaging, and accessibility.
- **Desks and desk equipment:** Offer standing desks, and if possible, walking stations. If the budget is limited, provide devices to encourage more movement at workstations, such as reminder apps, monitor risers, exercise balls, or even music stands (to prop up reading materials at eye level while standing).
- **Second spaces:** Create second spaces (in addition to break rooms) with equipment and instruction to facilitate more movement, such as high-top tables, mats, stretch bands, stationary bikes, and stretch guides.
- **Reconfiguration of meeting room spaces:** Add environmental prompts to get people standing (and even moving) during meetings.
- **Internal walking paths:** Create internal "trails" to encourage more walking meetings or walking breaks (demarcated with masking tape).

Cues = Cultural prompts → it's normal to . . .

- **Policies:** Implement policies that support more movement and less sitting in the workplace, such as a policy that meetings shorter than 30 minutes should be stand-up meetings.
- **Rituals:** Integrate rituals that get people moving, such as company-wide morning stretches, team-based or department-based morning huddles, company-wide "10 and 2" (everyone stands or moves for 2 minutes at 10 AM and at 2 PM).

- **Communication:** Infuse communication (especially from executives and managers) with ongoing tips on well-being and reminders of upcoming wellness events.
- **Recognition:** Encourage regular recognition from the top, such as recognition of managers who empower their teams to move more.
- **Modeling:** Ensure that leaders and managers are modeling more movement practices, such as taking the stairs instead of the elevator.
- **Integration:** Devise practices that fully integrate movement into the fabric of the culture, such as an inclusion of wellness and getting people moving into performance reviews.

ORGANIZATIONS CAN NUDGE AND CUE PEOPLE INTO GREATER WELL-BEING—BEYOND PHYSICAL

The power of nudges and cues can be leveraged beyond getting people to move more and eat healthier food. Nudges and cues can also be used to improve well-being in emotional, financial, social, career, environmental, spiritual, and even creative dimensions.

A growing number of organizations now design their offices to maximize social interactions. The goal is to generate ideas and promote camaraderie. Pixar Animation Studios, based in Emeryville, California, has a large atrium designed to encourage employees to "bump" into one another. Square, a Bay Area-based technology company that is "making commerce easy," has designed their office in the likeness of city blocks, with streets (running perpendicularly) and avenues (running diagonally), with the kitchen in the center. Any time an employee is hungry, he or she takes the avenue to the kitchen and is likely to run into a colleague. To encourage impromptu meetings, the designers smartly placed convenient and attractive meeting spots along the way. IDEO has also experimented with increasing social interactions. Instead of working in designated cubicles, desks, or offices, employees work out of rotating locations.

Eileen Fisher, a New York-based fashion company that proudly embraces its nontraditional culture, has taken nudges and cues to a whole new level.

TAKING WELL-BEING NUDGES AND CUES TO A WHOLE NEW LEVEL

"We're pretty nontraditional and have been from the beginning," says Leslie Ritter, wellness leader at Eileen Fisher. For starters, Leslie refers to the founder and chief creative officer on a first-name basis. "Eileen," she explains, "takes holistic well-being very seriously for herself and for the people who work for her—and, always has."

Holistic well-being, one might say, is part and parcel in the culture at Eileen Fisher. About 15 years ago, Eileen decided that she wanted to make it easier for her employees to take advantage of holistic offerings by creating an employee benefit program that would cover nontraditional, alternative therapies like acupuncture, chiropractic, massage, and yoga. These were all things that she valued personally. So as a start, the company began offering $500 to employees that could be used toward any type of personal well-being. The money could go toward any of these alternative practices or toward more traditional wellness options such as a gym membership or a personal trainer. The amount was later upped from $500 to $1,000, along with an additional allowance of $1,000 to go toward education. Every employee in the three main corporate locations, along with all of the employees in the retail stores, has access to these benefits. Education can be defined as learning a new language, taking coursework to develop a new career, or even taking a cooking class. "It's totally your personal decision," says Leslie.

To increase the "nudge" factors that make it easier to make healthy choices, the company has continued expanding its on-site programs. The company's free programs include yoga, Pilates, and meditation classes, along with workshops on various well-being topics. In addition, employees can apply their annual wellness and education allowances to go toward any of the fee-based, on-site offerings, including massage, acupuncture, reflexology, facials, manicures and pedicures, Alexander technique lessons, cranial sacral therapy, hypnosis, allergy treatments, and chiropractic. Employees can even make an appointment with an astrologer or a medical intuitive/nutritionist. The company offers a "quiet room" in each of its three main corporate locations so that any employee can meditate, nap, or just regroup.

The company has also integrated a number of inspiring well-being cues into its daily work practices. A common ritual used to symbolize and reinforce a sense of equality is their "circle practice": conducting meetings sitting in a circle (rather than around a conference table where there is an obvious head of the table). This practice encourages everyone to share their ideas with the group. Meetings often begin with a check-in, a time when people share something that's on their mind—work-related or personal, and the company even promotes a Native American tradition of using a "talking stick" to facilitate more intentional listening.

Every meeting begins with a moment of silence. The person leading these moments of silence rotates, and anyone can volunteer to take the lead. There's also someone who is designated to "hold the space" for the group as they meet, making sure that a diversity of voices are heard—and not just the dominant ones. This is especially important when there are a lot of changes happening in the company. There's an "intention" set for every meeting, as opposed to just objectives.

Another important cue is the company's general practice of no meetings before 10 AM on Mondays and no meetings after 2 PM on Fridays. The common understanding is that people have the space and time they need to use this time for themselves. "All of these practices," Leslie explains, "build a culture of well-being and mindfulness."

The goal of all of these practices is to fully integrate physical health and happiness with building community, honoring diversity,

(*continued*)

(continued)

creating trust, fostering leadership, and supporting financial well-being. The important connections between culture, well-being, and smart business are fully embraced by Eileen Fisher. "We work hard to create transparency in relationships, encourage honesty, and help every person to find their purpose and find pleasure in the work that they're doing," says Leslie. A big piece of this is happiness—and this is something that Eileen takes seriously. "She is a firm believer that happy people create a successful company." And that right there is the value proposition for wellness at Eileen Fisher.

Source: Leslie Ritter, interview with author, December 16, 2014.

TAKING ACTION TO INCREASE THE NUMBER OF NUDGES AND CUES

The first step to build this culture of well-being is to assess what nudges and cues already exist. From there you can devise a simple action plan to build more nudges and cues to foster an environment of well-being.

ACTION ITEM

CONDUCT AN INVENTORY OF NUDGES AND CUES

Nudges. In terms of nudges, you'll want to focus on the built environment. What do you already have in place that nudges employees to make positive (or negative) choices? What are some additional environmental prompts you can put in place to make the positive choices the easy choices?

Cues. In terms of cues, you'll want to focus on the culture—and assess whether or not you have a culture of well-being in place. What do you already have in place that cues employees to make positive or negative choices? What are some cultural prompts you can put in place to cue employees to make more positive choices without having to "go after" them as individuals? What are the cues you can employ to make health and well-being "normal"?

Here are some ideas to consider:

- Policies
- Rituals
- Recognition
- Modeling by leaders and managers
- Encouragement by leaders and managers
- Peer-to-peer encouragement
- Mentorship and sharing between colleagues
- Integration of wellness into business decisions

Action Item

Implement Nudges to Foster More Movement and Healthier Eating

The following is a checklist of ways to create environmental prompts in order to promote more movement and healthier eating in the workplace.

MOVEMENT NUDGES

- Prominent, well-lit stairs
- Showers and lockers

(*continued*)

(continued)

- Place to lock up bikes
- Biking and walking paths
- On-site gym
- On-site fitness classes
- Time allotted for physical activity
- Walking meetings
- Walking groups
- Company-sponsored teams
- Posters promoting physical activity
- Stand-up and moving workstations
- E-mail-free days
- Stationary bike in the waiting area
- Slow elevators

HEALTHY EATING NUDGES

- Healthy options in the vending machines
- Healthy options in the cafeteria
- Nutritional labeling in the cafeteria
- Posters promoting healthy eating
- Available water station
- Refrigerator available for employees
- Healthy foods served at meetings
- Fruit bowl instead of candy bowl in the reception area
- On-site garden or farmers market

Action Item

Implement Nudges and Cues to Foster Well-Being

Here are a few examples of nudges and cues that can boost multiple dimensions of well-being:

Emotional	Financial	Social	Career	Community	Creative
Designated stress-free zones	Higher base pay, de-emphasize bonuses	Central atrium space	Career development plans	Community outreach projects	"Creative collisions" design
Buddy system	Financial pools to encourage more collaboration	Management "office hours"	Strengths assessments	Paid day for service	Brainstorming sessions
Work-life balance	Matching donations to charitable organizations	High-top tables that encourage gathering	Managers working with team members to leverage strengths	Promotion of neighborhood-based activities	Collaborative workshops
Benefits that support emotional well-being	Evaluation of current compensation strategies	Creation of more intimate spaces	Systems to help employees identify higher purpose in their work	Community service projects instead of typical team-building programs	Creative projects (linked with career development plan)
Wellness days instead of only sick days	Financial planning services	On-site childcare	Professional development opportunities	Mission focused on social and environmental responsibility	Bottom-up innovation campaigns
Mindfulness rituals		Morning huddle		Certifications, such as B Corp status or LEED certification	Learning culture
Icebreaker activities to kick off meetings		Benefits that support social well-being			
		Encouragement to bring family and friends to organizational events			
		Recognition rituals			

FINAL THOUGHTS

As we have discussed, framing wellness as a matter of "personal responsibility" is problematic. Forcing individuals to bear the burden of making lifestyle change calls for willpower, self-regulation, setting goals, and other actions that are difficult to sustain—and nearly impossible if the larger culture and environment do not support the desired change. By looking at the environment and the culture, employing nudges and cues, we're able to skirt around so many of the barriers that keep wellness from working. Nudges and cues create an oasis of vitality that make it *easy* and *normal* for individuals to make the healthy choices.

Step 9

Launch and Iterate

(The Experimentation Imperative)

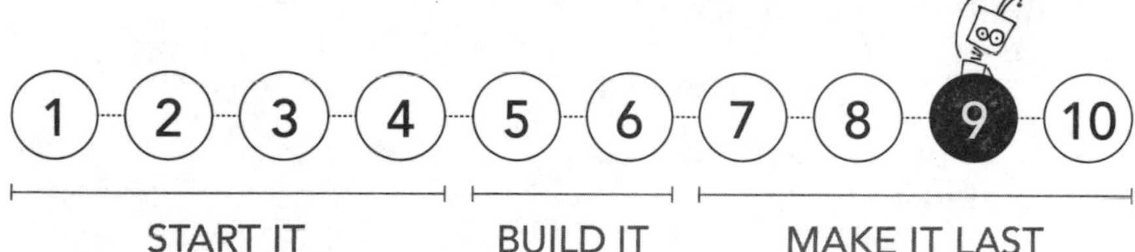

The story goes that Thomas Edison failed 1,000 times before he succeeded in inventing the lightbulb. When asked by a reporter how he felt about having failed so many times, Edison replied, "I didn't fail 1,000 times. The lightbulb was an invention with 1,000 steps." In other words, he launched and iterated a thousand times.

Similarly, a recent *Forbes* blog post describes how "it's not innovation that sets Silicon Valley apart from other centers of technological development—it's a willingness to iterate."[1] This iterative process—or launching a product into the marketplace *earlier*, seeing what happens and then making rapid iterations *after*—is the important, powerful process of embracing failures, learning from them, and then making improvements. This practice of experimentation and refinement happens in a participatory and collaborative fashion between different groups, and it's the often messy but productive heart of creativity, innovation, and, ultimately, success.

This is exactly the kind of spirit you should bring to your wellness movement—with individual employees, with the programs you develop or select, and with the organization as a whole. Very simply, the launch-and-iterate approach means *learning through doing*: Launching activities, programs, and strategies *before* they're perfect; evaluating and learning from the results and reactions; making adjustments; and then launching again. This approach can move your workplace wellness from check the box to out of the box. If there is no room for failure or experimentation, your wellness movement will become safer and smaller.

Conversely, if you can embrace failure as part of the process, you'll invent greatness, just as Edison did. Most important, perhaps, is that iterating will also demonstrate to the workers in your organization that management is committed to providing and collaborating with them to seek out effective solutions. This interactive experimentation and learning will get employees involved in the process, which will increase engagement. In workplace wellness, a launch and iterate approach is truly a win/win!

In this chapter, we'll focus on:

1. The iterative advantage,
2. How the scientific method can be blended with design thinking,
3. The research behind launch and iterate,
4. Defining a growth mind-set and how you can foster more of this kind of thinking,
5. Launch and iterate on an individual basis,
6. Launch and iterate on a program-by-program basis, and
7. Launch and iterate on an organizational level.

YOUR STEP 9 CHECKLIST

- ☐ Create a public forum around big questions to generate a growth mind-set
- ☐ Provide tools for peer-based evaluations
- ☐ Provide tools and resources to empower habit formation
- ☐ Cultivate learning labs
- ☐ Launch and iterate on a program-by-program basis
- ☐ Launch and iterate on an organizational level

THE ITERATIVE ADVANTAGE

Merriam-Webster defines iteration as "a procedure in which repetition of a sequence of operations yields results successively closer to a desired result." Some may consider the process of experimentation and iteration to be risky, but highly regarded, leading organizations like the research-based McKinsey Global Institute are advocating an iterative approach to improve our health and well-being. In their recent report on the international obesity epidemic, the authors wrote, "While investment in research should continue, society should also engage in trial and error."

I agree that trial and error can be productive in solving our wellness problems, and I believe that we need to couple our research efforts (which take time) with efforts in experimentation (which can be more immediately informative). The McKinsey authors continue with, "In many intervention areas, impact data from high-quality, randomized control trials (RCTs) are not possible to gather. So, rather than waiting for such data, the relevant sectors of society should be pragmatic with a bias toward action, especially where the risks of intervening are low, using trial and error to flesh out their understanding of potential solutions."[2]

SCIENTIFIC THINKING MEETS DESIGN THINKING

Scientific thinking applies a deductive, analytical, problems-based approach. What is the problem, and how do we solve it? In workplace wellness, we have strongly favored a scientific, evidence-based approach to improving employee health and well-being. Identify the risks (the problems) through HRAs and biometric screenings, feed this information back to the employee, and then offer programs to help reduce these risks (lessen the problems). This is a small, safe process designed to *avoid* failure.

Avoiding failure is not enough; we need to *imagine what's possible*, and this is what design thinking helps us do. Design thinking, as the name implies, means to think like a designer using a more creative, open-ended, solutions-focused approach (as opposed to analytical, problem-solving approach). Design thinking, by definition, is a methodology that is active and highly participatory, and draws upon imagination, intuition, and systems thinking. It is a process of identifying the desired future state, imagining how we might get there, and strategizing how we can launch some of these ideas.

Rather than converging on one "right" answer to avoid failure, as we were taught to do as test takers, a launch and iterate approach is divergent and about generating multiple ideas (applying tools like Edward de Bono's Six Thinking Hats®) and then experimenting with them in a trial-and-error fashion over and over again, just as Edison did.

In order to find the ideal nexus between scientific thinking, design thinking, and your wellness movement, your goal should be to combine best practices from evidence-based, research-oriented approaches with lots of experimentation to collect your own data along the way in order to discover what works best. Always keep your da Vinci hat on, and do not limit your research to what's available only in the field of workplace wellness. Best practices from outside the field of wellness, such as management, education, architecture and design, and even advertising, can help you gain a more balanced perspective, which is essential as the field increasingly embraces a more holistic approach toward wellness.

Launch and Iterate in Action: The Story of IDEO

The promise of rapid succession of experimentation and failure is central to IDEO's core beliefs. They call it "Fail faster!" IDEO employees "try early and often," which means lots of prototyping and trying out untested ideas, lots of seeing what went wrong, and lots of trying it again. In other words, it's a lot of good old-fashioned trial and error.

IDEO embraces big thinking and playfulness to achieve its vision, which is nothing short of "positively impacting the world through design," according to Duane Bray, head of talent. On its company website, IDEO speaks about "helping you find your inner adult" and "ensuring children everywhere thrive." "We help organizations grow," the website declares. "We help organizations innovate" and "We help organizations develop capabilities" and "We help organizations build businesses."

One look at IDEO's impressive roster of credentials shows that these are more than just words. IDEO and IDEO.org (its nonprofit branch) have received multiple international awards for designing an array of products and services from medical devices to Pilates equipment to food systems in K–12 schools to sanitation systems in Ghana. All of this has happened as a result of the company's undying commitment to experimentation and "failing faster."

Not only does IDEO's success illustrate the advantages of launching and iterating, and of creating and supporting a culture where this is encouraged, but the company's approach toward wellness is also a fantastic example of leveraging Maslow to redefine well-being at work. "For us," Duane explains, "well-being shows up in many places. Our definition of it is being able to bring your whole self to work. We can each be our best when we take care of the whole person."

IDEO opts for a playful, experimental, and emergent approach toward workplace wellness. As with all their projects, employees are encouraged to test out wellness ideas—any ideas. IDEO, as an organizational entity, simply creates the conditions for that and signals that it's okay to do so. The net result: Wellness at IDEO is truly about well-being and living with vitality, and it incorporates support for multiple dimensions of well-being, including physical, social, financial, career, and creative. Here are some examples of how IDEO does this:

Physical Well-Being. IDEO employees address physical well-being in a number of creative ways. A practice that started in the Palo Alto office but that has spread across the firm, is hanging up one's bike over one's desk, using a pulley system designed by employees. A lot of the employees are yoga instructors and will teach "pop-up" yoga classes to coworkers. Employees even encourage outsiders, like the UPS delivery people, to join them in fun movement activities like jumping rope. Many of these activities could fit into a wellness budget designed by Ebenezer Scrooge himself.

(*continued*)

(*continued*)

Social Well-Being. IDEO has a playful tradition of "redesigning" a coworker's space while they are away on vacation. On one occasion, an employee's workspace in the Palo Alto office was replaced with a VW camper while the employee was away traveling—fully stocked with a desk, computer, and a phone. The redesigned workspace was a hit. It became a popular gathering place for employees and is regularly booked for meetings. Later, to meet popular demand, a roof deck was installed on top of the camper to accommodate rooftop meetings and social gatherings.

This stunt is a great example of the power of imagining what's possible, and of the benefit of a culture that encourages employees to take risks.

IDEO fosters social well-being through fluid working arrangements like the VW camper and rotating workspaces, and the opportunity to do project-based work in different offices, even in different countries. This creative practice builds social well-being across global offices and also helps to further build and unify the culture.

Financial Well-Being. IDEO has developed a unique 401(k) system that does the work for employees. Since 80 percent of employees are what Duane refers to as "passive investors," IDEO's 401(k) system is *opt-out* in order to make investing easier for employees. In keeping with their culture of transparency and collaboration between organization and employees, company leaders solicited employee feedback on the 401(k) program and its goals.

Career Well-Being. IDEO uses an explicit "guided mastery" approach to promote and create career well-being. Employees are encouraged to perpetually cycle through a process of "learning mode" to "fluency mode" to "mastery mode." Growth is demonstrated through mastery, which they define as the ability to teach others.

Creative Well-Being. Creativity is king at IDEO—and play is the avenue to promote creativity. One of the bathrooms in the San Francisco office has a giant chalkboard. People post big open-ended questions like, "What things do I fancy learning? What things am I practicing? What am I teaching?" Duane says, "It's incredible seeing the energy around this."

Source: Duane Bray, interview with author, December 2, 2014.

The launch-and-iterate approach that IDEO uses is *great* for employees, as it offers a very real path for tapping into all of the key intrinsic motivators we discussed in Step 7: Create Meaning. Through IDEO's explicit support for experimentation and failure, employees get to flex their autonomy muscles on a daily basis. The guided mastery approach fosters a sense of competency. Employees are always encouraged to work together in teams (relatedness)—and in a playful manner (play). Finally, every activity and every project at IDEO is deeply tied to purpose on both an organizational level *and* on the individual level.

THE RESEARCH BEHIND LAUNCH AND ITERATE

Educational psychologist David Kolb suggests that we learn and grow through a process of trial and error—or what he refers to as the "experiential learning cycle," a model he developed in the 1980s. His findings showed that we learn through a continuous cycle of "concrete experience," or *doing*, that leads to "reflective observation," or *observing* without judgment, which in turn gives rise to "abstract conceptualization," or *evaluating* what worked and what didn't. All of this, according to Kolb, then leads to "active experimentation," in which we test out new understanding, applying what we have learned.[3] Kolb's theoretical model is a very useful tool for developing a better understanding of how to apply a launch and iterate approach toward workplace wellness.

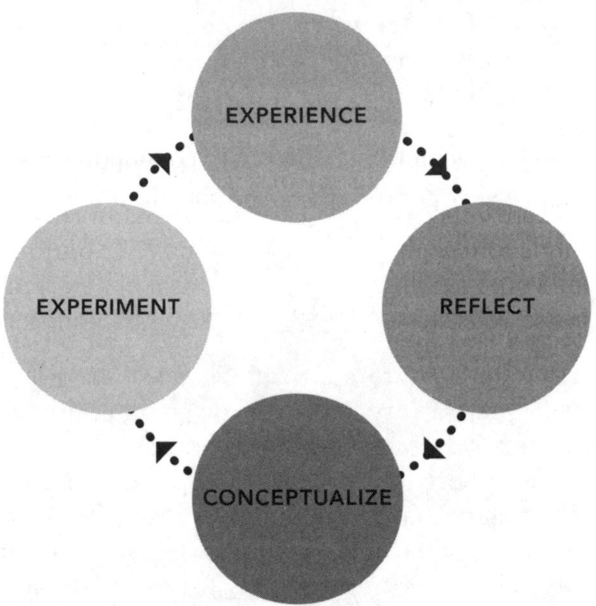

Source: Adapted from David Kolb, "Experiential Learning Cycle." Used with permission.

To bring this launch-and-iterate spirit to your wellness movement, your focus should be on creating opportunities for practice, feedback, evaluation, and application. Your goal is to get employees, managers, and leaders to experience (and actually do something), make *meaning* of their experience (through impactful reflection and evaluation exercises), and then try again, based on what they learned. This will help accelerate learning and real innovation through a dynamic process of doing, then reflecting, and then doing again.

Peer-based evaluations are a great way to foster this process of active learning, support the wellness movement, and evolve the culture.

ACTION ITEM

PEER-BASED EVALUATION

Implementing systems for peer-based evaluation is a critical step toward building a *learning* organization that supports a launch and iterate process: learning through doing, followed by feedback to deepen the learning process. Below is a very simple tool you can share with employees:

Colleague A observes Colleague B performing some type of work activity (facilitating a meeting, conducting a sales call, delivering a talk) and then provides feedback using three prompts. Be sure to rotate roles.

+: What did Colleague B do well?

Δ: What would you suggest that he/she change?

Action steps: Are there any specific action steps you'd recommend he/she do?

+	Δ
Suggested Action Steps:	

MORE RESEARCH THAT CALLS FOR A LAUNCH AND ITERATE APPROACH

Carol Dweck, psychology professor at Stanford University and author of *Mindset: The New Psychology of Success*, has focused her research on the power of our beliefs and how these shape our ability to make positive change in our lives. She distinguishes between what she calls fixed mind-set versus growth mind-set. As the term implies, a fixed mind-set is based on the belief that our capabilities are set and cannot be changed. It is the belief that one either is or is not skilled or talented at something, and that this skill or talent cannot be learned or improved without great effort and risk.

When we operate from a fixed mind-set we get stuck, because we tend to engage in catastrophic thinking such as "I'll never lose weight" or "I'm unhealthy, so why even bother?" and "I'm stuck in my job."

This mind-set is exactly the *opposite* of what we're trying to foster in the people we're trying to reach with wellness programming.

A growth mind-set, on the other hand, is the sense that it's never too late, and that *all* of us can *always* make change. A growth mind-set is critical as it encourages action, progress, possibility, and creativity. Growth mind-set is more likely to translate into persistent effort and continual improvement. A growth mind-set is also more conducive to learning something new or, in our case, building a new habit.[4] Obviously, this is exactly what we want in wellness and, ideally, in entire organizations. An overarching growth mind-set is what helps great companies like IDEO build thriving, highly engaged groups of employees, and it can help you succeed in your wellness movement.

Coauthors Michelle Segar and Winifred Gebhardt advise cultivating a growth mind-set in their chapter "Pursuing Health-Related Goals," in Michael O'Donnell's *Health Promotion in the Workplace*, "Teaching people to take a learning-goal approach might help them enjoy the process of striving toward their health-related goals and view their setbacks and challenges as opportunities to learn, instead of failures, something that builds resilience toward challenges and fosters ongoing behavior."[5]

ACTION ITEM

USE QUESTIONS TO FOSTER A GROWTH MIND-SET

To foster a growth mind-set, ask more questions! Get people thinking! You can pose the questions in a number of different ways:

- **Bathroom talk.** In every stall, post a flyer that asks a big question. During their "private time," people can think of new ideas.
- **Big poster or chalkboard.** Create a space—say, in the break room—to generate a conversation.

- **Social media.** SmartCar has launched a "#WhatAreYouFOR" campaign, which has led to responses like "FOR having a dream." You can generate a similar discussion within your organization, leveraging social media platforms.
- **Meetings.** A practice at Eileen Fisher is to start off meetings with a moment of silence to reflect. You could start your meetings with a moment of silence—followed up by a provocative and open-ended question.

Tip: *It's important that you ask the* right kinds *of questions and in the* right way *to generate engagement and critical thinking. Below are a couple of guidelines for asking good questions:*

- **Use open-ended questions.** Too often we pose a question that's really a statement: a "right/wrong" question that only has one answer. This type of question is called a "closed question." An open-ended question, on the other hand, has no one right answer and therefore is much more conducive to an interesting conversation that promotes critical thinking.
- **Prompt further discussion.** If you are facilitating a discussion, try following up responses people share with "yes, and . . ." as opposed to "yes, but . . ." or, "tell me more . . ." instead of "why?"

LAUNCH AND ITERATE ON AN INDIVIDUAL BASIS

Now, let's talk about how we can apply some of these big ideas like learning through doing and growth mind-set to actually change habits. In Step 7: Create Meaning, we examined the "M," or motivation, and to a certain degree, "S," or skills, in Michael O'Donnell's AMSO model on behavior change. In Step 8: Design Nudges and Cues, we addressed the "O," or opportunities. Now, we're going to go deeper into some of the skills that are useful in changing habits.

Charles Duhigg, author of *The Power of Habit*, proposes the notion of a habit loop in which a trigger leads into a routine, which in turn delivers some kind of reward, which in turn leads us right back into the loop. This process usually happens automatically.

For example, every time I go to the movies (trigger), I order a box of popcorn (routine), and while I'm craning my neck to look up at the big screen and fill my mouth with another kernel of popcorn, I get a big hit of butter and salt (reward). I am rationally aware of the fact that the popcorn is stale, the butter is probably fake, and it really doesn't even taste that good, but here's an example of a routine that's well etched into my brain. Over time, my cravings get even sharper—and I'm pretty much in a cycle of addiction.

Here's the good news: My habit—or anyone else's—doesn't have to stay that way. The research shows that we can make big changes through an accumulation of small, iterative steps. The goal is to build a repertoire of small wins that can eventually lead to larger transformations. "Small wins," writes Duhigg, "fuel transformative changes by leveraging tiny advancements into patterns that convince people that bigger achievements are within reach."[6] In other words, small victories can help reinforce a growth mind-set, which in turn is essential for triggering lasting behavior change.

B. J. Fogg, founder and director of the Persuasive Technology Lab at Stanford University and named by *Fortune* magazine as one of "10 gurus you should know,"[7] advocates a convergence of three key elements to change habits: motivation, ability, and trigger. With the right amount of motivation, the appropriate level of ability (easier is better), and a trigger (or reminder) to activate the behavior, we can each take action to convert ideas into action. Fogg suggests that we break down big goals into not just manageable steps, but "tiny habits," and then slowly build from there.

ACTION ITEM

SIMPLE STRATEGIES TO FORM NEW HABITS

Goals can motivate us if we're on track—or they can deplete us if we're having a hard time staying on track. Pulling together elements from the steps we've explored so far, here are some strategies you can share with employees. The key here is to emphasize that changing habits should be viewed as a *learning* process, above all.

1. **Identify a "keystone" habit.** This is a trick that Duhigg suggests we use. What's the one change that will effectively create a chain reaction or domino effect on all of your other habits that play into your health and well-being?
2. **Identify "tiny habits."** Try out B. J. Fogg's recommended "tiny habits" to break down the desired keystone habit. The idea is to build big successes through an accumulation of mini-successes.
3. **Triggers.** A growing number of employers are enabling employees to leverage mobile technology and apps to help trigger healthy behaviors.
4. **Keep track.** Just monitoring your progress increases your chances for success. There are millions of mobile apps out there to help you keep track. If you prefer, pen and paper will work just fine.
5. **Organize your environment.** Just as organizations can nudge their employees into better wellness choices, we can do the same for ourselves! One simple step is to rearrange your refrigerators and cupboards to make the healthy choice the easy choice.
6. **Find a friend.** Any time you partner up with a friend to work toward a goal, you're more likely to succeed. This is one of the most powerful techniques we can use to stay on track. Even pets can help keep us on track.
7. **Reflect.** Simply observing how we're doing, how we're feeling, and above all, being kind to ourselves and others, can help us to stay in the game of learning, and, ultimately, making change. Journaling is a great tool to use, as well as loving and kindness meditation, or even conversations with a friend.

LAUNCH AND ITERATE ON A PROGRAM-BY-PROGRAM BASIS

Now, let's consider how you can bring this launch and iterate approach to your programs. As we have discussed at length, you should be thinking about leading a movement—not just another program. That said, you certainly want to have programs *within* this larger movement, and a great way to launch and iterate on a program-by-program basis is to incorporate "learning labs"—or mini-centers of experimentation—in your program design. This can be particularly useful if you're working in an organization like IDEO with multiple locations or departments.

Patty de Vries, wellness manager for HealthySteps, and her team have launched a program to support department-based experimentation: Departments can apply for a grant to support a novel idea. The Center for Healthy Weight at Lucile Packard Children's Hospital is using the funds from their awarded grant to adapt a weight-control curriculum designed for kids and design the curriculum for adults. Their plan is to then pilot the program with another department. Small-scale prototypes such as this one can provide terrific insights into which programs should be implemented or modified on a larger scale.

Another way to promote a launch and iterate approach in developing programs is to form ad hoc teams of employees tasked with taking a design-thinking approach for gathering information and testing out new ideas. According to Jennifer Pitts, cofounder of Edington Associates and coauthor of *Positive Health as a Win-Win Organizational Philosophy*, "These ad hoc teams can work collaboratively with their peers to iteratively prototype and test solutions and ultimately develop successful and sustainable approaches. This helps build empathy, trust and engagement in the process from employees throughout the organization."[8]

ACTION ITEM

CULTIVATE LEARNING LABS

Each team or each location can launch and iterate its own experiment in promoting employee well-being. The goal is to learn from the process, begin distilling what works, and then share results with the larger organization.

Now, let's break down the actual process of building an iterative program. To capture the spirit of a movement, I often like to segment programs, such as learning labs, into three phases: "get ready" (analyze, ideate, design, and develop); "go" (implement); and "keep going" (evaluate and iterate).

Get Ready: Analyze, Ideate, Design, and Develop. Getting ready is a combination of analyzing the collected data and stories, designing the program, and then developing the materials needed to actually launch the program. Let's take a brief look at each of these elements.

- **Analyze:** In keeping with a design-thinking approach to assessing, go beyond the standard surveys through shadowing, collecting stories, and observing trends. You've already done a lot of assessing and analyzing: Let's briefly recount everything you've already accomplished. In Step 2: Imagine What's Possible, you created the vision for your movement. In Step 3: Uncover the Hidden Factors, you examined the culture of the organization, by gathering the quantitative data, as well as the qualitative data (the stories). In Step 4: Start With What's Right, you identified what's right, and you identified the key metrics for your wellness movement.

ACTION ITEM

REFLECT FIRST

Here are some questions for you and your da Vinci team to consider—before launching your program:

- Based on the data and stories we have so far, what are we expecting?
- How will we know that the program has been a success?

- **Ideate and Design:** Having gathered the information during the analysis phase and created a vision in Step 2, now it's time to start ideating. Beginning with the end in mind, which road will take you where you want to go? Or, do you need to build a new one? How will the program—or the stops along the way—help move employees and the organization toward the vision you created in Step 2? What would you like people to know, do, think, or feel as a result of the program? What are the key objectives for the program, and how are you going to ensure they're met?

- **Develop:** Once you've created your design, you can start moving into actual production phase. What materials, resources, and tools will you need for delivery?

Go: Implement. The implementation phase is when the actual delivery of the wellness program takes place. You should always use a "bias for action" over lengthy, cumbersome assessments. Recall that it's the *doing* part that matters most.

"Doing a thorough assessment, creating an elegant design, and developing a quality program are certainly necessary," explains Lance Dublin, CEO of Dublin Consulting and a recognized leader in the field of learning and development. "But these preparatory activities pale in comparison to the importance of the actual implementation. This is when the rubber hits the road."[9] Do sooner—and learn from it.

Keep Going: Evaluate and Iterate. To keep your movement going, you'll need to evaluate and refine on a continuous basis. This is where the iteration takes place. Very simply, what are the lessons learned? What worked, and what needs to be changed? A helpful model to use in this stage is the Four Levels™ Training Evaluation Model, developed by Professor Donald Kirkpatrick, a leader in the field of learning and development. The four levels are reactions, learning, behavior, and results.[10]

- **Reactions:** What are people's immediate reactions to the program? Were they satisfied with the program? Typically, these are measured by post-program surveys, which are sometimes referred to as "smile sheets" in the field of learning and development. While these evaluations do provide insights into whether or not the participants enjoyed the program, they don't necessarily measure impact on learning outcomes or the application of knowledge.

ACTION ITEM

EVALUATE REACTIONS

To evaluate a program on this first level, you and your da Vinci team should consider the following questions:

- Is there evidence that people actually liked the wellness program? If so, why?
- Is there evidence that people disliked the program? If so, why?
- Is there evidence that people perceived value in the wellness program?
- Is there evidence that the modes of delivery were effective and met the needs of employees?

To gather this evidence, you can conduct post-program satisfaction surveys, track participation rates, conduct ongoing polls, ask people directly, and tune into sideline conversations. This type of evaluation should be initiated immediately after the wellness program is implemented.

- **Learning:** What are the participants actually taking away from the program? Did they gain knowledge or skills? Did they experience a change in attitude?

ACTION ITEM

EVALUATE LEARNING

To evaluate on this second level, you and your da Vinci team should consider the following questions:

- Is there evidence that people acquired new information that could be useful?

(*continued*)

(continued)

- Is there evidence that people acquired new skills?
- Is there evidence that people are more motivated?
- Is there evidence that people have a positive attitude toward what they learned?

This information can be gathered through a post-program survey, post-program discussion, demonstration, or test. This level of evaluation also initiates immediately after the program.

- **Behaviors:** Are the participants now able to translate what they learned in the program into a change in behavior outside of the program? Are they maintaining these new behaviors over time? Do they have the capability to translate the new knowledge, skills, and values into action? Are there any changes in attitude toward the behavior?

ACTION ITEM

EVALUATE BEHAVIORS

To evaluate on this third level, you and your da Vinci team should examine whether or not there is now evidence of actual behavior changes. To do so, you should consider:

- Is there evidence that people are applying what they learned in the program?
- Is there evidence that people—on all levels—are practicing behaviors that are likely to improve their health and well-being?
- Is there evidence that managers are practicing behaviors that cue their teams into engaging in their health and well-being?

- Is there evidence that senior leaders are practicing behaviors that set the tone for the entire organization to practice health and well-being at work?
- Is there evidence that people—on all levels—are teaching others what they learned, in terms of new knowledge, skills, and attitudes?
- Is there evidence that people are aware of practicing new behaviors?

For this information, you should measure impact 3–6 months after the wellness program is implemented. You are looking for changes in behavior on the job and over time, and this data can be collected through observation, interviews, and focus groups, as well as through reporting from supervisors. You might even consider integrating these types of questions into performance evaluations, especially for managers. Before-and-after assessments are useful tools to measure changes in behaviors over time.

Keep in mind that upon reaching this level, organizational evaluation is essential. Keep asking the questions, "Does the larger organization support well-being in the workplace? Are there nudges and cues in place that reinforce the desired behaviors?"

SAMPLE QUESTIONS AND COMMENTS (POST-PROGRAM)

Level One: Do people *genuinely* like the wellness program? Do they seem motivated and excited? Or do they resent it?

Sample prompt (for a participant survey): I would recommend this program to a coworker.

Level Two: Did people learn useful information and skills during the specific programs?

Sample prompt: I learned information that is useful.

(*continued*)

(continued)

Sample prompt: I have a more positive attitude toward improving my personal well-being, as a result of this program.

Level Three: Are people actually adopting new behaviors (healthy habits) as a result of the program? Are people adopting new attitudes as a result of the program?

Sample prompt: I am taking steps to address my personal well-being.

Sample prompt: I am noticing new behaviors in my team as a result of this program.

Sample comment: "I was out of the office the day of the workshop. I have noticed that the team is conscientious of their physical well-being (participating in fitness breaks and walks)."

Informal Evaluation. In addition to formal evaluations, it is essential that you gather feedback *along the way*, evaluate and refine if necessary, and then make rapid iterations. Using informal evaluations is a great way to do this—and can serve as a tool to get people thinking and more involved. Collectively, these increase engagement and commitment.

INFORMAL EVALUATION TOOLS

Here are two very simple informal evaluation tools that I often use to get some feedback from participants at the end of a session. These can also be used to assess a strategy or session along the way (instead of waiting until the end).

ACTIVITY 1: HIGHLIGHTS

Ask each participant to turn to a partner and share highlights. Then, ask for volunteers to share one highlight with the larger group. If the larger group is already comfortable with one another, you can start immediately asking participants to share with the full group. I generally encourage people to share only one highlight, to keep the activity moving. If it's a larger group, don't feel compelled to ask for everyone's highlight.

ACTIVITY 2: WHAT ARE YOUR THOUGHTS?

- Organize participants into small groups, and ask each group to assign roles: recorder (takes notes), facilitator (makes sure everyone in the group participates in the discussion), and reporter (presents the findings to the larger group at the end).
- Give each group a flip-chart sheet and markers.
- Ask each group to divide the sheet into four quadrants.
- Ask each group to write in the following four questions (one per quadrant):
    - What were you expecting?
    - What did you get?
    - What did you love?
    - What would you change?
- Allow 5–10 minutes (depending upon how much time is available) for the groups to discuss the questions.
- If there's time, ask each group's reporter to present their findings to the larger group.
- Collect the flip-chart sheets at the end so that you can transcribe them and report the results back to the participants. By doing so, you close the feedback loop to generate an active and iterative learning process.

LAUNCH AND ITERATE ON AN ORGANIZATIONAL LEVEL

You are now ready to ascend to the fourth level of Donald Kirkpatrick's Four Levels™ Evaluation Model: measuring impact on organizational outcomes. Just as you have with levels one through three, you'll find it valuable to evaluate both formally and informally to gain a full picture. Here are the four areas to consider: (1) organizational culture shifts, (2) employee engagement in relation to wellness, (3) actual well-being outcomes, and (4) organizational outcomes.

ACTION ITEM

EVALUATE RESULTS

Evaluating on this fourth level requires a higher level of resources, in terms of time and cost and is the most difficult to measure. For this level, you and your da Vinci team might consider the following questions:

INDIVIDUALS

- Is there evidence that people are healthier?
- Is there evidence that people are experiencing higher levels of well-being and vitality—in multiple domains?
- Is there evidence that people are more energized?

ORGANIZATION

- Is there evidence that the organization is healthier?
- Is there evidence that there's a higher level of safety at work?
- Is there evidence of a higher level of employee engagement?
- Is there evidence of improved retention and recruitment?
- Is there evidence of a higher level of productivity?
- Is there evidence of a higher level of performance?
- Is there evidence that customer service has improved?
- Is there evidence that the bottom line has improved?

1. **Evaluate organizational culture shifts.** If enough time has passed (generally a year), I recommend that you break out your Maslow Meets Mallory Culture Audit again to evaluate whether the culture has evolved, especially in relation to these well-being needs. Are there any measurable improvements? If so, gather your da Vinci team to *ideate* on these improvements and how you can iterate even *more* improvements!

   Here are some additional indicators that will give you a sense of whether or not the culture is shifting:

   - Employee satisfaction scores
   - Employee engagement scores
   - Employee reviews (coming from external sources)
   - Absenteeism rates
   - Turnover rates
   - Employee comments (coming from focus groups, interviews, and informal conversations)
   - Management engagement
   - Leadership engagement
   - Customer loyalty and evangelism
   - A feeling of humanity
   - Clear sense of a higher purpose—on an organizational level and on the individual level

2. **Evaluate employee engagement in well-being.** The most obvious way to measure engagement in your wellness movement is by tracking participation rates. This is a great place to start, but I encourage you to go deeper to get a better sense of whether or not people are truly engaged. Employees will know the difference between a thoughtful evaluation that will have real impact, and one that is haphazard and unlikely to help them in any meaningful way.

ACTION ITEM

CREATIVE WAYS TO ASSESS ENGAGEMENT IN WELLNESS

- **Observe.** Go to any wellness event or program and take a look. Do people seem happy? It's pretty easy to tell if people are engaged or if they're just "checking the box."
- **Tune into the sideline conversations.** Listen to what people are saying on the sidelines. Tap into your da Vinci team, as well as your extended network, to find out the real "scuttlebutt" on your wellness program.
- **Check in with your challengers.** This is the group you're depending on to keep you on track and to give you honest feedback. What are they saying and hearing?
- **Conduct frequent "pulse surveys."** What do employees, managers, and leaders think of what's being offered? Find out through short surveys that include prompts like, "My organization is helping me to achieve my wellness objectives in ways that are meaningful."
- **Simply ask people.** Ask people you run into: What do you think? Are we reaching people? Are people engaged with the wellness movement? Is this an example of Workplace Wellness That Works—or not? Can you tell me more?
- **Be on the lookout for "pop-up" advocates.** An office administrator attended a session of mine that was part of a series. She was so excited about the session that she sent out an e-mail to all of the company office administrators encouraging them to attend the next session. She was definitely a pop-up advocate!
- **Observe what happens "after the show is over."** Is there evidence that the activities are continuing after the wellness program has ended? If you staged and completed a walking challenge, are groups and individuals continuing to walk?

- **Engage in ongoing reflection with your da Vinci team.** Here are some questions to prompt some discussion:
  - Do people seem to like the programs or do they seem resentful?
  - Is there a perception among employees that wellness is being done *to* them—or that wellness is being done *for and with* them?
  - Are people learning new skills—that apply outside of a strictly wellness or well-being context?
  - Do you hear people talk about sharing what they've learned with their family and friends?
  - Are people asking for more—or are they running away?
  - Are people doing things that are wonderfully unexpected?
  - Is there evidence that people are adopting healthy well-being habits on all levels?
  - Is there a change in the language that people are using, reflecting that they are embodying the larger messaging about well-being and vitality?
  - Are people showing up, especially when there are no strings attached?

3. **Evaluate employee well-being outcomes.** As we have discussed, HRAs and biometric screenings will only give you information specific to physical risk factors and may create negative fallout. Other measures that indicate improvement in health outcomes include reductions in both medical claims and health care utilization rates. Getting a sense of how employees perceive their well-being is a fantastic way to measure impact in the multiple domains of well-being. Research has consistently shown that one's perceived sense of well-being is a vital indicator of actual health and well-being.

ACTION ITEM

MEASURE PERCEIVED SENSE OF OVERALL WELL-BEING

Below are some questions to consider asking your program participants. Generally, a survey is created with prompts, with an option to respond with one of five levels: “strongly agree,” “agree,” “neutral,” “disagree,” and “strongly disagree.” Therefore, you’ll need to reword these questions as statements.

- **Physical:** Are you feeling more energy? Are you feeling more alert? Are you moving more? Are you sitting less? Are you getting more rest? Have you made improvements in your eating? Are you feeling more engaged in taking care of your health?
- **Emotional:** Are you feeling more resilient? Are you feeling a greater sense of confidence? Are you feeling more optimistic?
- **Social:** Are you engaging in more social activities with friends? Are you feeling more connected with your family? Has your social network expanded? Are you spending more time with people who bring positive energy into your life?
- **Financial:** Have you created default systems to better manage your finances? Do you have a better sense of feeling that you already have enough? Are you spending money on others (within reason)? Are you creating more resources toward meaningful life experiences?
- **Career:** Are you feeling more productive at work? Are you feeling a greater sense of purpose in your work? Are you using your strengths more often? Are you feeling more focused at work?
- **Community:** Are you engaged in more community outreach projects? Are you taking any leadership roles within your community? Are you connecting more often with your neighbors?

- **Creative:** Are you practicing your "creative habit" more often? Are you feeling more bursts of creative energy?

Tip: *I have participants complete surveys immediately after any wellness program I offer. This approach ensures the highest response level, but the drawback is that it requires a pen and paper survey—which means a lot of added work on your end to enter the data. For more tech-savvy groups that have moved completely to laptops or smartphones, sending survey links is great, but response levels may not be as high. For organization-wide evaluations, survey links and online tools are obviously the only practical option. I like using Survey Monkey, which is inexpensive, but there are plenty of other online surveys tools to use.*

4. **Assess organizational outcomes.** What is the impact on the larger organization? If you really want to be scientific, you should conduct very specific types of evaluations. According to the National Business Group on Health, these evaluations include (1) before and after comparisons with the same group over time (which is exactly what American Cast Iron Pipe Company did in measuring impact of their wellness initiative), (2) comparison using a control group, or (3) a randomized clinical trial (RCT). For most organizations, these types of evaluations are beyond their scope.

Measuring overall organizational impact brings us back to making the case for your wellness movement, discussed in Step 1: Shift Your Mind-Set from Expert to Agent of Change. Here are some guidelines in terms of how you might measure organizational impact:

1. Has there been a savings on costs *beneath* the surface, particularly presenteeism?
2. Has there been a positive return on *value* (ROV), looking at factors such as impact on productivity, retention, attraction, and morale?
3. Has there been a positive impact on identified needs, specific to the organization?

4. What has been the level of engagement and *emotional* buy-in from leaders, managers, and employees?
5. Has the wellness movement helped individuals and the organization to connect with a higher purpose?

ACTION ITEM

ASSESS ORGANIZATIONAL IMPACT

The following are areas to consider in measuring broader, organizational impact:[11, 12]

Productivity and performance:

- Absenteeism
- Presenteeism
- Productivity
- Performance

Workforce health and safety:

- Medical costs
- Disability costs
- Workers compensation costs
- Musculoskeletal claims
- Rate of injuries
- Recovery time

Employer of choice:

- Buzz and referrals for hire
- Collaboration and creativity
- Leadership engagement—on all levels
- Employee engagement
- Recognition
- Retention and attraction

- Internal promotions
- Quality of life for employees
- Connection with a higher purpose

FINAL THOUGHTS

Workplace Wellness That Works can foster a convergence between empowered individuals who thrive in their work and successful organizations that are "soulful" and "simply irresistable."[13] A launch and iterate approach can be a powerful platform for evolving an organization to this higher level, *because launching and iterating is a virtuous cycle that can actually increase engagement on its own.* This is great news for you, as you and your da Vinci team now have a new tool to accelerate levels of engagement. In addition, by applying a launch and iterate approach to wellness, you and your team will be more empowered and engaged yourselves, and this excitement will provide the self-sustaining energy you'll need to Start the Movement, Build the Movement, and Make It Last.

STEP 10

Go Global

(The International Imperative)

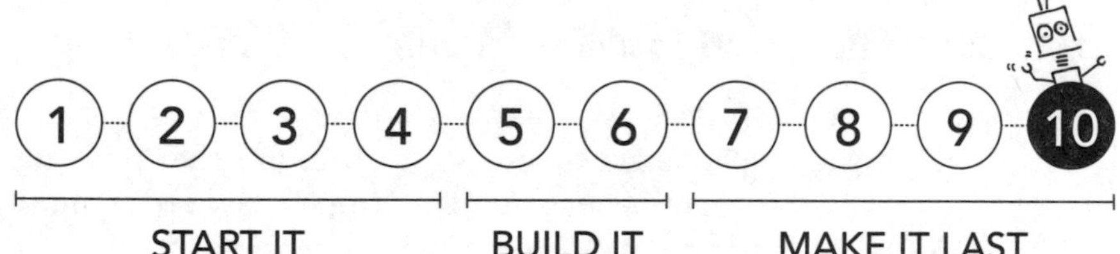

When I was very young, my family lived in Ethiopia. My dad, an epidemiologist, was hired by the U.S. government to fight malaria. Malaria is an *infectious* disease. If we were to telescope forward to today, my family might have moved to another country to fight a different kind of epidemic: obesity. In our altered reality, the world is waging a battle against obesity and correlated *chronic* diseases, such as heart disease and diabetes. Now, in countries like South Africa, you're more likely to die of heart disease than you are of AIDS or tuberculosis.[1]

You've already started a wellness movement, built it, and taken steps to make it last. Now, you need to *grow* the movement on a global scale—keeping in mind these shifts in global health challenges.

In this chapter, we'll discuss the following:

1. Why the need for wellness is now an international issue,
2. Why the need for well-being, especially emotional well-being, is also a rising international issue,
3. Examples of global bright spots,
4. The importance of sharing best practices across borders, and
5. Steps you can take to build an effective global strategy.

YOUR STEP 10 CHECKLIST

- ☐ Clarify your organization's overarching strategy (refer to Pull It All Together addendum). Encourage each global office to customize and localize this template.
- ☐ Look for ways to integrate efforts across global offices.
- ☐ Share best practices across borders—and within borders.

CHANGING TRENDS IN GLOBAL HEALTH

Up until just a couple of decades ago, most of the world was battling infectious diseases like cholera, hepatitis, influenza, measles, typhoid, and yellow fever. While some persist (and continue to escalate), most notably HIV/AIDS, malaria, tuberculosis, and, more recently, Ebola, a bigger epidemic is eclipsing these diseases. In less than four decades, the rate of obesity has doubled and in some cases tripled for many countries. Obesity has even spread to developing countries, especially fast-growing, emerging economies. In only two decades, obesity rates have increased by *82 percent* around the world, creating a massive shift in global health trends. The Middle East has seen a startling 100 percent rise in obesity, just since 1990.[2]

"The whole world is fat!" screamed a recent NPR story on global obesity.[3] Another headline proclaimed, "America no longer world's fattest nation!"[4] The latest reports show that nearly 35 percent of the U.S. population is now obese, followed closely by Mexico, Saudi Arabia, and South Africa.[5] Mexico's obesity rates actually outpace obesity rates of the United States, and the problem is only worsening.[6] According to a recent McKinsey report, 30 percent of the world's population is overweight, and if trends continue, 40 percent will be overweight by 2030.[7]

In 2010, researchers published a study that tracked this trend in more than 50 different countries. Says Ali Mokdad, coauthor of the study and professor at the University of Washington, in an interview with CNN: "We discovered that there's been a huge shift in mortality. Kids who used to die from infectious disease are now doing extremely well with immunization." But, unfortunately, these gains are now countered by the rise in obesity. "The world is now obese," he warns, "and we're seeing the impact of that."[8]

While the obesity epidemic and correlated conditions continue to grow at a rapid rate in the United States, they appear to be happening at *light speed* in other parts of the world, particularly in emerging economies. What we're seeing is that fast economic growth equals fast obesity growth. There is evidence to suggest that the rates of increase of obesity and related conditions like diabetes are growing *faster* in emerging economies than they are in more developed countries. What we're seeing is a "perfect storm" in place: a coupling of lifestyle factors along with genetic predispositions, as research has shown that obesity and diabetes disproportionally impact some ethnicities more than others.

In countries like China, the obesity rates are only 3 percent in rural areas, but in some urban areas the rate is 50 percent.[9] India, another fast-growing economy, is divided into halves—in terms of wealth and in terms of weight. Half of the country is malnourished and the other half, one might say, is *overnourished*—or more accurately, overfed. If current trends continue, 57 percent of the Indian population will be diabetic by year 2025. Brazil, another emerging economy, is experiencing one of the highest rates of increase in diabetes in the world. In parts of the Middle East, the rates of diabetes are already close to 25 percent.[10]

Just as we've seen in the United States, the primary drivers of these alarming health changes are social changes, like reductions in food prices, less physical activity on the job, and availability of fast food. While Kentucky Fried Chicken (KFC) plays second string to McDonald's in the United States, abroad it rules—especially in Asia. Beginning in 1987, the parent company Yum opened its first KFC restaurant in China. By 2011, the number was already up to 3,200—with a reach of more than 650 cities throughout China.[11]

THE RISING NEED FOR WELL-BEING

In addition to the spike in global health issues, there's a parallel jump in other well-being issues, particularly stress. Just like in the United States, the workplace has become a leading source of stress for individuals across the globe. These rising rates of stress correlate with fast economic growth. According to a recent survey of 11,000 companies in 15 countries, conducted by the Regus Group, the rates of stress in the workplace are exploding. On average, twice as many workers in large organizations (more than 1,000 employees) are reporting stress, and workers in China showed the highest rate of increase (86 percent). Overall, 58 percent of workers report feeling stress on the job. A growing impingement on work-life balance appears to be the biggest driver of these rising levels of workplace stress.[12]

These rising rates of stress go hand in hand with growing rates of social isolation, particularly among younger people. Increases in chronic disease and conditions, stress, and loneliness all seem to be part of the package as third-world economies catch up with first-world economies. According to Dr. Andrew McCulloch, chief executive of the Mental Health Foundation, "We have data that suggests people's social networks have gotten smaller and families are not providing the same level of social context they may have done 50 years ago."[13] McCulloch attributes this breakdown in the social fabric to modern-day dilemmas, such as increased divorce rates, juggling childcare and eldercare responsibilities, and an increase in work hours.

ACTION ITEM

ENCOURAGE A GLOBAL MIND-SET

All of us are global citizens—and framing wellness in an international context is a helpful way to spur action and thoughtful debate. Every time I conduct a workshop related to the topic of stress, I usually begin by posing questions to encourage participants to engage with the topic. The first question below examines the issue from a *global* perspective. This question always generates great conversation.

Directions: Organize participants into small groups (usually by table). Assign one to three questions to each group, depending on the time available. After each smaller group has had time to discuss their question, ask each to share findings with the full group.

Questions to consider:

1. There is an epidemic of stress, anxiety, and depression that is growing exponentially around the world. WHY?
2. How can we begin to address what many consider to be a taboo topic in the workplace?
3. What can we each do to make a difference?

Tip: *Any time you ask people to work in small groups, it is essential that you provide plenty of directions. Tell them exactly how much time they have to discuss the question and let them know exactly what the task is at hand. Ask participants to assign roles within the group: facilitator (makes sure that everyone is participating in the conversation), recorder (records the discussion—usually on a flip chart, to be used during the presentation to the larger group), and presenter (presents to the larger group).*

Inevitably, this activity leads to a discussion about the role of technology and living in a world that is "always on"—and how these contribute to mental health challenges. The age of hyper-connectivity brings many benefits, but also challenges that are affecting our well-being at work and at home. There's growing evidence to suggest that computers and mobile technology are even changing the way we think—especially for kids.

In addition to the physical and emotional well-being issues affecting economies around the world, career well-being is also in jeopardy. While lack of engagement in the workplace is a pressing issue in the United States, the rates of engagement at work are even lower in other parts of the world. Globally, only 13 percent of workers report feeling "highly engaged" in their work, according to Gallup. Out of the remaining pool, 63 percent are "disengaged" and 24 percent are "highly disengaged"—which means that these workers are going out of their way to disengage and take their coworkers down with them. Parsing this out further, rates of disengagement are even lower in China, India, the Middle East, and Africa, where only 6 percent are highly engaged. Fortunately, there are bright spots of engagement in Australia and

New Zealand: A full 25 percent of their workers report feeling highly engaged.[14]

These low levels of engagement are likely due to the soul-crushing work environments that we have collectively created. "Too many of us leave our lives—and, in fact, our souls—behind when we go to work," writes Arianna Huffington in *Thrive*.[15] Your job, as an agent of change for workplace wellness and in partnership with your da Vinci team, is to find effective ways to unravel this current state of the workplace and start creating workplaces that are infused with vitality and well-being. And if your organization has a global presence, your challenge is to figure out how to scale up these efforts internationally.

START, BUILD, AND MAKE IT LAST

Throughout this book, we've explored the theme of a wellness movement: starting it, building it, and then making it last. Your task is about changing the world. This may sound daunting, but this is exactly what Chade-Meng Tan, former Google engineer, had in mind when he first began contemplating his mindfulness and emotional intelligence leadership-training course known as "Search Within Yourself."

THE STORY OF MENG

Chade-Meng Tan, Google engineer turned world-renowned mindfulness leader and now part of a team nominated for the Nobel Peace Prize, started a movement, built the movement, and gave over 1,000 of his fellow employees the tools to engage with this movement. He has even grown the movement beyond Google, giving thousands of individuals around the world a guide for increasing their level of mindfulness, emotional intelligence, and overall well-being.

In the Start a Movement phase, Meng had a great idea: Bring mindfulness to his fellow Googlers. His personal why behind his movement was nothing short of creating world peace.

"For as long as I can remember," he recalled in an interview, "I have had a desire to do something big and important for humanity."[16] After making his fortune in 2004, this is exactly what he set out to do. Taking advantage of the 20 percent time given to engineers at Google to research any area of interest, Meng began looking for ways to make a difference in the world. Sparked by a belief that the world needed to take more of an "inside out" approach to solve global problems, he started building a corporate mindfulness and emotional intelligence program for his fellow Googlers, later named "Search Inside Yourself."

Next, Meng began to Build the Movement. He had the idea and the passion behind the idea, but he didn't have the expertise. So he called upon others who did—to build his da Vinci, multidisciplinary team. First, he brought in Mirabai Bush, founding director and senior fellow at the Center for Contemplative Mind in Society, based in Northampton, Mass. She, in turn, invited Norman Fischer, poet, Zen Buddhist priest, and teacher, to join the movement. Soon, Daniel Goleman, author of *Emotional Intelligence*, joined in the effort.

Meng also took steps to Build the Movement *within* the organization. He was able to recruit Peter Allen, director of Google's education program, to join as a supporter and a participant. Meng and Peter along with another Googler, Monika Broeker, launched the School of Personal Growth within Google University.

Then Meng thought about what he would need to do to actually engage his fellow Googlers in the program to Make It Last. The first step was to carefully think about ways to demonstrate the business value of meditation and mindfulness to employees. He needed to show that these contemplative practices could be productive in a corporate context.

Next, Meng knew that he would need to test out his plan before fully launching it. So he took a launch and iterate

(*continued*)

(*continued*)

approach—proposing his plan to small groups, getting extensive (and honest) feedback, and then trying it again.

Finally, he knew that he needed to make the program accessible to the everyday kind of person at Google—not just to the types who already understood the value of mindfulness and meditation. He cleverly marketed the program by allowing other Googlers to watch the mindfulness in process. Eventually, these iterations turned into a three-month program that kicked off with a day-long intensive workshop.

Ultimately, Meng grew the program beyond Google. As the program gained momentum within Google, other organizations were already taking note. Leading organizations like SAP, Genentech, McKesson, Ford, Rotman School of Management at the University of Toronto, Farmers Insurance, and even the Federal Reserve Bank of New York have signed on to take part in the Search Inside Yourself Leadership Institute's training sessions. Meng's personal influence has spanned the globe. A worldwide speaker, he's met with almost as many dignitaries as a leader of a country. Meng's story is a great reminder that any of us have the capacity to Start a Movement, Build a Movement, and Make It Last.[17]

THE BRIGHT SPOTS

While the trends in obesity and chronic disease are a wake-up call to the world, there's also some good news to share. Most notably, we've seen an increased awareness of the importance of well-being on an international level. The country of Bhutan, to a large extent, led this shift in awareness.

THE STORY OF BHUTAN

In 1972, the newly anointed king of Bhutan, King Wanchuk, declared that his country would shift its primary focus from gross national product (GNP) to gross national happiness (GNH). He pronounced, "If at the end of the plan period, our people are not happier than they were before, we should know that our plans have failed."[18]

Amazingly, this focus on a nobler cause (happiness over making money) led to dramatic changes in wealth, health, and levels of education. Pre-GNH, the gross per-capita income was one of the lowest in the world; today it exceeds India's. Life expectancy used to be 43 years; now it is 66. Infant mortality rates were 163 out of every 100,000 births; now they have dropped to 40 out of every 100,000 births. The literacy rate used to be 10 percent and is now 66 percent. And, according to the World Bank, Bhutan went from having one of the most repressive governments in the world to one whose openness exceeds countries like India and Nepal.[19]

While Bhutan is still the only country that has an official national policy dedicated to the pursuit of happiness, other countries are taking note. Bhutan is certainly an inspiration for the benefits of happiness and well-being—and is a country that we can all learn from.

We can also take note of the world's "Blue Zones," or fountains of longevity, originally tracked by demographers Gianni Pes and Michel Poulain. In his book *The Blue Zones*, Dan Buettner picks up on this theme and unpacks the key reasons why people are living longer and more vibrantly in places like Okinawa, Japan; Sardinia, Italy; Loma Linda, California; Nicoya, Costa Rica; and Icaria, Greece. In addition to the basics—staying active throughout the day, eating mostly a plant-based diet, eating in moderation, and enjoying red wine in moderation—the remaining keys revolve around quality of life issues, bringing us back to what we discussed in Step 2: Imagine What's Possible. These additional elements include (1) having a strong sense of life purpose, (2) taking time out to restore, (3) being part of a spiritual community, (4) prioritizing family, and (5) spending time with people who uplift us.[20] The Blue Zones underscore the importance of taking a global perspective to find unexpected answers in wellness. We need to be studying these hotspots of well-being so that we can continue to improve upon our current workplace wellness strategies.

CROSSING BORDERS TO SHARE BEST PRACTICES

In the 1920s, a group of Japanese postal insurance workers took a tour of the United States. During their trip, the Japanese visitors came across an exercise radio station, sponsored by Metropolitan Life Insurance, that played in six major American cities. The group took to the exercise radio station idea and brought it back to Japan, where the idea was quickly embraced and instituted in 1928 as a way to honor the newly crowned Emperor Hirohito.[21] While many assume this national practice got its start in Japan, it was, in fact, a practice learned from the United States—and a great example of opportunities to gain ideas by crossing borders.

Whether your organization is a multinational corporation or a small nonprofit, your wellness movement can gain some real advantages if you're tuned into what's happening globally. You can learn from the international community—and in turn, you can share your own discoveries globally. In this age of interconnectivity, *any* organization can go global. If the workplace wellness field is going to move forward, we need to be sharing our successes, our failures—and what we learned from both—and share these findings across borders.

THE STORY OF SHARING BEST PRACTICES IN EDUCATION

Allison Rouse, CEO of EdVillage, a nonprofit organization that supports innovation in education, has identified "Blue Zones" of educational excellence in unexpected pockets around the world. Now, he is helping educators in these different areas to distill their best practices and then *share* these best practices across national boundaries—from the United States and the United Kingdom to India and South Africa.

In the United States, "no excuses" schools like KIPP and Uncommon Schools understand the pivotal role that school culture plays in determining academic performance. These schools have worked tirelessly to build cultures of excellence through extensive training for emerging school leaders. These schools have had success where most schools in these areas have not in America's historically underserved neighborhoods. What if more schools around the world could adopt some of these practices?

In the United Kingdom, another educational Blue Zone is OFSTED (Office for Standards in Education, Children's Services and Skills). A core group of principals have joined together to assess and evaluate one another. They have discovered that the best way to improve a school is through peers giving feedback and support. What if there were a way to help educators in other communities to create similar networks of peer evaluation and support?

In India, the Akanksha Foundation developed innovative teaching programs, by supplementing after-school childcare centers with training and development for educators. What if more communities developed day care centers that served children and trained future teachers at the same time?

In South Africa, LEAP (Langa Educational Advancement Program) is a Blue Zone of socioemotional excellence. Most of the students enrolled in these schools come from rural and township communities that are still suffering from the legacy of apartheid: lack of infrastructure, lack of opportunity, endemic violence, economic hardship, and an enduring history of institutionalized racism. While the focus of study at LEAP is math and science, the cornerstone of the curriculum is a class called "Life Orientation," or "LO"—a *nonacademic* class that focuses solely on emotional well-being and resiliency. Every day, students and teachers come together in a circle of trust engaging in a direct and often emotionally charged conversation. The students are reaping the benefits. Last year, 94 percent passed the National Senior Certificate—exceeding the national average by 20 percent. What if schools in America could create a similar program?

It turns out some schools in America are doing exactly that. Colleen Green, director of High Tech High School in San Diego, California, got a firsthand look at Life Orientation while working as a resident teacher at LEAP through a San

(*continued*)

(*continued*)

Francisco-based organization called Teach with Africa, founded by Marjorie Schlenoff. Green explains, "The principles of LO have influenced my work with all of my students. The primary goal of LO is to provide a safe place to process emotional aspects of adolescence, which can be difficult. Left unchecked, these challenges can impede a young person's capacity to learn and focus on academics. It is imperative that I get to know my students—and they each other. And, not just on the surface." Now, Green gives all of her students the space and encouragement to engage at this deeper level, which she admits, takes time and an extraordinary amount of patience. This work has led to a mind-shift for her. "It helps me to recognize that my students are, after all, people first and students second."

Source: Allison Rouse, interview with author, January 14, 2015; Colleen Green, interview with author, January 20, 2015.

In each of these cases, country-specific initiatives are distilling and honing their best practices. Through organizations like EdVillage and Teach with Africa, educators are forming a global community to share, integrate, and incorporate these best practices into their respective schools. This is exactly what we need to be doing more of in the field of workplace wellness—sharing ideas, discoveries, and distilled best practices among organizations and across national boundaries.

FOSTERING AN INTERNATIONAL GROWTH MIND-SET

What we really need to be doing on a global level is *co*innovating to address the pressing issues at hand. This can only happen through a process of collaborative experimentation and active sharing of ideas across borders.

Any organization that has global offices needs to figure out its international wellness strategy sooner, rather than later. Companies like IBM, Citrix, Chevron, Hewlett-Packard, American Express, CEMEX, and Dow Chemical are bringing wellness to their employees around the world—and finding that taking an iterative approach is key to finding solutions that work. Johnson & Johnson, for example, has applied an approach of continual improvement in its wellness strategy, using a global tracking instrument that measures progress in participation, engagement, and health outcomes in 400 different locations—across 60 countries![22]

Dow Chemical is committed to providing health promotion services for all locations, regardless of size, and across the globe. Company policy requires that every employee have access to Dow's health and wellness services. A relatively easy way for Dow to reach across borders is to extend its "Dow Health Days" globally. These health days cover the basic themes: "Dow No-Tobacco Day," "Walk at Dow Day," "Dow Preventative Care Day." These are easy and low cost wellness programs that employees can engage with—whether they're remote or in the main corporate office.

Dow also extends longer lasting challenges, called their "12 Percent Solution," across their global offices. Twelve percent of every year (44 days), the company conducts a more concentrated outreach to employees on specific areas of health. These intensive efforts often bring in up to 5,000 employees at a time. Both of these strategies feed into changing behaviors and evolving the culture, across borders.[23]

BROCADE BRINGS WELLFIT TO ITS OFFICES AROUND THE WORLD

Brocade's WellFit programming extends beyond its San Jose, California corporate headquarters. Jacqueline Szeto, wellness program manager, along with the WellFit Council is actively seeking solutions to promote employee well-being across their 90 global offices—from Singapore and Brazil to India and France.

Each global office embraces the corporate strategy and then creates region-specific activities. The India office, for example, recently held a monthlong challenge to increase physical activity levels at work through morning and afternoon mini-stretch sessions. Employees were also challenged to take the message

(*continued*)

(*continued*)

home and walk with their families in the evening. To better localize the initiative, the organizers gave the challenge a name in Bangalore's local language, Kannada—"Kursi biDu, Stretches maaDu." To create a sense of cohesion across these disparate global efforts, Brocade uses a gamification platform that allows employees to compete against one another, share stories, and encourage one another, even if they're in different countries. Through this platform, employees can read about monthly features across all sites, including a recent event in which an employee swam across the English Channel to raise money for a friend's child who was battling cancer.

Source: Jacqueline Szeto, interview with author, November 11, 2014.

While organizations like Brocade localize the bulk of their wellness efforts, others try to create systems that unify these efforts across global offices.

THE STORY OF OZFOREX GROUP

OzForex Group, an Australian-based company with offices in the United Kingdom, Canada, United States, Europe, and Asia Pacific, has coupled its rapid growth with efforts to launch wellness campaigns across its global offices. They've set up a "Good Vibes" Committee—which spans the globe. Each office also has its own local Good Vibes team, generally two or three people. To promote a mentorship opportunity, these teams generally consist of a senior employee partnered with a junior employee.

Each local team is given a budget and creates a calendar of weekly, monthly, and quarterly events. To keep the offices linked, the Good Vibes teams try to foster connections. While a cricket pool may be happening in the Australia office, there may be a soccer pool happening in the United Kingdom and a football pool in North America at the same time. Each Good Vibes team gets to decide how they'd like to use their allotted budget. It might go toward a larger event like a holiday party—or an office may choose to spread out the funds for a happy hour every Friday.

The company organizes participation in global races, such as Tough Mudder, a race that uses obstacles to challenge participants beyond their normal limits. Employees from different locations are able to virtually challenge one another in these competitions.

OzForex coordinates fun across the global offices to build international social connections, but it also coordinates business operations across the different offices. Unlike operational strategies of most global companies, the work at OzForex is not siloed by region. Instead, it's organized around business objectives. This approach, the leaders have found, has led to significant improvements in processes, internal communication, and customer experience.

"Whatever we do for one, we want to do for the other," explains Mike Ward, CEO of Europe and North America. For example, four-week vacation is the norm in Australia. Despite the fact that it's not the norm in North America, OzForex has implemented a four-week vacation policy across the organization to maintain consistency, foster a better culture, and promote enhanced emotional well-being. To promote financial well-being, they've made efforts to keep compensation models consistent, striking a parity across global offices but also allowing for flexibility relative to the local market. In an effort to break down the old broker culture that fosters competition over collaboration, OzForex pays a higher base salary and lower bonuses and commissions.

In the area of community well-being, OzForex supports employee involvement with charitable events and organizations by providing matching funds. The company also encourages employees to volunteer. Like many organizations, OzForex

(*continued*)

(*continued*)

holds a Charity Day that extends across all offices. "All of the revenue we make that day—as a company—goes toward giving back to local organizations," Mike explains.

The core business strategies for OzForex and how they're applied toward well-being and camaraderie for their employees can be categorized as follows:

- **Smart:** Everything is well thought out and framed in the context of how the company can differentiate. The company pays careful attention to its strategies around benefits, retention, customer experience—and employee well-being.
- **Simple:** "What we do," Mike explains, "is a simple business. We never want to overcomplicate. Rather, we want to leverage technology and design processes to create a great experience for the customer that is simple, not complicated." The company also applies the same "simple is better" strategy toward its employee well-being efforts.
- **Focused:** "Every year, we set the vision for a one-year period for our business strategy, and we couple this with our *human* strategy." The human strategy is seen as being *bottom up*—and is dictated by employee surveys and building on strengths (in addition to recruitment expectations and talent escalation). In other words, OzForex is working hard to be both a smart organization and a *healthy* organization.

Source: Mike Ward, interview with author, January 6, 2015.

GETTING STARTED ON GOING GLOBAL

As illustrated in the cases discussed above, what works internationally requires the same basic building blocks that we've been exploring throughout the book: committed leaders and management engagement; sense of employee ownership, purpose, and meaning; positive energy; holistic and integrated strategy; healthy organization and culture of well-being; ongoing communication; a willingness to experiment; and effective ways of gauging success.

While the organizations mentioned above are examples of success, most international organizations are falling short on their efforts to bring wellness to their global offices, according to the National Business Group on Health and Towers Watson.

To help you avoid falling into this category, here are some ideas to ensure better impact on an international level. Several of these points are also relevant to organizations that have multiple locations:

Acknowledge that lifestyle-related issues are now global in nature. The first step in expanding your wellness movement globally is to acknowledge that lifestyle-related issues are no longer restricted to Western countries. These are global issues, particularly in countries with fast-growing economies.

Adapt the strategies, practices, and programs to the local culture. Different locations have different demographics, cultural norms, and practices. Fitting your strategies and programming to meet these cultural differences is a key factor—and one that organizations have really fallen short on. For starters, use the local language for key messages (as Brocade did in their recent India office campaign), and whatever you do, don't make the mistake of using images of people who don't look like the people who actually live there! Keep in mind local customs and cultural mores when designing any program. In some cultures, for example, it's considered taboo to talk openly about mental illness, such as depression.

Different regions have both shared and distinct health and wellness issues. Research shows that chronic diseases like heart disease and diabetes seem to affect people in other countries, especially in countries with emerging economies, at a younger age than in Western countries. In Mexico, for example, many of those who are affected by heart disease are dying at ages as young as 40 years old.[24] According to the 2013/2014 Staying@Work Survey Report, heart disease and diabetes are top health concerns for countries like India, Mexico and the United States, whereas smoking and alcohol abuse are more pressing issues in the United Kingdom.[25] According to a 2014 survey conducted by Buck Consultants at Xerox, the top health and wellness issues identified by a group of over 1,000 employers worldwide include stress and the need for physical activity. Nutrition and healthy eating is the third leading area of concern. In regards to differences, workplace safety is a top concern for Africa, the Middle East, Asia, and Latin America; physical activity is the top concern for Australia, New Zealand, and the United States; and stress is the leading wellness concern for Canada and Europe.

Top Health and Wellness Issues by Region

	ALL REGIONS	AFRICA/ MIDDLE EAST	ASIA	AUSTRALIA/ NZ	CANADA	EUROPE	LATIN AMERICA	UNITED STATES
1	Stress	Workplace Safety	Workplace Safety	Physical Activity	Stress	Stress	Workplace Safety	Physical Activity
2	Physical Activity	Stress Work/Life Balance Infectious Disease	Physical Activity	Stress	Physical Activity	Physical Activity	Stress	Healthy Eating
3	Healthy Eating		Personal Safety	Healthy Eating	Chronic Disease Healthy Eating	Healthy Eating	Psychosocial Work Environment	Stress

Source: Working Well: A Global Survey of Health Promotion, Workplace Wellness and Productivity Strategies, 6th ed., July 2014, Buck Consultants LLC.

Different regions have both shared and differing organizational priorities. According to the 2013/2014 Staying@Work Survey Report, organizations in Asia primarily are focused on retention and attraction; European employers are zeroing in on issues related to safety and social responsibility; and companies in the United States, along with Brazil and Mexico, are more focused on rising health care costs.[26] Buck Consultants at Xerox found that while cost containment continues to be the top priority for employers in the United States, leading organizational priorities globally include reducing presenteeism and absenteeism due to poor health, along with increasing employee morale and engagement.[27] Across the board, stress in the workplace and lack of employee engagement are chief concerns.

Top Organizational Objectives by Region

	ALL REGIONS	AFRICA/ MIDDLE EAST	ASIA	AUSTRALIA/ NZ	CANADA	EUROPE	LATIN AMERICA	UNITED STATES
1	Morale/ Engagement	Reduced Absenteeism	Workplace Safety	Morale/ Engagement	Reduced Absenteeism	Morale/ Engagement	Morale/ Engagement	Reduced Health Care Costs
2	Reduced Absenteeism	Workplace Safety	Reduced Absenteeism	Mission/ Values	Productivity/ Presenteeism	Productivity/ Presenteeism	Workplace Safety	Productivity/ Presenteeism
3	Workplace Safety	Work Ability	Work Ability	Workplace Safety	Morale/ Engagement	Reduced Absenteeism	Reduced Absenteeism	Reduced Absenteeism

Source: Working Well: A Global Survey of Health Promotion, Workplace Wellness and Productivity Strategies, 6th ed., July 2014, Buck Consultants LLC.

Shift your business case away from cost containment to productivity and performance. Controlling health care costs is less of an issue internationally, since medical care is generally supported by government funding and not covered by employers. Just as we've already discussed in shifting from a discussion of simplistic return on investment to a more nuanced return on value, you'll definitely want to focus more on other selling points such as productivity. Another issue to keep in mind is that you're likely to have a lot less data at your disposal, especially data related to health risks.

Steer away from financial incentives. The practice of using incentives, especially negative incentives, is less common outside of the United States. As a rule of thumb, you are better off applying a more intrinsically based approach to change. Globally, companies are more focused on selling the inherent value of wellness programs on an individual and organizational level—counting on individuals to then make their own choices. The international financial services company American Express avoids the use of any penalties and instead focuses on "nurturing and encouragement" through free offerings—from vitamins and preventative care to health coaching.[28]

Account for different levels of resources. Every location will experience vast differences in terms of availability of resources, such as access to technology and budgets. You'll have to adjust accordingly—and get creative! Employ the same mind-set of starting with what's right and identifying the bright spots—and then build on these.

Many of the issues are shared. Culture, engagement, tackling stress—these are issues that transcend national boundaries. According to the National Business Group on Health and Towers Watson, "The key themes across markets are the need to create a workplace culture of health, improve employees' engagement in their health, and better manage employee mental health (i.e., stress and anxiety)."[29]

Continue to focus on the key role of leaders at all levels. As we have discussed at length, managers play a critical role in employees' levels of engagement at work—and their level of well-being. In addition, top leaders play a key role in shaping the culture of the organization, which in turn greatly impacts individuals' workday experiences and levels of well-being.

Just as we've discussed—and as the McKinsey Report on global obesity urges—all of these examples illustrate a launch and iterate approach: Leverage evidence-based practices and be willing to experiment and try out new ideas on a small scale—and then scale up the ideas that have legs.

ACTION ITEMS

- On a modified scale, go through each of the 10 steps to build a Workplace Wellness That Works strategy for each location.
- Encourage brainstorming, experimentation, and a commitment to continual improvement at each site.
- Empower each location to customize solutions.
- Find ways to integrate well-being efforts across global sites.
- Share findings and build an emerging battery of best practices—specific to the larger organization and to each location.

EVERY WORKPLACE, EVERY COMMUNITY

Workplace wellness, as we have discussed, is for any organization, any size, in any industry, anywhere. The workplace is a key point of entry for impacting health and well-being—in the United States and around the world. We can literally start to impact global well-being one workplace at a time. It can happen in corporate offices, manufacturing sites, nonprofits, startups, universities, and even public schools. This is exactly what Jim Golden, superintendent of the Sisters School District in Central Oregon, is doing: creating the conditions to enable teachers and students to engage with their well-being.

THE STORY OF SISTERS SCHOOL DISTRICT

Educational leader Jim Golden is bringing well-being to teachers with simple but effective practices—many of which are free. While workplace wellness does often require an investment, especially in terms of staffing, it is important to remember that each organization can make a difference in the well-being of their employees through easy and low-cost practices.

Jim is committed to changing cultural norms around how we learn—and how we teach. He shares, "We have this perception that when kids are sitting, they're learning. That's not always true." Rather, Jim believes that we learn best when we are doing—and this means getting out of our seats and moving. Movement, he explains, generates discussions and better thinking—for kids as well as for teachers. A simple practice he uses to get teachers on the move—and thinking more creatively—is to distribute professional development trainings across multiple locations. Each location features a different topic of discussion. So moving on to the next topic of discussion requires that teachers walk to the next site. During this transit time, he explains, teachers deepen social ties, get energized, and gain a fresh perspective—enabling them to tackle the next topic with a heightened level of engagement and insight.

(*continued*)

(*continued*)

Jim is creating professional development opportunities that promote teacher well-being. He's investing in workshops that are focused on enhanced emotional well-being through a practice of active listening and thoughtful reflection, as well as trainings on how to infuse movement into the classroom. The teachers love it—and they're passing it along to the kids. The kids, in turn, are bringing messages of well-being and vitality back home. These transformations demonstrate how wellness within the workplace can lead to a larger community transformation.

Source: Jim Golden, interview with author, January 5, 2015.

Ultimately, we will be better off taking a more integrated strategy among the various points of entry: workplace, school, family, community, society—as each can reinforce the other. Ryan Picarella, president and CEO of the Wellness Council of America (WELCOA), the largest resource for workplace wellness, believes that this cross-sectional approach is the next step in the evolution of workplace wellness. In his view, workplace wellness efforts need to spill over into the community. "We all need to work together collaboratively to create healthier places to live, work, and be." In concert with moving organizations forward, he explains, we can move local communities—and even our global communities—forward by aligning efforts in "shaping our schools and our kids and our communities and the places we work and the green spaces we protect."[30]

This evolution is the next level for workplace wellness. Every employer has the opportunity to redefine itself in this vein to become an essential contributor in improving the health and well-being for every stakeholder. And we have the opportunity to create a larger and more holistic view of who really counts beyond the shareholders: customers, employees, suppliers, environment, community groups, governments, and even families.

FINAL THOUGHTS

Every time I travel to remote parts of the world, I am reminded of living a simpler life—and one in which wellness is a way of being that is infused into daily activities. People walk instead of using cars, tasks are manual instead of electronic, food is grown locally, people go to bed when the sun sets and awake when it rises, and people live and work together as a tight-knit community. This simpler life is, in essence, a reminder of what's possible—and how we might better bridge the gap between what we are culturally mandated to do versus what we are biologically programmed to do, bringing us back to where we started at the beginning of the book. The task that lies ahead for all of us is to find ways to integrate these time-tested and wise practices back into our rapidly changing, techno-charged world. Maintaining this global perspective—and remembrance of cultural traditions—may be our greatest hope in coming up with creative solutions to launch and sustain Workplace Wellness That Works in our workplace, in our homes, in our communities, and in our world.

Workplace Wellness That Works Strategy

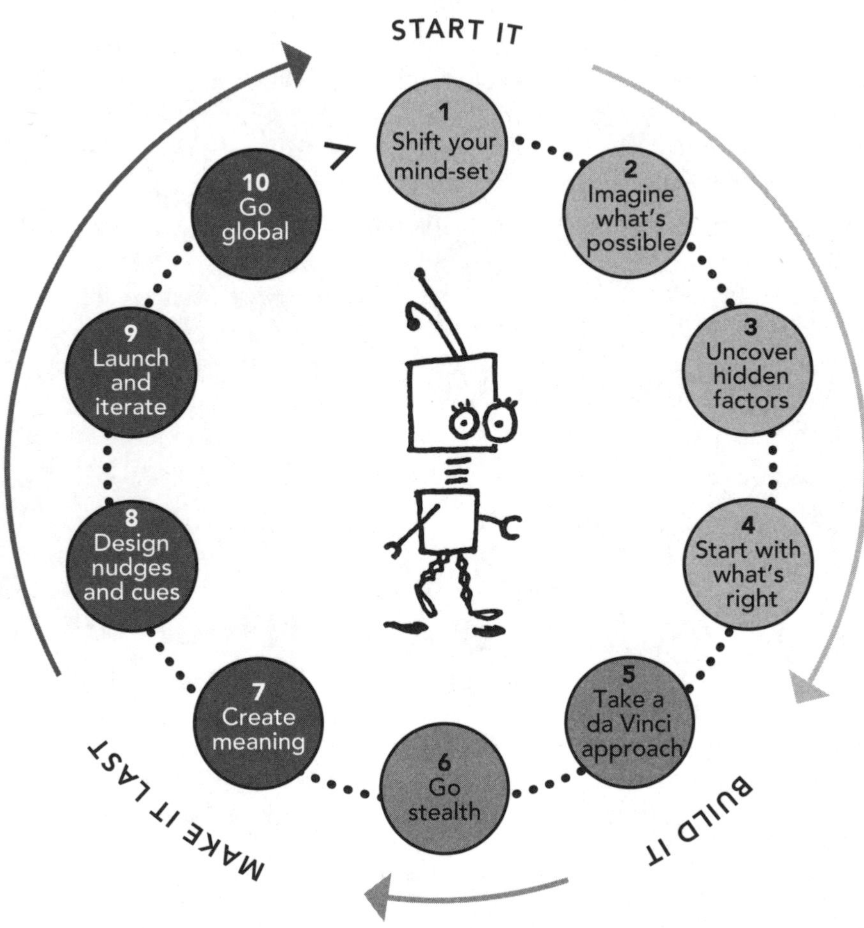

Pull It All Together

Over the course of this book, we explored 10 steps to Start a movement, Build the Movement, and Make It Last. Now, it's time to put it all together. This final section recaps the chapters and gives a checklist for each step to provide a framework for the wellness strategy that works for *your* workplace. As we have discussed, having a clearly articulated and well-communicated strategy in place is critical for any movement, especially for a wellness movement.

This strategy is the blueprint that shows the vision, and can serve as an excellent starting point. Every organization is different, so I encourage you to view this section and this entire book as a guide, but certainly not as the absolute rule. Although the steps are listed in a linear fashion, feel free to pick and choose from the steps as you see fit for your organization and your budget. Get creative, make adjustments, and then experiment! If nothing else, my hope is that you feel emboldened to try things you wouldn't have before.

Let's take a look at the information we've covered.

Start It: Workplace Wellness That Excites

In Step 1: Shift Your Mind-Set from Expert to Agent of Change, we discussed how the movement starts with you, giving you the opportunity to reflect on your potential as a leader and influencer. As an agent of change you'll strive to get top leaders on board from the outset, but you may need to take a more bottom-up approach to launch your wellness movement.

Checklist:

- ☐ Sharpen your changemaker skills.
- ☐ Form your core action team.
- ☐ Make the business and the emotional case for your movement.
- ☐ Issue an initial call to action—to leaders and employees.

In Step 2: Imagine What's Possible, we discussed leveraging Maslow to expand the conversation from wellness to well-being and living with vitality. In this step, your goal is to think big to create a powerful vision that's worth working toward. We also explored ways to measure the impact of your wellness movement.

Checklist:

- ☐ With the core action team, begin creating the vision for your wellness movement.
- ☐ Identify the key areas of focus for your well-being platform.
- ☐ Create a tracking system to make sure you're covering key elements of well-being.

In Step 3: Uncover the Hidden Factors, your first task is to better understand the organizational culture you're working in. Ideally, you'll be able to leverage the inherent strengths of your organization's culture to start your wellness movement. You'll also need to identify the cultural elements that may undermine your efforts, and find ways to start slowly evolving the workplace culture in a positive direction.

Checklist:

- ☐ Conduct a Maslow Meets Mallory Culture Audit to assess the culture.
- ☐ Collect the stories behind the data to get a better picture.
- ☐ Identify the organization's cultural strengths and challenges.
- ☐ Share results and initiate a dialogue with leaders and your core action team.

In Step 4: Start with What's Right, we discussed the power of an optimistic mind-set on an individual level and an organizational level. You also learned how to tap into bright spots of your organization.

Checklist:

- ☐ Employ activities and campaigns that start with what's right.
- ☐ Empower individuals to identify their well-being strengths.
- ☐ Identify the organizational bright spots.
- ☐ Identify the key well-being metrics for your wellness movement.

BUILD IT: WORKPLACE WELLNESS THAT GROWS

In Step 5: Take a da Vinci Approach to Change, we discussed the power of the interdisciplinary approach and how important it is to reach out to unexpected voices to nurture the seeds of a movement that everyone buys into. By breaking down silos, a spirit of creativity and collaboration will infiltrate your wellness strategies and will provide the opportunity to create a network of alliances within your organization.

Checklist:

- ☐ Form your da Vinci team.
- ☐ Strategize on interdisciplinary strategies.
- ☐ Start building the brand for your movement.
- ☐ Get everyone involved—leaders, managers, employees.
- ☐ Brainstorm next steps with your da Vinci team.

In Step 6: Go Stealth, your task is to leverage your interdisciplinary da Vinci team to "sneak" well-being throughout the organization, even in unlikely places. Your goal is to use unusual points of entry and if need be, to *not* call it a wellness initiative. This step provides a perfect opportunity to align with the organizational top priorities.

Checklist:

- ☐ Identify top priorities of the organization.
- ☐ Based on these, identify top opportunities for going stealth.
- ☐ Devise stealth language to rename your wellness efforts.
- ☐ Devise "go stealth" programming.

MAKE IT LAST: WORKPLACE WELLNESS THAT WORKS

In Step 7: Create Meaning, we explored tangible ways to shift away from incentives and go deeper by connecting with our intrinsic, human needs. These include our needs for competency, autonomy, relatedness, purpose, and play. The goal in this step is also to create alignment between individual purpose and organizational purpose.

Checklist:

- ☐ Minimize extrinsic motivators.

- ☐ Create your motivation plan.
- ☐ Devise activities and programs that leverage intrinsic motivators.

In Step 8: Design Nudges and Cues, we discussed tangible ways to shift the focus from the individual to changing the organization as a whole. We explored different environments that nudge teams into better choices. We looked at cues that make wellness the *norm*, laying the foundation for a culture of well-being and vitality.

Checklist:

- ☐ Assess current baseline of nudges and cues.
- ☐ Implement nudges and cues.

In Step 9: Launch and Iterate, we discussed the importance of fostering a growth mind-set—as individuals, as teams, and as an organization. While research is essential, we also need to experiment more, iterate faster, do more, and learn more.

Checklist:

- ☐ Get ready: Reflect on the data and stories you've gathered.
- ☐ Go: Launch programs.
- ☐ Keep going: Assess along the way and evaluate.
- ☐ Promote a growth mind-set—as an organization, team by team, and on an individual level.
- ☐ Give leaders, managers, and employees strategies to form new habits.

In Step 10: Go Global, we explored how to grow the movement across the different branches of your organization—and connect with others across national boundaries. Chade-Meng Tan has become the leader of a global movement—and there's no reason you can't do the same.

Checklist:

- ☐ Encourage each global office to customize and localize the organizational strategy.
- ☐ Look for ways to integrate efforts across global offices.
- ☐ Share best practices across borders.

FINAL THOUGHTS

You've got the information. You've got the tools. There's a whole world of wellness waiting for you! Here are some final tips to bear in mind as you set forth:

- Workplace Wellness That Works is more than a program. It's a *movement* that affects all aspects of the workplace.
- The key is *infusion*, or a full integration of well-being and vitality, into daily conversations, daily work rituals, and core business objectives so that wellness is woven into every aspect of business as usual within the organization.
- Workplace wellness truly is for organizations of any size, of any industry, anywhere in the world. Each workplace is unique and requires the customization that you and your da Vinci team will devise.
- Well-being in the workplace is largely dependent upon the larger culture, which can be a challenge to address, though not an insurmountable one. Evolving a culture takes patience and deliberate thinking. You may find a door in from the top, but you may need to take more of a bottom-up approach to effect change.
- Workplace Wellness That Works begins with a strategy—but definitely does not end there. Remember that the doing part is what matters most. Don't be afraid to experiment and learn from your actions—and encourage others to do the same.
- Finally, don't lose sight of yourself as an agent of change and the *leader* of this movement. Just like Chade-Meng Tan, Julie Shipley, Flip Morse, or Oprah Winfrey, you too can Start a Movement, Build the Movement, and Make It Last.

About the Author

Laura Putnam is founder and CEO of Motion Infusion, a well-being consulting firm that provides creative solutions in the areas of engagement, behavior change, human performance improvement, and building healthier, happier, and more innovative organizations. As a consultant, trainer, and keynote speaker, Laura has worked with a range of organizations from Fortune 500s and government agencies to academic institutes, schools, and nonprofits. She also serves as the chair of the American Heart Association's Greater Bay Area 2020 Task Force.

Laura has a diverse background in education and educational reform, organizational learning and development, public policy, competitive gymnastics, and professional dance. Her wide range of experiences includes teaching in urban public high schools, organizing community development projects in Africa, facilitating corporate learning and development initiatives, leading a nationally recognized youth leadership organization, and working as a staff member on the United States Senate Subcommittee on Antitrust. Laura was also a nationally competitive collegiate gymnast and a professional dancer, and is a certified Pilates instructor, a skier, and a yoga practitioner.

A graduate of Brown University School of Education and Stanford University, she lives in San Francisco with her fiancé and two amazing cats.

Notes

Introduction

1. Centers for Disease Control and Prevention, "Overweight and Obesity," accessed October 23, 2014, http://www.cdc.gov/obesity/data/adult.html.
2. Eric A. Finkelstein, et al., "Obesity and Severe Obesity Forecasts through 2030," *American Journal of Preventive Medicine* 42, no. 6 (2012): 563–570.
3. Centers for Disease Control and Prevention, "Chronic Diseases and Health Promotion," accessed October 5, 2014, http://www.cdc.gov/chronicdisease/overview/.
4. Centers for Disease Control and Prevention, "Leading Causes of Death Overview Page," accessed January 2, 2015, http://www.cdc.gov/nchs/fastats/leading-causes-of-death.htm.
5. Centers for Disease Control and Prevention, "CDC Newsroom Overview Page," accessed February 5, 2015, http://www.cdc.gov/media/releases/2011/p0126_diabetes.html.
6. Centers for Disease Control and Prevention, "CDC Newsroom Overview Page."
7. Eric Pianin and Brianna Ehley, "Budget Busting U.S. Obesity Costs Climb Past $300 Billion a Year," *The Fiscal Times*, June 19, 2014, accessed January 12, 2015, http://www.thefiscaltimes.com/Articles/2014/06/19/Budget-Busting-US-Obesity-Costs-Climb-Past-300-Billion-Year.
8. Centers for Disease Control and Prevention, "Rising Health Care Costs Are Unsustainable," accessed December 4, 2014, http://www.cdc.gov/workplacehealthpromotion/businesscase/reasons/rising.html.
9. World Health Organization, "The World Health Report 2000," accessed on December 10, 2014, http://www.who.int/whr/2000/en/whr00_en.pdf.
10. The Advisory Board Company, "Bloomberg Ranks the World's Most Efficient Health Care Systems: United States Ranks 46th in a List of 48 Nations," August 23, 2013, accessed January 4, 2015, http://www.advisory.com/daily-briefing/2013/08/28/bloomberg-ranks-the-worlds-most-efficient-health-care-systems.
11. Centers for Disease Control and Prevention, "Childhood Obesity Facts," accessed December 15, 2014, http://www.cdc.gov/healthyyouth/obesity/facts.htm.
12. Centers for Disease Control and Prevention, "Number of Americans Living with Diabetes Projected to Double or Triple by 2050," accessed

December 15, 2014, http://www.cdc.gov/media/pressrel/2010/r101022.html.
13. S. Jay Olshansky, et al., "A Potential Decline in Life Expectancy in the United States in the 21st Century," *The New England Journal of Medicine* 352 (2005): 1138–1145.
14. Centers for Disease Control and Prevention, "Chronic Disease Prevention and Health Promotion," accessed February 21, 2015, http://www.cdc.gov/chronicdisease/overview/index.htm.
15. American Heart Association, "My Life Check—Life's Simple 7," accessed October 15, 2014, http://www.heart.org/HEARTORG/Conditions/My-Life-Check---Lifes-Simple-7_UCM_471453_Article.jsp.
16. Mary Cushman et al., "Abstract 13062: Life's Simple 7 in 2003–2007 and Mortality in Blacks and Whites: The REasons for Geographic and Racial Differences in Stroke (REGARDS) Cohort," Circulation 122 (2010): A13062.
17. David L. Katz, "I Love You, Have Another Helping: Why It's Time to Update the Way We Show Love in This Country," *U.S. News & World Report*, July 18, 2012, accessed November 5, 2014, http://health.usnews.com/health-news/blogs/eat-run/2012/07/18/i-love-you-have-another-helping.
18. American Nurses Association, "An Issue of Weight," *The American Nurse*, accessed January 7, 2015, http://www.theamericannurse.org/index.php/2013/03/01/an-issue-of-weight.
19. Olivia Katrandjian, "Study Finds 55 Percent of Nurses Are Overweight or Obese," January 30, 2012, accessed January 7, 2015, http://abcnews.go.com/Health/study-finds-55-percent-nurses-overweight-obese/story?id=15472375.
20. John Lehrer, "Blame It on the Brain," *Wall Street Journal*, December 26, 2009, accessed January 5, 2014, http://www.wsj.com/articles/SB10001424052748703478704574612052322122442.
21. American Psychological Association, "What Americans Think of Willpower: A Survey of Perceptions of Willpower & Its Role in Achieving Lifestyle and Behavior-Change Goals" (2012), accessed December 4, 2014, http://www.apa.org/helpcenter/stress-willpower.pdf.
22. Roy R. Baumeister, et al., "Ego Depletion: Is the Active Self a Limited Resource?" *Journal of Personality and Social Psychology* 74, no. 5 (1998): 1252–1265.
23. John Lehrer, "Blame It on the Brain."
24. B. J. Fogg's Website, accessed December 2, 2014, http://www.bjfogg.com.
25. Joshua C. Klapow and Sheri D. Pruitt, *Stop Telling Me What, Tell Me How!* (New York: iUniverse, Inc., 2005).
26. Charles Duhigg, *The Power of Habit: Why We Do What We Do in Life and Business* (New York: Random House, 2012).

27. Kelly McGonigal, *The Willpower Instinct: How Self-Control Works, Why It Matters, and What You Can Do to Get More of It* (New York: Penguin Group, 2012).
28. John J. Ratey and Eric Hagerman, *Spark: The Revolutionary New Science of Exercise and the Brain* (New York: Little, Brown and Company, 2008).
29. Retrieved from "Fed Up" documentary, http://fedupmovie.com/#/page/home.
30. Anthony Brino, "Striving for 'Well-Being' Amid the Wellness Backlash," *Healthcare Payer News*, January 23, 2015, accessed March 15, 2015, http://www.healthcarepayernews.com/content/striving-well-being-amid- wellness-backlash#.VS9R86YXqAZ.
31. Rachel M. Henke, et al., "Recent Experience in Health Promotion at Johnson & Johnson: Lower Health Spending, Strong Return on Investment," *Health Affairs* 30, no. 3 (2011): 490–499.
32. John Tozzi, "Employers Love Wellness Programs. But Do They Work?" *Bloomberg Business*, May 6, 2013, accessed December 6, 2014, http://www.bloomberg.com/bw/articles/2013-05-06/employers-love-wellness-programs-dot-but-do-they-work.
33. David Hilzenrath, "Misleading Claims about Safeway Wellness Incentives Shape Health-Care Bill," *Washington Post*, January 17, 2010, accessed December 10, 2014, http://www.washingtonpost.com/wp-dyn/content/article/2010/01/15/AR2010011503319.html.
34. Austin Frakt and Aaron E. Carroll, "Do Workplace Wellness Programs Work? Usually Not," *New York Times*, September 11, 2014, accessed November 4, 2014, http://www.nytimes.com/2014/09/12/upshot/do-workplace-wellness-programs-work-usually-not.html?abt=0002&abg=0&module=ArrowsNav&contentCollection=The%20Upshot&action=keypress®ion=FixedLeft&pgtype=article.
35. Soeren Mattke, et al., "Workplace Wellness Programs Study" (Santa Monica: RAND Corporation, 2013), accessed October 20, 2014, http://aspe.hhs.gov/hsp/13/WorkplaceWellness/rpt_wellness.pdf.
36. Soeren Mattke, et al., "Workplace Wellness Programs Study."
37. Jessica Grossmeier, "The Influence of Worksite and Employee Variables on Employee Engagement in Telephonic Health Coaching Programs: A Retrospective Multivariate Analysis," *American Journal of Health Promotion* 27, no. 3 (2013): e69–e80, doi:10.4278/ajhp.100615-quan-190.
38. Katherine Baicker, David Cutler, and Zirui Song, "Workplace Wellness Programs Can Generate Savings," *Health Affairs* 29, no. 2 (2010): 304–311.
39. John P. Caloyeras, "Managing Manifest Diseases, But Not Health Risks, Saved PepsiCo Money Over Seven Years," *Health Affairs* 33, no. 1 (January 2014): 124–131. doi:10.1377/hlthaff.2013.0625.
40. RAND Corporation, "Workplace Wellness Programs Can Cut Chronic Illness Costs; Savings for Lifestyle Improvements Are Smaller," January

6, 2014, accessed January 4, 2015, http://www.rand.org/news/press/2014/01/06/index1.html.

41. Mattke et al., "Workplace Wellness Programs Study."
42. Leonard L. Berry, Ann M. Mirabito, and William B. Baun, "What's the Hard Return on Employee Wellness Programs?" *Harvard Business Review* 12 (2010).
43. Jessica Grossmeier, "Influence of Worksite and Employee Variables."

STEP 1

1. PBS NewsHour Interview, "Oprah Winfrey vs. the Beef People," January 20, 1998, accessed November 3, 2014, http://www.pbs.org/newshour/bb/law-jan-june98-fooddef_1-20.
2. Michael Pollan, *In Defense of Food* (New York: Penguin Books, 2008).
3. Seth Godin, *Tribes* (New York: Portfolio, 2008), 14.
4. Tom Rath, *Eat Move Sleep* (Arlington, VA: Missionday, 2013).
5. Donna Arnett, "Where We've Been, Where We Are, and Where We're Going: Heart Disease and Stroke Statistics-2013 Update," American Heart Association, December 12, 2012, accessed October 20, 2014, http://my.americanheart.org/professional/Library/Commentary-Heart-Disease-and-Stroke-Statistics_UCM_447354_Article.jsp.
6. Daniel Goleman, *Emotional Intelligence* (New York: Bantam Books, 1995).
7. Brené Brown website, accessed December 3, 2014, brenebrown.com.
8. Greg J. Stephens, Lauren J. Silbert, Uri Hasson, "Speaker-Listener Neural Coupling Underlies Successful Communication," *Proceeding National Academy of Science USA* 107, no. 32 (2010), 14425–14430.
9. Howard Gardner and Emma Laskin, *Leading Minds* (New York: BasicBooks, 1995).
10. Arianna Huffington, *Thrive* (New York: Harmony Books, 2014).
11. Richard Feloni, "5 'Lemonade Lessons' from 10-Year-Old Entrepreneur Vivienne Harr," *Business Insider*, May 19, 2014, accessed December 3, 2014, http://www.businessinsider.com/make-a-stand-founder-vivienne-harr-2014-5.
12. ALS Association website, accessed February 15, 2015, http://www.alsa.org/fight-als/ice-bucket-challenge.html.
13. Paul Terry, "An Interview with Dr. Michael Roizen, Chief Wellness Officer at Cleveland Clinic," *American Journal of Health Promotion*, Jan/Feb 2014: 2–7.
14. Marc L Berger et al., "Investing In Healthy Human Capital," *Journal of Occupational and Environmental Medicine* 45 (2003): 1213–1225, accessed November 20, 2014, doi:10.1097/01.jom.0000102503.33729.88.
15. Ronald Loeppke et al., "Health and Productivity as a Business Strategy: A Multiemployer Study," *Journal Of Occupational And Environmental*

Medicine 49 (2007): 712–721, accessed November 1, 2014, doi:10.1097/jom.0b013e318133a4be.

16. Paul Hemp, "Presenteeism: At Work—But Out of It," *Harvard Business Review*, October 2004.
17. Ronald C. Kessler et al., "The Effects of Chronic Medical Conditions on Work Loss and Work Cutback," *Journal of Occupational and Environmental Medicine* 43 (2001): 218–225, accessed November 15, 2014, doi:10.1097/00043764-200103000-00009.
18. McKinsey & Company and Boston College Center for Corporate Citizenship, "How Virtue Creates Value for Business and Society: Investigating the Value of Environmental, Social and Governance Activities" (Boston: 2009), accessed November 21, 2014, http://commdev.org/files/2426_file_Boston_College_McKinsey_31909.pdf.
19. Celina Pagani-Tousignant and Asako Tsumagari, "Designing Effective Health and Wellness Strategy," *World of Work Journal*, Third Quarter (2014): 63–72, accessed November 6, 2014, http://www.worldatwork.org/waw/adimLink?id=75784.
20. Dee Edington, interview with author, December 15, 2014.
21. Robert Safian, "What Drives Generation Flux," *Fast Company* 190 (2014): 66.
22. Julia La Roche, "Here's the Memo Jamie Dimon Sent to JP Morgan Employees After His Cancer Treatment," *Business Insider* (2014), accessed on December 15, 2014, http://www.businessinsider.com/dimon-sends-memo-saying-no-cancer-2014-12.
23. Nicholas A. Christakis and James H. Fowler, *Connected: The Surprising Power of Our Social Networks and How They Shape Our Lives* (New York: Little, Brown and Co., 2009).

STEP 2

1. Randy Glasbergen, Glasbergen Cartoon Service, accessed December 4, 2014, http://www.glasbergen.com/diet-health-fitness-medical.
2. Robert Wood Johnson Foundation Commission to Build a Healthier America, "City Maps," accessed January 7, 2015, http://www.rwjf.org/en/about-rwjf/newsroom/features-and-articles/Commission/resources/city-maps.html.
3. Ellen Meara et al., "The Gap Gets Bigger: Changes in Mortality and Life Expectancy, by Education, 1981-2000," *Health Affairs* 27 (2008): 350–360.
4. Gina Kolata, "A Surprising Secret to a Long Life: Stay in School," *The New York Times*, January 3, 2007, accessed November 8, 2014, http://www.nytimes.com/2007/01/03/health/03aging.html?pagewanted=all&_r=1&.
5. Carla M. Perissinotto, Irena Stijacic Cenzer, I, and Kenneth E. Covinsky, "Loneliness in Older Persons: A Predictor of Functional Decline and

Death," *Archives of Internal Medicine* 172, no. 14 (2012): 1078–1084, doi:10.1001/archinternmed.2012.1993.

6. Julianne Holt-Lunstad, Timothy B. Smith, and J. Bradley Layton, "Social Relationships and Mortality Risk: A Meta-analytic Review," *Public Library of Science Medicine* 7, no. 7 (2010): e1000316, doi:10.1371/journal.pmed.1000316.
7. Juliet Chung, "Healthier Than You Might Expect," *Los Angeles Times*, August 28, 2006, accessed on October 12, 2014, http://articles.latimes.com/2006/aug/28/local/me-paradox28.
8. "Eliza Corporation Shares Additional 'Unmentionables' Data, Insights and Opportunities at the 2011 Health 2.0 Conference," *BusinessWire*, September 27, 2011, accessed November 7, 2014, http://www.businesswire.com/news/home/20110927006626/en/Eliza-Corporation-Shares-Additional-"Unmentionables"-Data-Insight#.VFkvEr44I70.
9. Dee Edington, interview with author, December 15, 2014.
10. Susan Sorenson, "Lower Your Health Costs While Boosting Your Performance," *Gallup Business Journal*, September 19, 2013, accessed January 3, 2015, http://www.gallup.com/businessjournal/164420/lower-health-costs-boosting-performance.aspx.
11. Richard Sandomir, "A Story of Perseverance: ESPN Anchor's Private Battle with Cancer Becomes a Public One," *The New York Times*, March 11, 2014, accessed on October 8, 2014, http://www.nytimes.com/2014/03/12/sports/espn-anchors-private-battle-with-cancer-becomes-a-public-one.html.
12. David L. Katz and Stacey Colino, *Disease Proof: The Remarkable Truth About What Makes Us Well* (New York: Penguin Press, 2013).
13. James Levine, "Non-Exercise Activity Thermogenesis (NEAT)," *Best Practice & Research Clinical Endocrinology & Metabolism* 16, no. 4 (December 2002): 679–702.
14. Neville Owen, Adrian Bauman, and Wendy Brown, "Too Much Sitting: A Novel and Important Predictor of Chronic Disease?" *British Journal of Sports Medicine* 43 (2009): 81–83.
15. Alpa V. Patel, et al., "Leisure Time Spent Sitting in Relation to Total Mortality in a Prospective Cohort of US Adults," *American Journal of Epidemiology* 172, no. 4 (2010): 419–429.
16. Randy Glasbergen, "Health and Medical Cartoons," accessed October 25, 2014, http://www.glasbergen.com/diet-health-fitness-medical/?album=2&gallery=26.
17. Anna Almendrala, "The Frightening Connection between Lack of Sleep and a Shrinking Brain," *The Huffington Post*, September 4, 2014, accessed November 18, 2014, http://www.huffingtonpost.com/2014/09/04/sleep-shrinking-brain_n_5739442.html.
18. Merriam Webster Online Dictionary, accessed February 5, 2015, http://www.merriam-webster.com/medical/resilience.

19. Viktor E. Frankl, *Man's Search for Meaning* (Boston: Beacon Press, 2006).
20. Firdaus S. Dhabhar, "Effects of Stress on Immune Function: The Good, the Bad, and the Beautiful," *Immunological Research* 58, no. 2 (2014): 193–210, doi:10.1007/s 12026–014–8517–0.
21. Tim Ryan, *A Mindful Nation: How a Simple Practice Can Help Us Reduce Stress, Improve Performance, and Recapture the American Spirit* (Carlsbad, CA: Hay House, Inc., 2012).
22. Jon Kabat-Zinn, *Wherever You Go, There You Are* (New York: Hyperion Books, 1994).
23. Stephen McKenzie, *Mindfulness at Work: How to Avoid Stress, Achieve More, and Enjoy Life* (Pompton Plains, NJ: Career Press, 2014).
24. Anne Fisher, "Is Mindfulness Just Another Management Fad?" *Fortune*, September 26, 2014, accessed December 18, 2014, http://fortune.com/2014/09/26/mindfulness-management.
25. Elizabeth W. Dunn, Lara B. Aknin, and Michael I. Norton, "Spending Money on Others Promotes Happiness," *Science* 319, no. 5870 (2008): 1687–1688.
26. AonHewitt, "Survey Highlights," *2014 Hot Topics in Retirement: Building a Strategic Focus*, accessed March 5, 2015, http://www.aon.com/attachments/human-capital-consulting/2014_Hot-Topics-Retirement_Highlights_vFinal.pdf.
27. Sonya Stinson, "Financial Wellness Gains Traction," *Bankrate.com*, accessed March 5, 2015, http://www.bankrate.com/finance/jobs-careers/financial-wellness-programs-gain-traction.aspx.
28. Betsey Stevenson and Justin Wolfers, "Economic Growth and Subjective Well-Being: Reassessing the Easterlin Paradox," *Brookings Papers on Economic Activity* (Spring 2008): 1–87, doi:10.1353/eca.0.0001.
29. Philip Brickman and Donald Campbell, "Hedonic Relativism and Planning the Good Society," in M. H. Apley, *Adaptation-Level Theory* (New York: Academic Press, 1971): 287–302.
30. Gretchen Anderson, "Loneliness among Older Adults: A National Survey of Adults 45+," *AARP The Magazine*, Sep. 2010, accessed October 30, 2014, http://www.aarp.org/personal-growth/transitions/info-09-2010/loneliness_2010.html.
31. Christakis and Fowler, *Connected*, 7.
32. Holt-Lunstad, Smith, and Layton, "Social Relationships and Mortality Risk: A Meta-analytic Review."
33. John Cacioppo and William Patrick, *Loneliness: Human Nature and the Need for Social Connection* (New York: W. W. Norton and Company, 2008), 7.
34. Jim Harter and Raksha Arora, "Social Time Crucial to Daily Emotional Well-Being in U.S.," Gallup Web site, accessed January 21, 2015, http://www.gallup.com/poll/107692/Social-Time-Crucial-Daily-Emotional-WellBeing.aspx.

35. Andrew E. Clark, Ed Diener, Yannis Georgellis, m and Richard E. Lucas, "Lags and Leads in Life Satisfaction: A Test of the Baseline Hypothesis," *The Economic Journal* 118, no. 529 (2008): F222–F243.
36. Rath and Harter, *Wellbeing*, 16–27.
37. Ibid., 21.
38. Ibid., 15.
39. Ibid., 93.
40. UnitedHealth Group, "Doing Good Is Good for You: 2013 Health and Volunteering Study," accessed November 4, 2014, http://www.unitedhealthgroup.com/~/media/UHG/PDF/2013/UNH-Health-Volunteering-Study.ashx.
41. William M. Brown, Nathan S. Consedine, and Carol Magai, "Altruism Relates to Health in an Ethnically Diverse Sample of Older Adults," *Journals of Gerontology, Series B: Psychological Sciences and Social Sciences*, 60B, no. 3 (2005): 143–152.
42. Peggy A. Thoits and Lindy N. Hewitt, "Volunteer Work and Well-Being," *Journal of Health and Social Behavior* 42, no. 2 (2001): 115–131, doi:10.2307/3090173.
43. Hui-Xin Wang, et al., "Late-Life Engagement in Social and Leisure Activities Is Associated with a Decreased Risk of Dementia: A Longitudinal Study from the Kungsholmen Project," *American Journal of Epidemiology* 155, no. 12 (2002): 1081–1087.
44. Bronnie Ware, "Top 5 Regrets of the Dying," *Huff Post Good News*, January 21, 2012, accessed November 15, 2014, http://www.huffingtonpost.com/bronnie-ware/top-5-regrets-of-the-dyin_b_1220965 .html.
45. Jennifer Robinson, "The Business Case for Wellbeing," *Gallup Business Journal*, June 9, 2010, accessed December 15, 2014, http://www.gallup.com/businessjournal/139373/business-case-wellbeing.aspx.

STEP 3

1. Chip Conley, "WINTER NEWS," Chip Conley Blog, December 10, 2014, accessed January 4, 2015, https://chipconley.com/blog/winter-news.
2. Rajendra Sisodia, David B. Wolfe, and Jagdish N. Sheth, *Firms of Endearment* (Upper Saddle River, NJ: Pearson Education, 2007).
3. Society for Human Resource Management, "2011 Employee Job Satisfaction and Engagement," accessed January 7, 2015, http://www.shrm.org/Research/SurveyFindings/Articles/Documents/11-0618%20Job_Satisfaction_FNL.pdf.
4. John M. Gibbons, "Employee Engagement: A Review of Current Research and Its Implications," *The Conference Board*, November 2006.
5. Kevin Kruse, "What Is Employee Engagement," *Forbes*, June 22, 2012, accessed December 7, 2014, http://www.forbes.com/sites/kevinkruse/2012/06/22/employee-engagement-what-and-why.

6. Gallup, "State of the American Workplace: Employee Engagement Insights For U.S. Business Leaders" (2013), accessed December 13, 2014, http://employeeengagement.com/wp-content/uploads/2013/06/Gallup-2013-State-of-the-American-Workplace-Report.pdf.
7. Ibid.
8. Bill Autlet, "Culture Eats Strategy for Breakfast," *Tech Crunch*, April 12, 2014, accessed December 15, 2014, http://techcrunch.com/2014/04/12/culture-eats-strategy-for-breakfast/.
9. Joel Peterson post, "Signs Your Company Suffers from a Toxic Culture," accessed January 20, 2015, https://www.linkedin.com/pulse/signs-your-company-suffers-from-toxic-culture-joel-peterson.
10. Tony Hsieh, *Delivering Happiness* (New York: Business Plus, 2010).
11. Chip Conley, *Peak: How Great Companies Get Their Mojo from Maslow* (San Francisco: Jossey-Bass, 2007), 38.
12. Gasparino, "Will Merrill Throw Thiel Out."
13. David Hunnicutt, "People and Possibilities: A Critical Examination of Why Some Health Interventions Work and Others Don't," *Art & Science of Health Promotion Conference*, March 20, 2013.
14. Jennifer Flynn, interview with author, December 18, 2014.
15. Rosie Ward, interview with author, November 20, 2014.
16. Nancy Shute, "Is That Corporate Wellness Program Doing Your Heart Any Good?" National Public Radio, April 14, 2015, posted response to article, accessed April 15, 2015, http://www.npr.org/blogs/health/2015/04/14/399574095/is-that-corporate-wellness-program-doing-your-heart-any-good.
17. Sheryl Niehbur, interview with author, December 17, 2014.
18. National Institute of Mental Health, http://www.nimh.nih.gov/statistics.
19. Ron Goetzel et al., "Health, Absence, Disability and Presenteeism Cost Estimates of Certain Physical and Mental Conditions Affecting US Employers," *Journal of Occupational and Environmental Medicine* 46, no. 4 (2004): 398–412, doi:10.1097/01.jom.0000121151.40413.bd.
20. Gary D. Sherman et al., "Leadership Is Associated with Lower Levels of Stress," *Proceedings of the National Academy of Sciences USA*, 109, no. 44 (2012): 17903–17907, doi:10.1073/pnas.1207042109.
21. Yvon Chouinard, *Let My People Go Surfing*.
22. Maria F. Durand, "Teachers Spend Own Money for Supplies," *ABC News*, August 31, 2014, accessed on October 20, 2014, http://abcnews.go.com/US/story?id=95922.
23. Elise Brown, "Teachers Spend Own Money on Supplies," *WMAZ*, July 26, 2014, accessed on October 20, 2014, http://www.13wmaz.com/story/life/2014/07/26/school-supplies-teachers/13198573.
24. Adrian Gostick and Chester Elton, *The Carrot Principle* (New York: Free Press, 2007).

25. "Employer Strategies: 7 Signs of a Toxic Culture," *Employee Benefit Advisor*, accessed on October 16, 2014, http://eba.benefitnews.com/gallery/ebn/7-signs-of-a-toxic-culture-2745012-1.html.
26. Max Chopovsky, "How Hyatt Uses Empathy to Drive Its Culture and Employee Engagement," *Chicago Creative Space*, accessed on November 17, 2014, http://chicagocreativespace.com/why-hyatt-uses-empathy-to-help-drive-its-culture.
27. Patrick Lencioni, *The Advantage* (San Francisco: Jossey-Bass, 2012), 1.
28. Douglas R. Conant, "Secrets of Positive Feedback," *Harvard Business Review*, February 16, 2011, accessed on November 9, 2014, https://hbr.org/2011/02/secrets-of-positive-feedback.
29. Christine Porath, "Half of Employees Don't Feel Respected by Their Bosses," *Harvard Business Review* (2014), accessed on November 26, 2014, https://hbr.org/2014/11/half-of-employees-dont-feel-respected-by-their-bosses.
30. Rath and Harter, *Wellbeing*, 41.
31. Beverly Kaye and Julie Winkle Giulioni, *Help Them Grow or Watch Them Go* (San Francisco: Berrett-Koehler Publishers, Inc., 2012).
32. Josh Bersin, "The New Model for Talent Management: Agenda For 2015," accessed on January 20, 2015, http://www.slideshare.net/jbersin/talent-management-revisited.

STEP 4

1. Marcus Buckingham and Curt Coffman, *First, Break All the Rules* (New York: Simon & Schuster, 1999).
2. Marcus Buckingham, *Go Put Your Strengths to Work* (New York: Free Press, 2007).
3. Gallup Strengths website, accessed November 15, 2014, http://strengths.gallup.com/110242/about-book.aspx.
4. Rachel Feintzeig, "Everything Is Awesome! Why You Can't Tell Employees They're Doing a Bad Job," *Wall Street Journal*, February 10, 2015, accessed February 20, 2015, http://www.wsj.com/articles/everything-is-awesome-why-you-cant-tell-employees-theyre-doing-a-bad-job-1423613936.
5. Reed Albergotti, "At Facebook, Boss Is a Dirty Word," *Wall Street Journal*, December 25, 2014, accessed December 26, 2014, http://www.wsj.com/articles/facebooks-millennials-arent-entitled-they-are-empowered-1419537468.
6. Susan Sorenson, "How Employees' Strengths Make Your Company Stronger," *Gallup Business Journal*, February 20, 2014, accessed October 28, 2014, http://www.gallup.com/businessjournal/167462/employees- strengths-company-stronger.aspx.

7. National Business Group on Health and Towers Watson, "The Business Value of a Healthy Workforce: United States," *2013/2014 Staying@ Work™ Survey Report.*
8. Robin Soler, et al., "A systematic review of selected interventions for worksite health promotion: the assessment of health risks with feedback," *American Journal of Preventive Medicine* 38 (2010): S237–S262.
9. Alan Goforth, "Wellness Incentive Spending Sets Record," National Business Group on Health website, March 27, 2015, accessed April 10, 2015, https://www.businessgrouphealth.org/pressroom/pressClipping.cfm?ID=1607.
10. Willis, *The Willis Health and Productivity Survey Report 2014* (New York: Willis North America Inc., 2014).
11. ShapeUp, *2011 Employer Wellness Survey: Understanding How Large, Self-Insured Employers Approach Employee Wellness* (Providence, RI: ShapeUp, Inc., 2011).
12. Kelly McGonigal, *The Willpower Instinct: How Self-Control Works, Why It Matters, and What You Can Do to Get More of It* (New York: Avery, 2012).
13. Steven G. Aldana et al., "Cardiovascular Risk Reductions Associated with Aggressive Lifestyle Modification and Cardiac Rehabilitation," *Heart & Lung* (Nov/Dec 2003): 380.
14. Ornish Spectrum Web site, accessed December 12, 2014, http://ornishspectrum.com.
15. Dean Ornish, "Statin and the Soul of Medicine," *The American Journal of Cardiology* 89 (June 1, 2002): 1287.
16. Vic Strecher, interview with author, November 19, 2014.
17. Martin E. P. Seligman, et al., "Positive Psychology Progress: Empirical Validations of Interventions," *American Psychologist*, July/August (2005): 410–421.
18. Laura D. Kubzansky, et al., "Is the Glass Half Empty or Half Full? A Prospective Study of Optimism and Coronary Heart Disease in the Normative Aging Study," *Psychosomatic Medicine* 63 (2001): 910–916.
19. Harvard Health Publications, "Optimism and Your Health," May 1, 2008, accessed December 24, 2014, http://www.health.harvard.edu/newsletters/Harvard_Mens_Health_Watch/2008/May/optimism-and-your-health.
20. Sheldon Cohen et al., "Positive Emotional Style Predicts Resistance to Illness after Experimental Exposure to Rhinovirus or Influenza A Virus," *Psychosomatic Medicine* 68 (2006): 809–815.
21. Sonja Lyubomirsky, Laura King, and Ed Diener, "The Benefits of Frequent Positive Affect: Does Happiness Lead to Success?" *Psychological Bulletin* 131 (2005): 803–855.
22. Andrew J. Oswald, Eugenio Proto, and Daniel Sgroi, "Happiness and Productivity," University of Warwick Research Study, accessed January

28, 2015, http://www2.warwick.ac.uk/fac/soc/economics/staff/eproto/workingpapers/happinessproductivity.pdf.

23. Shawn Achor, *The Happiness Advantage* (New York: Broadway Books, 2010).
24. Barbara Fredrickson, "The Impact of Positivity on Health," Presentation, Annual Art & Science of Health Promotion Conference, San Diego, CA, March 30–April 3, 2015.
25. Seligman et al., "Positive Psychology Progress," 410–421.
26. Achor, *The Happiness Advantage.*
27. Albert Bandura, "Self-Efficacy Mechanism in Physiological Activation and Health-Promoting Behavior," in *Adaptation, Learning and Affect*, ed. J. Madden et al. (New York: Raven Press, 1987).
28. David Hunnicutt, "Five Things You Can Do to Take Your Program to the Next Level," *WELCOA Webinar*, May 23, 2013.

STEP 5

1. Blue Shield of California, "Leading by Example: Wellvolution—Blue Shield Of California," accessed November 25, 2014, https://www.blueshieldca.com/producer/largegroups/premier-accounts/total-health/wellvolution.sp.
2. Blue of California, "Blue Shield Wellness Program Case Study," accessed April 13, 2015, http://mrktoa.blueshieldca.com/rs/blueshieldofcalifornia/images/Blue_Shield_Wellness_Program_CaseStudy_A44130_5-12.pdf.
3. The Henry J. Kaiser Family Foundation, "Employer-Sponsored Family Health Premiums Rise 3 Percent In 2014," accessed November 24, 2014, http://kff.org/health-costs/press-release/employer-sponsored-family-health-premiums-rise-3-percent-in-2014/.
4. Willis, "The Willis Health and Productivity Survey Report 2014."
5. Dana Miller, interview with author, January 5, 2015.
6. Matthew Coan, interview with author, January 4, 2015.
7. American Heart Association Blog, "CEO Roundtable Tackling Health in the U.S. Workplace," accessed December 21, 2014, http://blog.heart.org/ceo-roundtable-tackling-health-in-the-u-s-workplace.
8. Casey Chosewood, interview with author, December 3, 2014.
9. "2012 Total Worker Health Symposium," *Journal of Occupational & Environmental Medicine* 55 (2013): S1-S7, doi:10.1097/JOM.0000000000000047.
10. Casey Chosewood, interview with author, December 3, 2014.
11. Victoria Weisfeld and Tracy A. Lustig, *Promising and Best Practices in Total Worker Health: Workshop Summary* (Washington, DC: The National Academies Press, 2014).
12. The Wellness Council of America, "A WELCOA Case Study with Performance pH: Optimizing Business Performance," accessed April 12,

2015, http://www.performph.com/wp-content/uploads/2013/08/PPH-OPTIMIZING-BUSINESS-PERFORMANCE-8-28-20132.pdf.
13. Ed O'Boyle and Jim Harter, "Why Your Workplace Wellness Program Isn't Working," *Gallup Business Journal*, May 13, 2014, accessed December 7, 2014, http://www.gallup.com/businessjournal/168995/why-workplace-wellness-program-isn-working.aspx.
14. Ibid.
15. Ibid.
16. Jessica Grossmeier, interview with author, November 15, 2014.
17. Paul E. Terry, "Tapping Passion: The Untold Talents of Wellness Champions, Ambassadors and Peer Educators," *American Journal of Health Promotion*, September/October 2013, TAHP-1–TAHP-12.
18. Edward de Bono, *Six Thinking Hats* (New York: Back Bay Books, 1999).
19. 2013/2014 Staying@Work™ Survey Report, 2.

STEP 6

1. American Society for Training and Development, *2013 State of the Industry Report* (Alexandria, VA: 2013).
2. Ibid.
3. Willis, "The Willis Health And Productivity Survey Report".
4. Ibid.
5. Stanford Medicine News Center, "Stealth Leads to Healthy in Effort to Improve Diet, Study Shows" April 26, 2010, accessed October 3, 2014 http://med.stanford.edu/news/all-news/2010/04/stealthy-leads-to-healthy-in-effort-to-improve-diet-study-shows.html.
6. Deloitte, "Global Human Capital 2014 Top 10," Deloitte University Press, accessed January 4, 2015, http://www2.deloitte.com/us/en/pages/human-capital/articles/human-capital-trends-2014-top10.html.
7. Joel Goh, Jeffrey Pfeffer, and Stefanos A. Zenios, "The Relationship Between Workplace Stressors and Mortality and Health Costs in the United States," Submitted to *Management Science*, manuscript MS-12-01264.R3 (2014).
8. The Energy Project Web site, accessed November 5, 2014, http://theenergyproject.com/?gclid=CMTcucGo1sMCFYKUfgodWZMALg.
9. Brigid Schulte, "Working Smarter, Not Longer," *The Bulletin*, Feb. 7, 2015.
10. Ibid.
11. 2013/2014 Staying@Work™ Survey Report.
12. Tony Schwartz and Jim Loehr, *Power of Full Engagement* (New York: The Free Press, 2003).
13. Human Performance Institute Web site and The Energy Project Web site, accessed November 25, 2014, https://www.hpinstitute.com and

http://theenergyproject.com/?gclid=CMTcucGo1sMCFYKUfgodWZ MALg.

14. Towers Watson 2012 Global Workforce Study.
15. Ibid.
16. Virgin Pulse, "3 Trends for 2015: What's Ahead for Employee Engagement and Well-Being," accessed February 4, 2015, http://connect.virginpulse.com/files/TipSheet_StateoftheIndustry.pdf.
17. Maggie Spicer, interview with author, December 15, 2014.
18. Ryan Scott, "Three Stellar Examples of Corporate Community Involvement Programs," Causecast Blog, July 17, 2012, accessed February 25, 2015, http://www.causecast.com/blog/3-stellar-examples-of-corporate-community-involvement-programs/.
19. Lynn Vojvodich, chief marketing officer, *Salesforce*, interview with author, March 4, 2015.
20. Lynn Vojvodich, interview with author, January 17, 2015.
21. Chipper Bro, interview with author, April 13, 2015.

STEP 7

1. David A. Asch and Kevin Volpp, "Use Behavioral Economics to Achieve Wellness Goals," *Harvard Business Review*, December 1, 2014, accessed January 6, 2015, Retrieved from https://hbr.org/2014/12/use-behavioral-economics-to-achieve-wellness-goals.
2. Niteesh K. Choudhry, et al., "Full Coverage for Preventive Medications after Myocardial Infarction," *New England Journal Of Medicine* 365 (22): 2088–2097, doi:0.1056/nejmsa1107913.
3. Michelle Segar, interview with author, December 4, 2014.
4. The Huffington Post, "Golden Gate Bridge Suicide Prevention: CHP Sergeant Kevin Briggs on Saving Lives over the Railing," December 11, 2012, accessed December 15, 2014, http://www.huffingtonpost.com/2012/12/11/golden-gate-bridge-suicide_n_2278973.html.
5. Mikaela Shiffrin, "World's Best Slalom Skier Prepares for Olympic Event," *NPR*, February 21, 2014, accessed December 15, 2014, http://www.npr.org/2014/02/21/280528551/worlds-best-slalom-skier-prepares-for-olympic-event.
6. Hyungshim Jang, John Marshall Reeve, and Edward L. Deci, "Engaging Students in Learning Activities: It Is Not Autonomy Support or Structure but Autonomy Support and Structure," *Journal of Educational Psychology*, 102, no. 3 (2010): 588-600, doi:10.1037/a0019682.
7. Daniel H. Pink, *Drive: The Surprising Truth about What Motivates Us* (New York: Riverhead Books, 2009), 41.
8. Alan Goforth, "Wellness Incentive Spending Sets Record," National Business Group on Health website, March 27, 2015, accessed April 10,

2015, https://www.businessgrouphealth.org/pressroom/pressClipping.cfm?ID=1607.

9. Sharon Begley, "Coming Soon to a Workplace Near You: 'Wellness or Else'," Reuters, January 13, 2015, accessed April 10, 2015, http://www.reuters.com/article/2015/01/13/us-usa-healthcare-wellness-insight-idUSKBN0KM17C20150113.
10. The Henry J. Kaiser Family Foundation, "Employer-Sponsored Family Health Premiums Rise 3 Percent in 2014," September 10, 2014, accessed January 7, 2015, http://kff.org/private-insurance/press-release/employer-sponsored-family-health-premiums-rise-3-percent-in-2014.
11. Adrian Gostick and Chester Elton, *The Carrot Principle: How the Best Managers Use Recognition to Engage Their People, Retain Talent and Accelerate Performance* (New York: Free Press, 2009), 18.
12. Kate Cahill and Rafael Perera, "Competitions and Incentives for Smoking Cessation," *National Business Group on Health*, July 16, 2008, accessed December 6, 2014, http://www.ncbi.nlm.nih.gov/pubmed/18646105?itool=EntrezSystem2.PEntrez.Pubmed.Pubmed_ResultsPanel.Pubmed_RVDocSum&ordinalpos=6.
13. Victoria Weisfeld and Tracy A. Lustig, *Promising and Best Practices in Total Worker Health: Workshop Summary* (Washington, DC: The National Academies Press, 2014).
14. Lauren Weber, "Wellness Programs Get a Health Check."
15. Posted response to Nancy Shute, "Is That Corporate Wellness Program Doing Your Heart Any Good?" NPR, April 14, 2015, accessed April 15, 2015, http://www.npr.org/blogs/health/2015/04/14/399574095/is-that-corporate-wellness-program-doing-your-heart-any-good.
16. Helen Darling and Karen Marlo, "Perceptions of Health Benefits in a Recovering Economy: A Survey of Employees," *National Business Group on Health*, July 26, 2012, accessed 3 March 2015 at http://www.businessgrouphealth.org/pub/f314a3d7-2354-d714-51ed-4alcf9fc4990.
17. Liz Hamel, Jamie Firth, and Mollyann Brodie, "June 2014 Health Tracking Poll," Henry J. Kaiser Family Foundation website, accessed April 7, 2015, http://kff.org/health-reform/poll-finding/kaiser-health-tracking-poll-june-2014/.
18. Natasha Singer, "Health Plan Penalty Ends at Penn State," *New York Times*, Sept. 19, 2013.
19. Todd F. Heatherton et al., "A 10-Year Longitudinal Study of Body Weight, Dieting, and Eating Disorder Symptoms," *Journal of Abnormal Psychology*, 106 (1997): 118.
20. Kaiser Permanente Website, accessed March 5, 2015, http://weighandwin.com/blog/index.php/kaiser-permanente-supported-weigh-and-win-pays-coloradans-to-maintain-weight-throughout-2014-holiday-season.
21. Pink, *Drive*, 39.

22. Michelle L. Segar, Jacquelynne S. Eccles, and Caroline R. Richardson, "Rebranding Exercise: Closing the Gap between Values and Behavior," *International Journal of Behavioral Nutrition and Physical Activity*, 8, no. 1 (2011): 94. doi:10.1186/1479-5868-8-94.
23. Eric Barker, "How Do We Find Meaning in Life?" *Time*, November 17, 2014, accessed December 3, 2015, http://time.com/3584646/find-meaning-in-life.
24. Aaron E. Black and Edward L. Deci, "The Effects of Instructors' Autonomy Support and Students' Autonomous Motivation on Learning Organic Chemistry: A Self-Determination Theory Perspective," *Science Education* 84, no. 6 (2000): 740–756.
25. Cindy Strickland, "The Five Entry Points of Howard Gardner," accessed March 1, 2015, http://dilangley.wikispaces.com/file/view/bENTRY+POINTS+2009+sec.pdf.
26. Barry See, "How to Stop Jaywalking? Hire Mimes . . ." *The Journal.ie*, August 6, 2012, accessed December 10, 2014, http://www.thejournal.ie/how-to-stop-jaywalking-hire-mimes-543388-Aug2012.
27. Ibid.
28. Laura Young, interview with author, December 18, 2014.
29. Gregory Walton and Clifton B. Parker, "Working Together Boosts Motivation Stanford University Research Shows," Biospace.com, September 22, 2014, accessed December 10, 2014, http://www.biospace.com/News/working-together-boosts-motivation-stanford/347243.
30. Eric Stein, interview with author, November 25, 2014.
31. "John Travolta Explains That 3 AM Gym Visit," *Yahoo! Celebrity*, accessed January 19, 2015, https://celebrity.yahoo.com/news/john-travolta-explains-3-am-gym-visit-165020079.html.
32. Vic Strecher, interview with author, November 19, 2014.
33. AMERICAN News, "ACIPCO Receives Prestigious National Health Award," October 7, 2014, accessed November 2, 2014, http://news.american-usa.com/2014/10/07/acipco-receives-prestigious-national-health-award.
34. Ibid.
35. Julie Appleby, "Companies Step Up Wellness Efforts," *USA Today*, July 31, 2005, accessed December 16, 2014, http://usatoday30.usatoday.com/money/workplace/2005-07-31-wellness-usat_x.htm.
36. Stuart Brown, *Play: How It Shapes the Brain* (New York: The Penguin Group, 2009).
37. Claire Bates, "Scaling New Heights: Piano Stairway Encourages Commuters to Ditch the Escalators," *DailyMail.com*, October 11, 2009, accessed October 30, 2014, http://www.dailymail.co.uk/sciencetech/article-1218944/Scaling-new-heights-Piano-stairway-encourages-com muters-ditch-escalators.html.

STEP 8

1. Richard H. Thaler and Cass R. Sunstein, *Nudge: Improving Decisions about Health, Wealth and Happiness* (New Haven, CT: Yale University Press, 2008).
2. Laura Anderko et al., "Promoting Prevention Through the Affordable Care Act: Workplace Wellness," *Preventing Chronic Disease* 9 (2012): 120092. doi:http://dx.doi.org/10.5888/pcd9.120092.
3. Centers for Disease Control and Prevention, *Trends in Current Cigarette Smoking among High School Students and Adults, United States, 1965–2011*, accessed November 18, 2014, http://www.cdc.gov/tobacco/data_statistics/tables/trends/cig_smoking.
4. Centers for Disease Control and Prevention, *Adult Cigarette Smoking in the United States: Current Estimates*, accessed November 18, 2014, http://www.cdc.gov/tobacco/data_statistics/fact_sheets/adult_data/cig_smoking.
5. Willis Health and Productivity Survey Report.
6. Simon Chapman et al., "The Impact of Smoke-Free Workplaces on Declining Cigarette Consumption in Australia and the United States," *American Journal of Health Promotion*, 89 no. 7 (1999): 1018–1023.
7. Nicole Angelique Kerr, et al., "Increasing Stair Use in a Worksite Through Environmental Changes," *American Journal of Health Promotion* 18, no. 4 (2004): 312–315.
8. Aaron Taube, "3 Ways Google Tricks Its Employees into Eating Healthy," *Business Insider*, November 10, 2014, accessed February 26, 2015, http://www.businessinsider.com/how-google-gets-employees-to-eat-healthy-2014-11.
9. Arianna Huffington keynote, ASTD International Conference and Exposition 2014.
10. Julia Gifford, "We Tested Standing Desks—Here's Proof They Make You More Productive," *ReadWrite*, Sept. 26, 2013, accessed October 30, 2014, http://readwrite.com/2013/09/26/standing-desks-productivity#feed=/series/body&awesm=~orDzJwsJ77Jw0s.
11. Stanford Center on Longevity, "Pilot Study Shows Way to Less Sitting in Workplace," accessed November 15, 2014, http://longevity3.stanford.edu/pilot-study-shows-the-way-to-sitting-less-in-the-workplace.
12. Michelle Pekarsky and Kerri Stowell, "Walking While They Work: Treadmill Desks Installed for 911 Dispatchers in Johnson County," Fox4kc.com Kansas City, Jan. 6, 2014, accessed January 4, 2015, http://fox4kc.com/2014/01/06/walking-while-they-work-treadmill-desks-installed-for-911-dispatchers-in-johnson-county.
13. Berry et al., "What's the Hard Return on Employee Wellness Programs?"
14. Philip Kendall, "Your Morning Workout: Japanese Library Staff Show Us How to Stretch in Hilarious/Cute Video," *Rocketnews24*, December 3,

2012, http://en.rocketnews24.com/2012/12/03/your-morning-workout-japanese-library-staff-show-us-how-to-strech-in-hilarious-cute-video.

15. Joshua Hammer, "Stretching Their Productivity As Well As Their Limbs, Autoworkers in Tennessee Go Japanese," *People*, October 24, 1983, accessed December 5, 2014, http://www.people.com/people/archive/article/0,20086211,00.html.
16. Jane E. Brody, "It's Time for Recess: Just Keep on Moving," *New York Times*, November 22, 2010, accessed January 4, 2015, http://www.nytimes.com/2010/11/23/health/23brody.html?_r=1.
17. Jeff Weiner, "Where I Work: I'll Take Walking 1:1's Over Office Meetings Any Day," January 29, 2013, accessed January 4, 2015, https://www.linkedin.com/pulse/20130129033750-22330283-where-i-work-i-ll-take-walking-1-1s-over-office-meetings-any-day.
18. Bloomberg, "A Walk with LinkedIn's CEO Jeff Weiner," *Bloomberg.com*, June 4, 2014, accessed January 20, 2015, http://www.bloomberg.com/news/videos/b/249713a0-0ced-4513-8d77-52941c1f4b05.
19. Charles Montgomery, "The Secrets of the World's Happiest Cities," *The Guardian*, November 1, 2013, accessed November 15, 2014, http://www.theguardian.com/society/2013/nov/01/secrets-worlds-happiest-cities-commute-property-prices.
20. Kate Abbey-Lambertz, "People Are Skiing in Detroit's Abandoned Buildings Now," *The Huffington Post*, December 10, 2013, accessed December 20, 2014, http://www.huffingtonpost.com/2013/12/10/detroit-skiing_n_4419564.html.
21. Christopher Jobsen, "An Interactive Dancing Pedestrian Signal by Smart," *Colossal*, September 17, 2014, accessed December 21, 2014, http://www.thisiscolossal.com/2014/09/interactive-dancing-traffic-light-by-smart.
22. Ron Z. Goetzel et al., "First-Year Results of an Obesity Prevention Program at The Dow Chemical Company," *Journal of Occupational and Environmental Medicine* 51, no. 2 (2009): 125–138, doi:10.1097/JOM.0b013e3181954b03.
23. Ilse De Bourdeaudhuij, James F. Sallis, and Brian E. Saelens, "Environmental Correlates of Physical Activity in a Sample of Belgian Adults," *American Journal of Health Promotion* 18, no. 1 (2003): 83–92, doi:10.4278/0890-1171-18.1.83.
24. Patricia A. Sharpe et al., "Association of Environmental Factors to Meeting Physical Activity Recommendations in Two South Carolina Counties," *American Journal of Health Promotion* 18, no. 3 (2004): 251–257.
25. Nancy Humpel et al., "Associations of Location and Perceived Environmental Attributes with Walking in Neighborhoods," *American Journal of Health Promotion* 18, no. 3 (2004): 239–242.
26. Nancy Humpel, Neville Owen, and Eva Leslie, "Environmental Factors Associated with Adults' Participation in Physical Activity: A Review,"

American Journal of Preventative Medicine 22, no. 3 (2002): 188–199, doi:10.4278/0890-1171-18.3.251.

27. Richard J. Jackson with Stacy Sinclair, *Designing Healthy Communities* (San Francisco: Jossey-Bass, 2012).
28. Goetzel et al., "First-Year Results of an Obesity Prevention Program at The Dow Chemical Company," 125–138.

STEP 9

1. Vinnie Lauria, "Silicon Valley Isn't Innovative, It's Iterative: Four Proof Points," *Forbes*, April 8, 2014, accessed December 4, 2014, http://www.forbes.com/sites/ciocentral/2014/04/08/silicon-valley-isnt-innovative-its-iterative-four-proof-points.
2. McKinsey Global Institute, "Overcoming Obesity: An Initial Economic Analysis," November 2014, 7.
3. David Kolb, *Experiential Learning: Experience as the Source of Learning and Development* (Upper Saddle River, NJ: Prentice Hall, Inc., 1984).
4. Carol S. Dweck, *Mindset: The New Psychology of Success* (New York: Ballantine Books, 2007).
5. Michelle Segar and Winifred Gebhardt, "Pursuing Health-Related Goals," ed. Michael O'Donnell, *Health Promotion in the Workplace*, 4th ed. (Troy, MI: American Journal of Health Promotion, 2014).
6. Charles Duhigg, *The Power of Habit* (New York: Random House, 2014).
7. Jennifer Reingold and Christopher Tkaczyk, "10 Gurus You Should Know," *Fortune*, accessed November 21, 2014, http://archive.fortune.com/galleries/2008/fortune/0811/gallery.10_new_gurus.fortune.
8. Jennifer Pitts, interview with author, January 15, 2015.
9. Lance Dublin, interview with author, January 20, 2015.
10. Donald L. Kirkpatrick, *Evaluating Training Programs: The Four Levels*, 2nd ed. (San Francisco: Berrett-Koehler, 1998).
11. National Business Group on Health and Institute on Health, Productivity and Human Capital, *Value of Investment in Employee Health, Productivity and Well-Being: A National Business Group on Health Toolkit.*
12. 2013/2014 Staying@Work™ Survey Report.
13. Josh Bersin, "Simply Irresistible: Engaging the 21st Century" Keynote Presentation, Bersin by Deloitte, May 7, 2014.

STEP 10

1. Anthony Mbewu and Jean-Claude Mbanya, "Chapter 21: Cardiovascular Disease." In *Disease and Mortality in Sub-Saharan Africa*, 2nd ed., ed. Dean T. Jamison, et al. (Washington, D.C.: World Bank, 2006).

2. Danielle Dellorto, "Global Report: Obesity Bigger Health Crisis Than Hunger," *CNN*, December 14, 2012, accessed December 5, 2014, http://www.cnn.com/2012/12/13/health/global-burden-report.
3. Jason Beaubien, "The Whole World Is Fat! And That Ends Up Costing $2 Trillion a Year," *NPR*, November 20, 2014, accessed November 25, 2014, http://www.npr.org/blogs/goatsandsoda/2014/11/20/365514156/the-whole-world-is-fat-and-that-ends-up-costing-two-trillion-a-year.
4. Dylan Stableford, "America No Longer World's Fattest Developed Nation, UN Report Says," *Yahoo! News*, July 19, 2013, accessed November 20, 2014, http://news.yahoo.com/blogs/news/america-fattest-obese-un-144341236.html.
5. McKinsey Global Institute, "Overcoming Obesity: An Initial Economic Analysis," November 2014.
6. Food and Agricultural Organization of the United Nations, "The State of Food and Agriculture" (Rome, Italy, 2013), accessed January 3, 2015, http://www.fao.org/docrep/018/i3300e/i3300e.pdf.
7. McKinsey Global Report, "Overcoming Obesity."
8. Dellorto, "Global Report: Obesity."
9. McKinsey Global Institute, "Overcoming Obesity."
10. International Diabetes Federation Website, accessed January 5, 2015, International Diabetes Federation, "IDF Diabetes Atlas," 6th ed., accessed February 15, 2015, http://www.idf.org/sites/default/files/DA-regional-factsheets-2014_FINAL.pdf.
11. William Mellor, "McDonald's No Match for KFC in China as Colonel Rules Fast Food," *BloombergBusiness*, January 26, 2011, accessed December 15, 2014, http://www.bloomberg.com/news/articles/2011-01-26/mcdonald-s-no-match-for-kfc-in-china-where-colonel-sanders-rules-fast-food.
12. PRNewswire, "Regus-Commissioned Survey Reveals Stress Levels Rising among US Workers," accessed December 10, 2014, http://www.prnewswire.com/news-releases/regus-commissioned-survey-reveals-stress-levels-rising-among-us-workers-71658307.html.
13. Vanessa Barford, "Is Modern Life Making Us Lonely?," *BBC News Magazine*, April 3, 2013, accessed December 2, 2014, http://www.bbc.com/news/magazine-22012957.
14. Steve Crabtree, "Worldwide, 13% of Workers Are Engaged," Gallup, October 8, 2013, accessed December 15, 2014, http://www.gallup.com/poll/165269/worldwide-employees-engaged-work.aspx.
15. Arianna Huffington, *Thrive*.
16. "Google Searches," Mindful.org, accessed December 4, 2014, http://www.mindful.org/at-work/in-the-workplace/google-searches.
17. Chade-Meng Tan, *Search Inside Yourself: The Unexpected Path to Achieving Success, Happiness (and World Peace)* (New York: HarperOne, 2012).
18. Quoted in Vijay K. Shrotryia, "Happiness and Development: Public Policy Initiatives in the Kingdom of Bhutan," in Yew-Kwang Ng and Lok

Sang Ho (eds.), *Happiness and Public Policy: Theory, Case Studies, and Implications* (New York: Palgrave Macmillan, 2006), 193, 201.

19. Derek Bok, *The Politics of Happiness* (Princeton, NJ: Princeton University Press, 2010).
20. Dan Buettner, *The Blue Zones* (Washington, DC: National Geographic Society, 2010).
21. Sloan Center on Aging & Work at Boston College, "The MetLife Study of Global Health & Wellness: A Look at How Multinational Companies Are Responding to the Need for a Healthier Workforce," *MetLife*, accessed December 15, 2014, https://www.metlife.com/assets/institutional/products/benefits-products/MetLifeGlobalHealthWellness_exp0116.pdf.
22. Natsuko Fukue, "Wake Up, Hike Out, Tune In, Move It," *The Japan Times*, June 22, 2009, accessed December 1, 2014, http://www.japantimes.co.jp/news/2009/07/22/reference/wake-up-hike-out-tune-in-move-it/#.VQKJuCk4I70.
23. "Dena Pflieger, Global Health Promotion Leader, Dow Chemical," The Commonwealth Fund Web site, April 30, 2010, accessed December 10, 2014, http://www.commonwealthfund.org/publications/newsletters/purchasing-high-performance/2010/april-30-2010/interview/dena-pflieger-global-health-promotion-leader-dow-chemical.
24. Sloan Center on Aging & Work at Boston College, "The MetLife Study of Global Health & Wellness: A Look at How Multinational Companies Are Responding to the Need for a Healthier Workforce," MetLife, accessed December 15, 2014, https://www.metlife.com/assets/institutional/products/benefits-products/MetLifeGlobalHealthWellness_exp0116.pdf.
25. World Heart Federation website, "Workplace Wellness in Mexico," August/September/October 2009, accessed November 5, 2014, http://www.world-heart-federation.org/?id=2393.
26. *Working Well: A Global Survey of Health Promotion, Workplace Wellness and Productivity Strategies*, 6th ed., July 2014, Buck Consultants LLC.
27. 2013/2014 Global Workforce Survey Report.
28. *Working Well: A Global Survey of Health Promotion, Workplace Wellness and Productivity Strategies.*
29. 2013/2014 Staying@Work Survey Report, 7.
30. Ryan Picarella, interview with author, November 19, 2014.

INDEX

A
absenteeism, 17
accountability, 12
Achor, Shaun, 93
action, call to, 22, 23, 25
action items
  Create Meaning (Step 7), 163, 182, 185, 189
  Design Nudges and Cues (Step 8), 205–207, 210–212, 213
  Go Global (Step 10), 248–249, 264
  Go Stealth (Step 6), 139, 156
  Imagine What's Possible (Step 2), 28–29, 44, 49–50, 54–55
  Launch and Iterate (Step 9), 224–225, 226–227, 228, 231–233, 236, 238–239, 240–241, 242
  Shift Your Mind-Set (Step 1), 10–11, 12
  Start with What's Right (Step 4), 94, 97–98, 100, 101–102
  Take a da Vinci Approach to Change (Step 5), 114–115, 121, 122, 123, 126–127, 128, 129, 130–132
  Uncover the Hidden Factors (Step 3), 67–68, 79, 80–81, 82–83
activist-based approach, to health promotion, 4
Advantage, The (Lencioni), 75
Aetna, 116
Affordable Care Act, 112, 167
agents of change
  elements of, 7–11
  experts *versus*, 4, 5–6
  overview, 3–5
  possibilities imagined by (*See* Imagine What's Possible (Step 2))
  See also Shift Your Mind-Set (Step 1)
Airbnb, 59
Akanksha Foundation, 255
Alice in Wonderland, 191
Allen, Peter, 251
Alles, Wesley, 120
American Cast Iron Pipe Company (AMERICAN), 179, 185, 186–188
American Heart Association, xviii, 7, 119–120, 152, 163
American Journal of Health Promotion, xxvii, 160
American Psychological Association, xx
AMSO model, 160, 225
Angelou, Maya, 74
Angus, Dylan, 181–182
Angus, Ross, 181–182
Anker, Conrad, 72
asa taisou, 201
Asch, David, 161
assessment
  data for, 70
  dialogue with leaders and, 81–83

assessment (*continued*)
  establishing baseline for, 100–102
  5 "F" Factors, 73–79
  impact of, xxxi
  Marbles technique, 71
  Maslow Meets Mallory Culture Audit, 72–73, 79
  monitoring progress of new habits, 176
  overview, 69–70
  peer-based evaluation, 222–223
  preliminary conclusions for, 70–71
  qualitative data for, 79–81
  Snow Day technique, 71–72
  See also Launch and Iterate (Step 9)
Athleta, 125–126
Autlet, Bill, 60
autonomy, 174, 177–178
awareness, behavior change and, 160–161

B
Banerjee, Sid, 201
Barker, Eric, 173
Basic Training, 204
Baumeister, Roy, xx–xxi
Baun, Bill, 8, 15
Beethoven, Ludwig van, 53
BeFit (Virgin America), 152
behavior
  behaviorist theory, 165–166
  changing, xx–xxi, 12, 161–163, 193 (*See also* Design Nudges and Cues (Step 8))
belonging, need for, 78
Bennett, Joel, 180
Bersin, Josh, 79
Bhutan, gross national happiness of, 252–253
"Biggest Loser" contests, 171–172
biometric screenings, 88–89
Blair, Charlotte, 186–188
Bloomberg, xviii
Blue Shield of California, 106–109, 115–116
Blue Zones, The (Buettner), 253
Blumenauer, Earl, 9, 11
book, organization of, xvi–xvii
Boston College Center for Corporate Citizenship, 19–20
bottom-up wellness movements, 15–16, 114
brain, willpower and, xx–xxi
brainstorming, 130–132
"brain to brain coupling," 8–9
brand, building, 114–115
Bray, Duane, 61–63, 218–221
Briggs, Kevin, 163
bright spots, identifying, 70, 97–100
Brocade, 36–37, 111, 195–196, 257–258
Broeker, Monika, 251
Brown, Brené, 8
Brown, Nancy, 119
Brown, Stuart, 188–189
Brown University, 176
Bruner, Jerome, 165–166
Buckingham, Marcus, 86, 87
Buettner, Dan, 253
Buffington, Scott, 76–78
Bullitt Foundation, 52
Burke, James, xxvi
Burnham, Douglas, 204

C

Cameron, Kim, 69
Campbell Soup, 75–76
career, as element of well-being, 47–51
Carney, Lloyd, 36
Carson, Ryan, 140
Center for Corporate Citizenship (Boston College), 19
Center for Mindfulness in Medicine, 44
Center on Longevity (Stanford University), 199
Centers for Disease Control and Prevention, xvii, 195
Challengers, on da Vinci team, 129–130
change. *See* Take a da Vinci Approach to Change (Step 5)
Changemaker Imperative. *See* Shift Your Mind-Set (Step 1)
checklists
  Create Meaning (Step 7), 159–160
  Design Nudges and Cues (Step 8), 192
  Go Global (Step 10), 246
  Go Stealth (Step 6), 134
  Imagine What's Possible (Step 2), 28
  Launch and Iterate (Step 9), 216
  Shift Your Mind-Set (Step 1), 5, 20–21
  Start with What's Right (Step 4), 86
  Take a da Vinci Approach to Change (Step 5), 106
  Uncover the Hidden Factors (Step 3), 58
Chesapeake Energy, 6, 99–100, 113
Chosewood, Casey, 120
Chouinard, Yvon, 13, 69
Cisco Systems, 20
Clarabridge, 200–201
#cleanstreets (Square), 154–155
Cleveland Clinic, 13
Clifton, Don, 86
coaching, 24–25, 183
Coan, Matthew, 117
Coffman, Curt, 86
Coles, Jeff, 181
Committee Encouraging Corporate Philanthropy, 153–156
communication
  agents of change as communicators, 8
  impact of, xxix
  persuading decision makers, 11–12, 17–21
community
  as element of well-being, 51–52
  external da Vinci teams and, 119–120
  outreach initiatives, 153–156
compensation and benefits, internal da Vinci team for, 112–113
competency, 174–176
Conant, Doug, 75
Con Edison, 19
Conley, Chip, 49, 59, 72–73, 75, 127
Connected (Cristakis, Fowler), 47
constructivism, 166
Cooked (Pollan), 4
core action team, forming, 12
Cosgrove, Toby, 13
Cossman, E. Joseph, 40

County of Solano (California), 150
Create Meaning (Step 7), 159–190
  autonomy and, 174, 177–178
  behavior change and, 160–163
  building competency, 174–176
  culture and, 64–65
  finding "your why," 163–164
  incentives and, 161
  incorporating intrinsic motivation, 173, 190
  key to lasting motivation, 174
  motivation, overview, 159–160
  motivation as extrinsic and intrinsic, 164, 165–170
  overview, 271–272
  participation *versus* engagement, 165
  play and, 174, 188–189
  purpose and, 174, 183–188
  relatedness and, 174, 178–183
  unintended consequences, 170–172
creativity, as element of well-being, 52–53
Cristakis, Nicholas, 47
critical thinking, 31
Csikszentmihalyi, Mihaly, 164
cues. *See* Design Nudges and Cues (Step 8)
Culture Imperative. *See* Uncover the Hidden Factors (Step 3)
Cushing, Elizabeth, 95–96

D

data, internal/external, 70. *See also* assessment
Davidson, Nick, 48–49
da Vinci Approach to Change. *See* Take a da Vinci Approach to Change (Step 5)
de Bono, Edward, 130–132
Deci, Edward L., 166, 177
decision makers
  obtaining buy-in from, 11–12, 17–21
  starting dialogue with, 81–83
  See also Go Stealth (Step 6)
Del Grande Dealer Group (DGDG), 117–118
Deloitte, 79, 139, 140
Denison Organizational Culture Survey, 69
Deresiewicz, William, 177
Design Nudges and Cues (Step 8), 191–214
  for behavior change, 193
  cues as cultural prompts, 201–203
  examples, 195–201
  increasing use of nudges and cues, 210–213
  nudges and cues, defined, 192
  overview, 191–192
  to reinforce well-being, 194–195, 207–210
  research about, 203–207
  using nudges and cues together, 193–194
  Welch and, 194
design thinking, xvi, 217–221, 229–230
de Vries, Patty, 91–92, 113, 228
Dhabhar, Firdaus, 41, 42
diet
  as element of well-being, 38–39
  food infrastructure, xxii
  See also Design Nudges and Cues (Step 8)

Dimon, Jamie, 20
Disciplined Entrepreneurship (Autlet), 60
Disney, 55
Dow Chemical, 120–121, 137, 169, 256, 257
Drane, Alexandra, 34
Drive (Pink), 166, 172
Duhigg, Charles, 175, 225–226
Duke University, 94
Dweck, Carol, 223

E
Eagan, John, 186
EAT (exercise activity thermogenesis), 39, 40
eating, health and. *See* diet
Eat Move Sleep (Rath), 5–6
Edington, Dee, 20–21, 35
Edington Associates, 228
Edison, Thomas, 215
education, life expectancy and, 33
EdVillage, 254
Eileen Fisher, 6, 150–151, 179, 208–210
Ekert, Kara, 124
"elevator confessions," 179
Eliza Corporation, 34
Emotional Equations (Conley), 127
emotional experience, creating, 23
Emotional Intelligence (Goleman), 7
emotional quotient (EQ), 7
employees
  employee engagement, 12
  focus of, 143–144, 163
  See also engagement; incentives; Take a da Vinci Approach to Change (Step 5)
Energy Project,76, 140, 145, 185
engagement
  employee engagement, 12
  global issues of, 249–250
  happiness and engagement in workplace, 93–94
  impact of, xxviii, xxix
  by management, 12
  organizational culture and, 64–65
  participation *versus*, 165
  See also assessment; Create Meaning (Step 7); Launch and Iterate (Step 9)
Envelope A+D, 204
environment
  as element of well-being, 52
  environmental prompts, 192
  mind-set and, 12
  See also Design Nudges and Cues (Step 8)
Equal Employment Opportunity Commission (EEOC), 171
Excellent Sheep (Deresiewicz), 177
Experimentation Imperative. *See* Launch and Iterate (Step 9)
experts, agents of change *versus*, 4, 5–7

F
facilities, internal da Vinci team for, 113
family members, da Vinci team and, 130
Fast Company, 20
fear, motivation *versus*, 89–90
Fed Up (documentary), xxii
financial issues
  financial fitness as element of well-being, 45–46
  financial incentives as motivation, 167–168

financial issues (*continued*)
of workplace initiatives, 136–138
"Fit-Friendly" Worksite, 119
Firms of Endearment (Sisodia, Wolf, Sheth), 59
First, Break All the Rules (Buckingham, Coffman), 86
5 "F" Factors
Feelings Factor, 74–78
Forward Factor, 78
Friendship Factor, 78–79
Fulfillment Factor, 79
Functioning Factor, 73–74
5 Pillars of Wellness (Brocade), 36–37
Flynn, Jennifer, 64
Fogg, B. J., 175, 226
food. *See* diet
Four Agreements, The (Ruiz), 92
Four Levels Training Evaluation Model™, 230
Fowler, James, 47
Frankl, Viktor, 41
Fredrickson, Barbara, 93
Friedman, Meyer, 42

G

Gallup, poll findings
Go Global (Step 10), 249
Imagine What's Possible (Step 2), 35, 47, 53
Start with What's Right (Step 4), 86, 87, 91, 97
Take a da Vinci Approach to Change (Step 5), 121, 124–125
Uncover the Hidden Factors (Step 3), 59, 76, 78
Gardner, Howard, 6
Gebhardt, Winifred, 224
General Electric (GE), 194
geographic factors, life expectancy and, 33
Gervais, Mike, 27
"Get Vitality" (Motion Infusion), 31
Giulioni, Julie Winkle, 78
Glasbergen, Randy, 32
Glass Door, 70
Global Workforce Study (Towers Watson), 149–150
goals
identifying, 156
setting, 176
Goetzel, Ron,187–188, 205
Go Global (Step 10), 245–267
changing trends in global health, 246–247
examples, 250–253
getting started for, 260–264
impact of, 265–266
mind-set for, 256–260
overview, 245, 272
rising need for well-being, 247–250
sharing best practices across borders, 254–256
Goh, Joel, 139
Golden, Jim, 265–266
Goldman Sachs, 143–144, 169, 175, 179, 199
Goleman, Daniel, 7, 251
Google, 19, 196, 250
Go Put Your Strengths to Work (Buckingham), 87
Go Stealth (Step 6), 133–156
encouraging healthy behavior and, 138–139
expense of workplace wellness and, 136–138

focus of business leaders and, 139
focus of employees and, 143–144
"going stealth," defined, 133
identifying goals and, 156
naming initiatives, 144–146
opportunities for "going stealth," 146–156
overview, 271
power of "going stealth," 134–136
stress in workplace and, 139–142
Green, Colleen, 256
Greenberg, Sarah Stein, 177
Groeppel, Jack, 145
Grossmeier, Jessica, xxvii

H

Power of Habit, The (Duhigg), 175, 225–226
habits, establishing, 175–176, 225–227
Haidt, Jonathan, 7, 91
happiness
engagement in workplace and, 93–94
financial fitness and, 45–46
gross national happiness, 252–253
Happiness Advantage, The (Achor), 93
Happiness Hypothesis, The (Haidt),7
Harr, Vivienne, 10
Harter, Jim, 35, 51
Harvard University, xxviii, 66, 93, 139
Hasson, Uri, 8–9
Hayes, Denis, 52
health
defined, 33, 35–36
types of, 32–34
See also wellness
health care
changing trends in global health, 246–247
diet and, xxii, 38–39
insurance carriers and external da Vinci teams, 116
"Most Efficient Health Care" (Bloomberg), xviii
obesity rates and, xvii, 246–247
positive approach to, 90
presenteeism and, 17
smoking cessation programs, 166, 193–194
Health Promotion in the Workplace (Segar, Gebhardt), 224
health risk assessments (HRAs), 87–89
HealthStream Research, 75, 168
HealthySteps, 91–92, 113, 228
Help Them Grow or Watch Them Go (Kaye, Giulioni), 78
Hettler, Bill, 35
hidden factors, uncovering. See Uncover the Hidden Factors (Step 3)
hierarchy of needs, 29–30, 32, 46–47, 51–52, 53–55, 78
Hillary, Sir Edmund, 72
Hilton, 75
Honda, 201
Honeywell International Inc., 171
How to Build a Thriving Culture at Work (Ward), 64
Hsieh, Tony, 49, 60
Huffington, Ariana, 9
Human Capital Media Advisory Group, 150
Human Performance Institute, 145, 184

human resources, internal da Vinci team for, 112
Hunnicutt, David, 63, 100–101

I
Identify Your Sphere of Influence (action item), 67–68
IDEO, 61–63, 196, 218–221
"I Have a Dream" (King), 8
image identification technique, 80
Imagine What's Possible (Step 2), 27–54
  creating vision, 28–29
  elements of well-being and, 37–52 (*See also* well-being)
  Imagine What's Possible Pyramid, 32
  living with vitality, 35–37
  Maslow's hierarchy of needs and, 29–30, 32, 46, 51–52, 53–54
  overview, 27–28, 270
  types of health and, 32–34
  visualizing possibilities, 30–31
In Defense of Food (Pollan), 4
incentives
  behavior change and, 161
  consequences of, 170–172
  as extrinsic motivation, 164, 165–170
  motivation as intrinsic *versus* extrinsic, 164, 165–170
  types of, 168–169
Infinite Jest (Wallace), 57
information technology (IT), internal da Vinci team for, 113
infusion, xxx, 273
inspiration,23, 31
internal resources, highlighting, 31–32
International Imperative. *See* Go Global (Step 10)
"Investing in Well-Being to Promote Sustainable Engagement" (County of Solano, California), 150
Irvine, Andrew "Sandy," 72
iteration. *See* Launch and Iterate (Step 9)
It's Just Lunch, 179

J
Jackson, Marianne, 106–109, 115–116, 179
Jackson, Richard J., 205
Japan, cues as cultural prompts in, 201
job, career *versus*, 47–51
Job Satisfaction and Engagement Survey (Society for Human Resources), 59
Johns Hopkins University, 52, 188
Johnson County (Kansas) Communication Center, 199
Johnson & Johnson, xxvi, 170
Joie de Vivre Hotels, 49, 127
Join the Movement model (Chesapeake Energy), 6, 113
journaling, 185
JP Morgan Chase, 20

K
Kabat-Zinn, Jon, 43–44
Kaiser Family Foundation, 110, 167, 171
kaizen, 201
Katz, David, xix
Kaye, Beverly, 78
KBI Benefits, 117–118
Kelley, David, 62

Kelly, Rebecca, 187
Kennedy, John F., 23
Kessler, David, 38–39
"keystone" habit, identifying, 175
Kids Cook with Heart (American Heart Association), 7
King, Martin Luther, Jr., 8
Kirkpatrick, Donald, 230
Kohn, Alfie, 169
Kolb, David, 221

L

Lang, Richard, 34
Langa Educational Advancement Program (LEAP), 255–256
Launch and Iterate (Step 9), 215–243
- design thinking, 217–221, 229–230
- on individual basis, 225–227
- iterative advantage, 217
- on organizational level, 236–242
- overview, 215–216, 272
- on program-by-program basis, 228–235
- research, 221–225

leadership
- development, 147
- focus of leaders, 139
- impact of, xxviii
- recruiting leaders for da Vinci team, 123–127

Leading Minds: Anatomy of Leadership (Gardner), 6
learning and development
- da Vinci teams and, 121–122
- workplace wellness cost compared to, 136–138

Lencioni, Patrick, 75
Leonardo da Vinci, 105. *See also* Take a da Vinci Approach to Change (Step 5)
Levine, James, 39
Lincoln Industries, 121, 168–169
LinkedIn, 202
Little Book of IDEO, The (IDEO), 61–63
L.L. Bean, 201
Lleras-Muney, Adriana, 33
Loehr, Jim, 144–145, 184
L'Oreal, 124
love, social well-being and, 46–47
Love Your Body campaign, 22
loving-kindness meditation, 93
Lucile Packard Children's Hospital, 228
lunch 'n' learn programs, 22–25

M

Make a Stand, 10
Make It Easy/Make It Normal Imperative. *See* Design Nudges and Cues (Step 8)
Mallory, George, 72, 79
management engagement, 12
management training, 149–150
Mandela, Nelson, 41
Man's Search for Meaning (Frankl), 41
Marbles (assessment technique), 71
marketing, internal da Vinci team for, 113–114
Markmann, Emily, 200
Martin Trust Center (MIT), 60
Maslow, Abraham, 28–30, 32, 47, 50–51, 53–54, 78, 79
Maslow Meets Mallory Culture Audit, 72–73, 79, 82–83, 237

Mayo Clinic, 39, 64
McCulloch, Andrew, 248
McDonald's, 3–4
McGonigal, Kelly, 89–90, 184
McKinsey & Company, 19, 217
MD Anderson Cancer Center, 8, 15, 195
Mead, Margaret, 6
meaning, creating. *See* Create Meaning (Step 7)
Mental Health Foundation, 248
Merrill Lynch, 63
Metropolitan Life Insurance, 254
MEvident, 19
Miller, Dana, 116
Mindful Nation, A (Ryan), 43
mindfulness, 176
  overview, 43–44
  tips for, 44
Mindset (Dweck), 223
mind-set shift. *See* Shift Your Mind-Set (Step 1)
mini-movements, 21–25
MIT, 60
Mockus, Antanas, 178–179
Mokdad, Ali, 246–247
Morgan Stanley, 139
Morse, Flip, 13–14, 197–198, 273
"Most Efficient Health Care" (Bloomberg), xviii
Motion Infusion, 15–16, 31–32
motivation
  autonomy for, 174, 177–178
  competency for, 174–176
  fear *versus*, 89–90
  finding "your why," 163–164
  incorporating intrinsic motivation, 173, 190
  intrinsic *versus* extrinsic, 164, 165–170
  overview, 159–160
  play for, 174, 188–189
  purpose for, 174, 183–188
  relatedness for, 174, 178–183
  "right why" *versus* "wrong why," 162
  See also Create Meaning (Step 7)
"My Life Check" (American Heart Association), 119

N

Nabors, Leo, 188
National Business Group on Health, 88, 121, 141, 166, 170–171, 241, 261–264
National Financial Partners, 112
National Institute for Occupational Safety and Health (NIOSH), 120
National Institute of Mental Health, 66
National School Supply and Equipment Association, 74
National Wellness Institute, 35
NEAT (nonexercise activity thermogenesis), 39, 40
negativity
  consequences of incentives as, 170–172
  flipping negative vortex for optimism, 91–92
  health risk assessments as problematic, 87–89
  terror tactics as problematic, 89–90
  in the workplace, 65–69
Niehbur, Sheryl, 65
Nintendo, 13–14, 196–198
Nissan, 201
Normisur International, 19

No Sweat: How the Simple Science of Motivation Can Bring You a Lifetime of Fitness (Segar), 162
Now, Discover Your Strengths (Buckingham, Clifton), 86
nudges and cues. *See* Design Nudges and Cues (Step 8)
Nudge (Thaler, Sunstein), 191

O
Obama, Barack, 53
obesity rates, xvii, 246–247
Occupational Safety and Health Act, 120
O'Donnell, Michael, 160–161, 225
Office for Standards in Education, Children's Services and Skills (OFSTED) (United Kingdom), 255
Omnivore's Dilemma, The (Pollan), 4
onboarding, 151–152
On Purpose (Strecher), 91, 183–184
Optimism Imperative. *See* Start with What's Right (Step 4)
organizational behavior. *See* Take a da Vinci Approach to Change (Step 5)
organizational culture. *See* Go Stealth (Step 6); Uncover the Hidden Factors (Step 3)
Organizational Culture Assessment Instrument (Cameron, Quinn), 69
organizational needs, 18
Organizational Wellness & Learning Systems, 180
Ornish, Dean, 90
Oxley, Robin, 152
OzForex Group, 258–260

P
Pagani-Tousignant, Celina, 19
Parks-Payne, Toni, 99–100
Parsons, Amanda, 99–100
Patagonia, 13, 20, 69
Pattee, Jenn, 204
Pavlov, Ivan, 165
PEAK (Conley), 72–73
peer-based evaluation, 222–223
Peñalosa, Enrique, 203
permission, waiting for, 9–10
persuasion, for Changemaker Imperative, 16–21
Persuasive Technology Lab (Stanford University), 226
Pes, Gianni, 253
Pfeffer, Jeffry, 140
PG&E, 121
physical activity. *See* Design Nudges and Cues (Step 8)
physical well-being, as element of well-being, 37–38, 39–41
Picarella, Ryan, 266
Pink, Daniel, 166, 172
Pitts, Jennifer, 228
Pixar, 207
play, 174, 188–189
Play (Brown), 188–189
Playworks, 95–96
"Please, *Don't* Have a Seat!" (workshop), 23
Pollan, Michael, 4, 38, 138
pop-up advocates, 238
Positive Health as a Win-Win Organizational Philosophy (Pitts), 228

positivity, 93
Poulain, Michel, 253
Power of Full Engagement, The (Loehr, Schwartz), 144–145
prefrontal cortex, xx–xxi
presenteeism, 17
Preserving Employee Wellness Programs Act, 167
Presidio Benefits Group, 116–117
PriMed Consulting Services, Inc., 40
Princeton University, 8–9
projective questioning, 80
Punished by Rewards (Kohn), 169
purpose, 19–21, 174, 183–188

Q
questions, fostering mind-set with, 224–225, 233–234
Quinn, Robert, 69

R
Radakovich, Mike, 117–118
RAND Corporation, xxii–xxvii, xxviii, 33
Ratey, John, xxi–xxii
Rath, Tom, 5–6, 35, 51
Raw Computing Power (Bennett), 180
reflection, 185
Regus Group, 247–248
relatedness, 174, 178–183
resilience, 41–44
rider-elephant metaphor, 8
risk factor assessment, as pessimistic, 87–89
Ritter, Leslie, 6–7, 150–151, 179, 208–210
Robert Wood Johnson Foundation, 33
Roering, Tess, 125–126
Roizen, Michael, 13
Rouse, Allison, 254
Ruiz, Don Miguel, 92
Ryan, Richard M., 166
Ryan, Tim, 43

S
Safety Odyssey (Motion Infusion workshop), 16
Safeway, xxvi–xxvii, 19
Safian, Robert, 20
San Francisco (California) Department of Public Works, 154, 155
SAS,199
Sawyer Effect, 172
scare tactics, as problematic, 89–90
Scarpulla, Fran, 48
Schein, Edgar, 65
Schindler Elevator Corporation, 15–16, 147–149, 180–181
Schlenoff, Marjorie, 256
Schwartz, Tony, 76, 140, 144–145, 185
scientific thinking, 217–221
Scott, Stuart, 37–38
"Search Within Yourself" (Tan), 250–252
Seattle Seahawks, 27
sedentary lifestyle, 39–40
Segar, Michelle, 162, 224
self-actualization, 51–52
self-determination theory, 177
self-efficacy, 94–95
self-expression, 52
Seligman, Martin, 93
Sexton, Bryan, 94
Sexton, Clair, 40
ShapeUp, 89

Sheth, Jagdish, 59
Shiffrin, Mikaela, 30, 164
Shift Your Mind-Set (Step 1), 3–25
  agents of change, elements, 7–11
  agents of change, overview, 3–5
  agents of change *versus* experts, 4, 5–7
  bottom-up wellness movements, 14–16
  challenges of, 11–12
  core action team formation, 12
  mini-movements for, 21–25
  overview, 273
  persuading decision makers about, 11–12, 16–21
  top-down wellness movements, 13–14
Shipley, Julie, 15, 148, 273
Shiv, Baba, xxi
"Simple Seven" (American Heart Association), xviii
Sioux Empire United Way, 202–203
Sisodia, Rajendra, 59
Sisters School District (Oregon), 265–266
Six Dimension Model (Hettler), 35
Six Hats Thinking, 130–132
Sizer, Ted, 176
Skansa, 180–181
Skinner, B. F., 165
sleep, 41
Smith, James, 33
Smith, Whitney, 23
smoking cessation programs, 166, 193–194
Smolensky, Debbie, 112
Snow, Sheri, 179, 187
Snow Day (assessment technique), 71–72
Snyder, Teresa, 31
social activism, encouraging, 23–24
social well-being
  as element of well-being, 46–47
  isolation and health consequences, 34
Society for Human Resources, 59
SOUL (seasonal, organic, unadulterated, local), 38
Southwest Airlines, 60, 189
Spark (Ratey), xxi–xxii
Spicer, Maggie, 151
Sport, Health, and Activity Research and Policy Center (SHARP) (University of Michigan), 162
Spurlock, Morgan, 3–4
Square, 154–155
staff meetings, 147
standing desks, 198–199
Stanford University
  on adopting healthy behavior, 138, 140
  Center on Longevity, 199
  Launch and Iterate (Step 9), 223, 226
  motivation research, 175, 176, 177, 180, 184
  on safety, 120
  Lucile Packard Children's Hospital, 91–92, 113
  Stanford Health Care, 91–92, 113
  on stress, 44
  on willpower and brain, xix
Staples, 45
Starbucks, 48

Start with What's Right (Step 4), 85–102
establishing a baseline for, 100–102
fear *versus* motivation, 89–90
flipping negativity for, 91–92
focusing on strengths, 86–87
happiness and, 93–94
identifying bright spots with, 97–100
overview, 270
risk factor assessment as pessimistic, 87–89
"start with what's right" approach, 8586
well-being advantage and, 94–97
"Staying on the Good Side of Stress Spectrum" (Dhabhar), 42
2013/2014 Staying@Work Survey Report (National Business Group on Health, Towers Watson), 88, 141, 261–264
StayWell, 128
stealthiness. *See* Go Stealth (Step 6)
Stein, Eric, 180
story bank, 9
Strecher, Vic, 91, 183–184
strengths, focusing on, 86–87
stress
as obstacle to resiliency, 41–42
"unmentionables," 34
Stress Reduction Clinic, 43
Sunstein, Cass R., 191
Super Size Me (documentary), 3–4
surveys. *See* assessment; Launch and Iterate (Step 9)
Szeto, Jacqueline, 36–37, 257

T

Take a da Vinci Approach to Change (Step 5), 105–132
advantage of, 106–107
building external da Vinci team for, 116–120
building internal da Vinci team for, 112–116
creating sense of ownership for, 127–130
da Vinci approach to change, overview, 105–106
example, 105–109
overview, 271
planning and, 130–132
recruiting leaders for, 123–127
unexpected team players for, 120–123
Tan, Chade-Meng, 250–252
"Tapping Passion: The Untold Talents of Wellness Champions" (Terry), 128
teachers, personal funds spent on school supplies, 74
Teach with Africa, 256
teams
development initiatives, 150
engagement, 34–35
fostering relatedness, 182–183
See also Take a da Vinci Approach to Change (Step 5)
terror tactics, as problematic, 89–90
Terry, Paul, 128
Thaler, Richard H., 191
Thiel, John, 63

third-party vendors, external da Vinci teams and, 119
Thrive (Huffington), 9
Time, 173
top-down wellness movements, 13–14
Total Care Wellness Program (Cleveland Clinic), 13
Total Worker Health™ (NIOSH), 120, 121
Towers Watson, 88, 121, 149–150, 261, 264
training and development. *See* learning and development
Travolta, John, 180–181
Treehouse LLC, 140–141
Tsumagari, Asako, 19
Type A and Your Heart (Friedman), 42

U
Uncover the Hidden Factors (Step 3), 57–83
  assessment of culture, 69–70
  assessment techniques, 71–81
  Cultural Ambassadors and change, 127
  culture, defined, 57–60
  dialogue with leaders and, 81–83
  engagement and culture, 64–65
  5 "F" Factors, 73–79
  investment in culture, 60–63
  negativity in the workplace and, 65–69
  overview, 57–58, 269–270
  understanding culture, 63–64
unions, da Vinci team and, 130
UnitedHealth Group, 51
University of California, Los Angeles, 33, 205
University of California, San Francisco, 76, 90
University of Michigan, 91, 162, 183–184
University of Oxford, 40, 167–168
University of Pennsylvania, 93
University of Washington, 246–247
"unmentionables," 34

V
Valentine, Shane, 7
Value Creation Framework (McKinsey & Company, Boston College Center for Corporate Citizenship), 18–19
value proposition, 18
Verity Analytics, xxvii
Virgin America, 151–152
Virgin Pulse, 150
Visa, 113
visual cues. *See* Design Nudges and Cues (Step 8)
visualization
  creating vision, 28–29
  visualizing possibilities, 30–31
  See also Imagine What's Possible (Step 2)
vitality, 34–37
Volpp, Kevin, 161
Volunteer Connect, 51

W
Wallace, David Foster, 57
Walton, Gregory, 180
Wanchuk (king of Bhutan), 252–253
Ward, Mike, 259–260
Ward, Rosie, 64
Warriner, Betsy, 50

Webb, Rob, 75
Weiner, Jeff, 202
Welch, Jack, 194
well-being
career and, 47–50
community and, 51
creativity and, 52–53
defined, 35–36
diet and, 38–39
emotions and, 41–44
environment and, 52
financial fitness and, 45–46
physical, 37–38
physical activity and, 39
reinforcing, 194–195, 208–210 (*See also* Design Nudges and Cues (Step 8))
rising need for, 247–250
social, 34, 46–47
well-being advantage, 94–96
See also wellness
Wellbeing (Rath, Harter), 35
WellFit (Brocade), 36–37, 111, 257–258
wellness
defined, xv, 35–36
elements of well-being and, 37–53
encouraging healthy behavior, 138
mismatch between culture and, 66
risk factor assessment of, as pessimistic, 93
types of health, 32–34
Wellness Ambassadors as advocates, 128–129
See also workplace wellness
Wellness Council of America (WELCOA), 64, 101, 120, 266
Wellvolution Campaign (Blue Shield of California), 106–109, 115–116
Whisk, 151
Willis Health and Productivity Survey, 89, 116, 119, 137, 194
willpower depletion, xx–xxi
Willpower Instinct (McGonigal), 89–90, 184
Winfrey, Oprah, 3
Wise, Judi Hennebry, 40
Wolf, David, 59
women, healthy aging for, 22
words on paper technique, 81
Workforce, 150
workplace initiatives
financial issues of, 144–145
naming of, 148–149
See also Go Stealth (Step 6)
workplace wellness
building, 103
classic model for, xxii–xxvii
defined, xv–xvi
key success factors of, xxviii–xxix
making it last, 157–158
as movement, xxxi, 273
need for, xvii–xviii, xix, xx–xxii
starting, 1–2
steps to, xxxi–xxxii
See also Create Meaning (Step 7); Design Nudges and Cues (Step 8); Go Global (Step 10); Go Stealth (Step 6); Imagine What's Possible (Step 2); Launch and Iterate (Step 9); Shift Your Mind-Set (Step 1); Start with What's Right (Step 4); Take

a da Vinci Approach to Change (Step 5); Uncover the Hidden Factors (Step 3)
World Health Report, xviii

Y

Yale University, xix, 177
Young, Laura, 143, 175, 179, 199
Yousafzai, Malala, 10
Yurchuk, Mike, 15–16, 149

Z

Zappos, 49, 60
Zenios, Stefanos A., 140
Zero Trends (Edington), 20
zip code, life expectancy and, 33